FINANCIAL INSTITUTIONS AND DEVELOPMENT IN CHINA

FINANCIAL INSTITUTIONS AND DEVELOPMENT IN CHINA

Revised Edition

Satyananda J. Gabriel

JEAE Books
Randwick, New South Wales, Australia

In memory of

Stephen A. Resnick

"… no ending is final, unless it is the end of all things …"

— Ian M. Banks, *The Algebraist*

CONTENTS

ACKNOWLEDGEMENTS

This text addresses the relationship between financial market reforms, rapid economic growth, and economic development in the People's Republic of China (PRC). The text is written for a broad audience that includes undergraduate students with basic training in introductory macroeconomics, individuals interested in a better understanding of the current transition taking place in the PRC, specialists in economic development, and professionals in the financial services sector.

I would like to thank Craig Freedman, editor of the Journal of East Asian Economies (JEAE), for his support on this project. In addition to data from common public sources, I am especially thankful for research and translations provided by Xinjia Zhu. I had a number of fruitful conversations with Jialu Chen, currently studying finance at Yale University. My conversations with Xinjia and Jialu were instrumental in shaping the text, although I am solely responsible for any errors of fact or logic.

PREFACE

This is the thirtieth anniversary of my first trip to China. By going back and forth over the past thirty years, I've had the privilege of witnessing one of history's most dramatic social transformations. Over those thirty years, the People's Republic of China (PRC) has gone from a relative economic backwater to a central node in an increasingly globalized network of capitalist economies. Change is happening so rapidly that there is very little resemblance between the China of my first visit in 1983 and the China of the present. It was during the Asian economic crisis of 1997-1998 that I had an experience that still serves as a sort of visual imprint of how quickly things change in contemporary China.

My family was living in Nanjing at the time, while I taught economics and finance at the Hopkins-Nanjing Center at Nanjing University (1996-1998). One summer we flew out of Nanjing's crowded, bustling airport in June and went to Vancouver, Canada for the summer, only to fly back into Nanjing in early September, landing at a completely new, much less crowded, and ultramodern airport. During one of Asia's worst economic crises, Chinese construction workers had completed and authorities had made operational an airport that would have been considered top notch in the United States or any OECD country.

How did the China I first visited in 1983 become the China where modern airports were being constructed, not just in Nanjing but in every major city? The China of 1983 was still mostly rural and agricultural. Rural incomes had risen since the early reforms of late 1978. The Household Responsibility System had demonstrated the vitality of self-employment and free markets, replicating prior successes with such reforms dating all the way back to Lenin's New Economic Policy (NEP) of the 1920s. Thus, conditions in 1983 were certainly better than they would have been prior to the early reforms, but still not sufficient to explain the rapidity of modernization in the 1990s and beyond. The roots of China's transformation are, nevertheless, to be found in a speech given by former Premier Zhou Enlai in 1963, twenty years before my first visit. It was in 1963 that Zhou Enlai first proposed modernization as the overarching goal of the Communist Party of China (CPC), rather than class struggle. This idea would be later refined and then labeled "The Four Modernizations," referring to the modernization of the military, industry, agriculture, and science and technology. Zhou Enlai died in January of 1976, about 8 months before the death of Mao. However, Zhou's Four Modernizations is the foundation of the post-Mao/Post-Zhou reforms that are responsible for the aforementioned transformation.

During my 1983 visit to China, the indications of the depth of the reform process were pervasive. Thanks to Unita Blackwell, who was then president of the U.S.-China People's Friendship Committee, as well as the first African-American woman elected mayor in the state of Mississippi, I attended a banquet hosted by Shanghai's mayor, Wang Daohan, who gave a speech that focused on the importance of the economic reforms championed by Deng Xiaoping and a coalition of reformers who had risen to leadership of the Communist Party of China (CPC).[1] Mayor Wang was emphatic that the reforms had done much to enrich the rural population but not enough for the cities. This was a sign of things to come, as it turned out.

The early reforms had focused on the countryside,[2] gradually

---

1 It was during the Third Plenary Session of the 11th Party Central Committee that Deng Xiaoping is credited with launching the economic reforms leading to a transition of China's economy to a form of state capitalism that has produced average rates of growth of nearly ten percent over the past thirty plus years. No country has ever produced such strong growth over a thirty year period. The second best record is Japan's twenty years of growth at an average rate of 9.2 percent.

2 During 1983, with the help of a young translator from Beijing University, I interviewed Dai farmers who had become primarily self-employed farmers and/ or artisans as a result of the reforms. They were quite vocal in their criticism of the commune system, which had not been completely dismantled at that time. From their standpoint, the commune system had been imposed on them by outsiders. The commune administrator was appointed from the outside (by the Party) and served the outsiders. According to more than one of those I interviewed, resistance to the commune system was passive but widespread. "People would pretend to work. Go to the fields and lean on their hoes." Since the reform process had started, output

giving rural producers more autonomy and weakening the so-called commune system. Wang Daohan's complaint that reforms benefited the countryside more than the cities would resonate within the CPC over the next several years. It is important to note that Wang was mentor to Jiang Zemin, who would become General Secretary of the CPC and President of China. Once he was in the top leadership position, Jiang would get the opportunity to follow through on the implications of Wang's speech and expand economic reforms to China's metropolitan areas. From 1993 to 2005, Jiang led the Party-state in executing a series of industrial and commercial reforms that are widely credited with continuing the rapid and previously thought to be improbable economic growth that provided the raw material for Zhou's Four Modernizations.

It was during the 1996-1998 teaching stint in Nanjing, a period during which I saw first-hand the impact of the Asian Economic Crisis, particularly on Hong Kong, which I visited frequently, that I came to realize that the Four Modernizations would ultimately stall if China's leadership could not solve the problem of generating an accelerating growth in capital availability. Capital was the raw material for modernization and it was precisely the failure of the pre-reform system to generate sufficient capital that caused several economic, political, and cultural crises during the Mao-era and the interregnum after Mao's death culminating in the rise to power of the current "modernization focused" leadership.

The old system had depressed the process of value creation, from which systemic value flows and capital accumulation could be achieved. The costs of the old system had been too great, its distribution of value too politically determined, and its overall value creation too weak to be an effective means for transforming China into a society strong enough to resist foreign domination and achieve "The Great Renewal of the Chinese Nation:"[3] the

---

in Xishuangbanna villages had increased dramatically. In addition, the variety of products available had increased. Households were buying more manufactured goods, like television sets and washing machines. Within two years, when I returned in 1985, the communes would be completely dismantled.

3 The CPC slogan "Great Renewal of the Chinese Nation" refers to the process of "self-strengthening," rejuvenating the relative economic, political, cultural, and

process of overcoming the weaknesses of the Qing (1644-1911) and the Nationalist (1911-1949) periods. Reform of agriculture and industry was only the beginning, however. Sustaining long-run economic growth and modernization would require such large amounts of capital that it was necessary to create a more effective financial system, a critical element in continuing the restructuring of China's economy, the functioning of an increasingly decentralized economic system, and the generation of rapid economic growth and the fundamental structural changes that define economic development.

The success of the Chinese reforms is, in no small part, a result of the flexibility of the modernist leadership in adapting institutional structures and relationships to meet the requirements for sustained growth. This is particularly evident in financial sector innovations, both in terms of the development of institutional structures and financial instruments. In addition to opening the path for innovative changes to banks, securities firms, wealth management funds, insurance companies, and other financial firms, regulatory and other public policies exist in a state of constant change, as the modernist leadership seeks to create an environment conducive to the development of domestic capital markets and to expanding access of domestic firms to foreign capital markets. These capital markets provide broader access of Chinese firms to the funding of expanding capital budgets. These capital budgets constitute the basis for investments in new projects and new technologies that embody the modernization of the Chinese economy, one of the key objectives of the current leadership. In order to sustain rapid economic growth, an accelerating growth in capital is a necessary, if not sufficient, condition. The bigger the Chinese economy grows, the more capital is required to sustain economic growth.

The source of new capital for Chinese firms was once exclusively the state but, under the reforms, has shifted to more autonomous banks and debt and equity securities sold in financial markets. The primary focus of this book will be the institutional, market, and policy innovations in the financial sector that have provided

---

military strength that epitomized China before the First Opium War (1840-1842).

for acceleration in the rate of growth of capital (and, therefore, a sustained high level of capital accumulation), particularly hard currency-denominated capital. It explores the connections between financial sector reforms and the various macroeconomic and ecological crises that threaten to derail rapid growth and potentially destabilize the PRC.

CHAPTER 1
THE PARTY-STATE AND VALUE CREATION

The roots of contemporary political struggles within the Communist Party of China (CPC) and resultant policies are located in the aftermath of the long period of national humiliations starting with the first Opium War (1839-1842) and culminating in the Japanese occupation of Chinese territories during World War II, with all of the intervening failures of the Qing and Nationalist governments to protect Chinese sovereignty. The response to these humiliations and related suffering of Chinese citizens was the so-called self-strengthening movement, when some elements of the national elite pushed an agenda of reform or modernization. In particular, the self-strengtheners believed that the adoption of Western technology combined with Chinese (Confucian) culture could turn the tide from defeat to victory over foreign forces.

However, the drive to modernity was short-circuited by conservative political forces, led by the Empress Dowager Cixi, who viewed modernization as a threat to their power within the dynasty and over the larger Chinese nation. Cixi and her cohorts successfully seized control of the dynasty (more than once) and punished those who had fostered modernization. Cixi also diverted funds that were to be used for military modernization to monumental conspicuous consumption, such as the rebuilding of the summer palace that had earlier been burned by the British and the building of a giant marble boat in nearby Kunmin Lake with funds that had been designated for naval vessels, an act which would contribute to China's defeat by the Japanese naval forces in the war of 1894-1895 that led to China's loss of Taiwan, the Ryukyu Islands, and its tributary relationship with Korea. The conservatives' suppression of modernization was also instrumental in China's loss to France of Indochina as a tributary region ten years earlier. Overall, the conservatives drained China of enormous value that might have gone to improving the economy and national defense, through corruption, wasteful spending, and reproduction of unequal relationships with foreign powers who extracted value from the Chinese economy in both direct and indirect ways. Precisely because the conservatives were so clearly a failure, the belief that modernization was the solution to the problems plaguing the Chinese nation would not die with the defeat of the self-strengthening movement. The eventual collapse of the Qing Dynasty and the consequent failure of the corrupt nationalist regime after the 1911 revolution would plant the seeds for a modernist revival within the CPC.

Why modernism?: The adoption of capitalism without refuting Marxism

Two years after the death of Mao Zedong and Zhou Enlai, a new coalition of political factions came to dominate the CPC. This coalition included most of the local-based party leadership, the powerful People's Liberation Army (PLA) leadership, and national party leaders who shared a common theoretical foundation that was, at its core, *modernist* (more commonly referred to, *ex post*, as pro-reform) and intellectually linked to the earlier self-strengthening movement, although the CPC modernists were, largely, more radical in their conception of the needs for modernization. These CPC modernists are described as modernist because of their agreement on a particular ontology (theory of cause and effect): the fundamental agreed upon *truth* of a linear path to progress, identifiable by global standards of comparison and measurement, such as GDP per capita, and the conviction that movement forward along this path requires that China be transformed into a "modern" society, defined as a society built upon a foundation of advanced technologies,[4] both tangible and intangible in nature. In other words, the CPC modernists

---

4 By advanced technologies is meant technologies that require relatively more embedded engineering to produce and are comprised of more complex technological components. In Marxian terms, the socially necessary abstract labor time (SNALT) required to produce these technics are relatively greater per hour of production time expended. Furthermore, it is generally assumed that advanced production technologies result in more output per hour and/or more complex output (more SNALT) per hour.

did not, for the most part, share the self-strengtheners belief that modernization could embody material technology alone, without fundamental changes in culture (the intangible aspect of modernity), as well. This progressive movement of both material technology and immaterial culture is, in the modernist way of thinking, the only path by which China can escape political weakness, the source of the previous humiliations under the Qing and the Nationalists, and achieve the "Great Renewal of the Chinese Nation."

In other words, in the modernist framework, technology (or the forces of production) is *the* key to progress but technology exists only in the context of a supportive culture. In symbolic representation, the modernist logic is simple, A → B, where A is advanced technologies in cultural context and B is transition to a *higher level* of society as determined by quantitative characteristics, such as GDP per capita. These factions also agree on a *modernist version of Marxian theory,*[5] which is the reason I refer to them

---

5 Modernist Marxian theories are a subset of the larger body of Marxian discourse. These theories are described as Marxist because they are based on the assumption that social evolution is either shaped by class processes (or class relations) or class processes are a direct consequence of social evolution or both. Either way, Marxian analysis has as its entry point into social analysis the concept of class. The modernist Marxist makes the additional assumption that human progress involves social transformation from lower to higher levels of class society, ultimately to a form of non-exploitative society labeled as communist (the adjective that is also used to describe the parties formed by Marxists to serve as an instrument for such transformation). The modernist assumes that this evolutionary movement from primitive to modern societies, from lower level class societies to higher level class societies, is inevitable, although the pace of this transition can be altered by concrete interventions by social groups. It is precisely the positing of this inevitability as a fundamental truth of progress that makes for modernist versions of Marxian theory. In China, the specific variation on the modernist theme that has risen to prominence is one in which this progressive movement is determined by the adoption of advanced "modern" technologies. This is also not new to Marxism. The notion that advanced technology drives the movement of societies from exploitative societies, such as feudalism and capitalism, to a non-exploitative communism of the future is associated with those Marxian theorists who give primacy to the "forces of production" (tangible and intangible forms of technology) over the "relations of production" (class relationships) in theorizing transition. Mao is often seen as representing the latter

collectively as "the modernist Marxists" (Gabriel 2006). Few Western economists have an understanding of Marxian theory and therefore falsely associate modernist reforms and the rise of capitalism with an abandonment of Marxism. Nothing could be further from the truth. The current leadership in China shares a Marxian interpretation of the class nature of society and the teleological necessity of capitalism as a stage in the evolution to communism. This is a long-held position among orthodox Marxists.[6] This return to the traditional teleological position that capitalism is a necessary but not sufficient condition[7] for eventual progress to communism contrasts the modernists to the Maoists, who believe that *class struggle* is the catalyst for social transformation and that the coming into existence of communism *does not* require first going through a capitalist phase. Mao's idea of a "Great Leap Forward" (leaping over the capitalist phase) was a social manifestation of this Maoist point of view. But one should remember that the Maoist vision was considered ultra-radical and, for many, utopian within the broader Marxian discourse. The modernists are, therefore, far more mainstream in the Marxian tradition and even their focus on market reforms is reminiscent of Lenin's New Economic Policy (NEP) of the 1920s.[8]

---

type of Marxist (one who focuses on class relationships as determinant of transition from one type of class society to another) and the reformers, such as Deng Xiaoping and the current CPC leadership (as well as Stalin), are understood as representing the former (modernist) type of Marxist.

6 Lenin would have felt very comfortable with the notion of transition embodied in the thinking of contemporary Chinese leaders, although he might have taken issue with their apparent abandonment of the international communist movement. China's leaders have made the pragmatic decision to drop Mao's aggressive promotion of revolutions in other poor countries in favor of cooperation with the advanced capitalist nations. The benefits to China from this cooperation are perceived to be greater than the perceived benefit of "Third World" revolutions. Thus, rejection of Mao's (Lenin's) internationalism is another example of modernist pragmatism.

7 If it were assumed that the progression from capitalism to communism was an evolutionary necessity, then the communist party would not be necessary as the instrument of that transition.

8 NEP was a successful policy, in terms of generating income growth, but Stalin terminated the experiment because he wanted the state to take greater control over the surplus value generated by direct producers, particularly rural farmers.

The success of the economic policies of the Communist Party of China and the mainland government it controls is the basis of the so-called Beijing Consensus, which is applauded as a model for other less developed countries and a counter to the so-called Washington Consensus. The Beijing Consensus is quite clearly not based on policy prescriptions generated within the most commonly taught neoclassical economic model, which is the basis for neoliberal policies, and epitomized by an idealized conception of markets and hostility to activist governmental policies (particularly with regard to actions that constrain or direct corporate economic decision making). What is less clear is the connection between Marxian economic theory and the Beijing Consensus. *Chinese Capitalism and the Modernist Vision* was, in part, an attempt to make this connection, and particularly to demonstrate the manner in which struggles over Marxian theory within the CPC led to the specific version of Marxian theory that was adopted by Deng Xiaoping and other so-called reformers.

However, the freedom to explore alternative theoretical frameworks or paradigms is highly limited within the American economics profession, even in the context of exploring the relationship between Marxian theory and the policies of a ruling Party-state that retains its link to Marxian theory. Therefore, the mainstream economics literature on China remains impermeable to any serious exploration of Marxian theory. Most economists do not perceive this as problematic, since there is an unspoken presumption that since China's leadership has implemented a successful set of policies then it must *necessarily* have abandoned Marxian theory. Understanding Chinese Party-state policies is presumed to be possible without a deep knowledge of Chinese Marxian debates (or the broader debates within Marxian theory globally) or Chinese history.

The neoclassical paradigm not only presumes that all other economic theories are irrelevant but also excludes the possibility

---

Interestingly, Stalin wanted this control over surplus value, in part, to finance industrialization, yet another form of modernization. It is possible, therefore, to place Stalin in the set of modernist Marxists, albeit from a very different temporal and spatial milieu and with his own unique characteristics.

that theory influences outcomes. In other words, even if neoclassical theory does not depict actual life, its presence (indeed, dominance), influences decisions and structures that shape social life. And the outcome of neoclassical theory's influence may even be in opposition to neoclassical theory's conception of economic dynamics. For instance, neoclassical theory implies that minimalist government is a condition for full employment. However, a government that fails to intervene in economic processes as employment and income falls may generate an even faster economic collapse. As Keynes and others have pointed out, the neoclassical prediction that minimalist government, in the context of perfectly competitive markets, leads to full employment may promote policies that result in higher unemployment.

George Soros, among others, has criticized the underlying ontology of the neoclassical paradigm for being unrealistic in its assumptions and downright wrong in it predictions. Soros, one of the world's most successful hedge fund managers, points out that markets are shaped by the trading behavior of human beings who are influenced by prevailing biases that have little or no basis in facts (people are sometimes slow to respond even to highly publicized information), resulting in unsustainable and not at all equilibrium prices and quantities at any given moment in the economic process. Thus, from a pragmatic standpoint, the neoclassical paradigm should come with a warning label for those who engage in market trading (and, perhaps, for anyone who engages in economic transactions of any kind).

Of course, neoclassical economists will protest that this criticism is too harsh, that their models are not meant to replicate reality but only to predict the outcome of trading under certain strict assumptions (which they will argue are necessary to construct mathematical models). Furthermore, the argument that the model does not take into consideration "changes in taste" (which is another way of saying "biases") fails to recognize that other variables (such as changes in taste) are allowed for as *autonomous shift variables*. In other words, only some factors are endogenous to the model (and therefore relevant) and everything else is, at best, exogenous). This is a form of reductionism, however, and presumes that there is an ontological A → B relationship that is independent of context. This text not only recognizes the significance of theory as a determinant but, in more general terms, is predicated on the assumption that context always matters and that everything is endogenous. In the case of China, the influence of a determinate version of Marxian theory upon the policy choice set and objectives of Chinese Party-state officials and the outcomes of those choices is a basic presumption. This commitment to ontological overdeterminism, the assumption that all economic, cultural, political, and environmental processes are implicated in observed outcomes, is a basic assumption of this text and one of the reasons for recognizing the inevitability of surprise.

Thus, when disequilibria can be identified, it becomes possible to expose potential outcomes that might not be recognized in a reductionist model (reducing the set of surprise outcomes), but it is rare in an uncontrolled social context to reduce the set of potential surprise outcomes to zero. The further we look into the future of a social formation, the larger the set of potential surprises. Indeed, it is assumed that eventually we will encounter, metaphorically speaking, one of Taleb's black swans, the completely unexpected phenomenon, such as occurs when a set of social and environmental processes comes into a configuration that triggers a tipping point that was not present in any of the "standard models." China (and, indeed, humanity) may be facing numerous potential paths to such tipping points, economic, political, and environmental.

One may not help wondering whether the Beijing Consensus will stand the test of time, particularly given the misunderstanding about the theoretical basis of the policies embodied in this approach to economic development. In any event, China largely escaped the negative consequences of the near cataclysmic break-down in the world of the Washington Consensus in the economic crisis of 2007-2009 and may do so yet again as the European economic crisis takes center stage.

Does this mean China's form of state directed capitalism is superior to more common private-corporate-centered versions of capitalism? Will this state-centered capitalism continue to protect China from the financial crises that have long beset the private-corporate-centered version? Is there some algorithm to be drawn from the Chinese model that could help us to understand the roots of this economic success and the path likely to be followed in future? This chapter includes an in-depth investigation of the relationship between China's financial institutions and markets and its economy, particularly the way these financial institutions and markets are shaping the trajectory of investment and innovation, the driving forces in all capitalist economies. If the financial sector is both a critical component of success in a capitalist economy and the source of many crises, then it may be helpful to understand the unique nature of financial arrangements in China.

In his book, *Capitalism with Chinese Characteristics*, Yasheng Huang pointed out that "the Chinese economy is so complicated that what appears to be straightforward and obvious on the surface is not at all so once we dig into the details." The structure and functioning of banks and other financial institutions, as well as other corporate structures, are the result of the complex interplay of social conditions, including internecine struggles within the CPC over Marxian theory and policies, market conditions, and external influences, e.g. from domestic institutions, trading partners, WTO, and overseas Chinese, as well as other economic, cultural, and political conditions. No single study can capture all of the relevant influences because corporate structures and the incentives shaping capital budgeting decisions are all overdetermined, meaning that every process in the social formation has some determinant impact on these structures and incentives.

In China, the dominant theoretical tradition since 1949 has been and continues to be Marxian theory. However, there is no single Marxian theory but a variety of versions of Marxian theory grounded in concepts introduced by Marx and elaborated by Engels and subsequent theorists. The version dominant in China has not remained constant over time. Struggles over the appropriate interpretation of these concepts, such as class, exploitation, and socialism are part of both the Marxian intellectual tradition and the internal struggles over policy within communist parties, including the CPC.

Since 1978, CPC strategies have been shaped primarily by a

version of Marxian theory closely associated with former Premier Zhou Enlai, whose preferred path to transition was captured in the phrase "Four Modernizations." In the post-Mao era, this modernist Marxian theory has become closely associated with Deng Xiaoping, who was noted for having said, "It doesn't matter if a cat is black or white, as long as it catches mice" – a clear statement in favor of an anti-dogmatic interpretation of the path to socialist transition. I describe this Zhou-Deng version of Marxian theory, which posits modernization as the driving force behind the transition to communism and rose to dominance at the end of the two-year interregnum following Mao's (and Zhou Enlai's) death, as *modernist Marxian theory* (or modernist Marxism).

Modernist Marxian theory shares the basic concepts and paradigmatic structure of other Marxian theories, as well as the teleology positing communism as the endpoint of historical evolution. However, the Maoist version of Marxian theory posits class struggle as the driving force behind the transition to communism (and modernization is defined as this transition). The modernist Marxian theory of Zhou-Deng assumes that any policy resulting in higher value creation and/or a rising organic composition of capital (an increase in the relative proportions of invested capital in technology vis-à-vis expenditures for labor) is necessarily more modern (and further along the teleological path to communism) than policies leading to lower value or more labor intensive production methods. In this modernist logic any change in social or material technology leading to higher value and/or a rising organic composition of capital is associated with progressive movement along the teleological road that ultimately culminates in the communist telos.

In the modernist framework, capitalist corporate structures are perceived as a necessary form of technology in the progressive teleological movement of society on this path to communism. Indeed, many social thinkers, including Adam Smith and Karl Marx, understood the corporation as a primarily social/collective institution. Smith was actually the most critical of corporations as diverging from his vision of "free enterprise" capitalism and Marx believed the corporate form a proto-socialist institution.

In addition to this social/collectivist nature, the modernist leadership recognized that corporate structures were good vehicles for generating higher value and/or a rising organic composition of capital. The reformers in the CPC were following in the footsteps of a long line of political leaders who recognized that corporate structures provided an effective and efficient means for raising capital and mobilizing work forces, particularly in the context of certain state granted advantages, such as limited liability for shareowners. For the CPC leadership and rank and file, the fact that corporate structures provided a means to attract capital from a wide range of sources, including foreign investors, and to allow the state to maintain an ownership interest were definite advantages.

The CPC leadership was not convinced that reforms needed to go so far as to remove the state from a position of exercising control or at least significant influence from most of the large corporate enterprises that remained critical to the Chinese economy but they wanted a means to modernize those same enterprises. The corporate structure, combined with participation in foreign financial markets and the development of domestic financial markets, including the stock markets in Shanghai and Shenzhen provided a successful resolution to this dilemma. The combination of advanced technologies (and related rising organic composition of capital within the corporate structure) with well-organized and highly specialized armies of wage laborers is perceived as the epitome of modern capitalism and the source of value creation for the society as a whole.

In other words, there is no contradiction between instituting capitalist economic relationships and socialism (where socialism is traditionally understood, within Marxism, as the stage linking capitalism to communism, and which is further assumed to be the period within which the wide scale adoption of advanced technologies will occur). Thus, modernist Marxian theory, as advanced by Deng Xiaoping and his successors in the Party, gives primacy to pragmatic policies that generate more value available for investment, more flexibility in the behavior and functioning of economic institutions to foster innovation, and a rising organic composition of capital wherein increasingly capital-intensive corporate structures come to dominate economic life in the most populous nation on the planet.

This path is justified on the basis of the belief that such changes push society further along a path to communism, a society that is poorly theorized but largely defined in terms of the ending of exploitative economic relationships. It is ironic that any version of Marxian theory would see corporate capitalism, which is understood in the Maoist framework as a particularly effective tool for maximizing exploitation, as the vehicle for achieving a society without exploitation.

Then again, "it doesn't matter if a cat is black or white, as long as it catches mice." The modernist leadership believes that capitalism, with its foundation of wage labor based exploitation, is a necessary moment in the life of any social formation, and rejects as absurd the Maoist idea of "a great leap forward" past capitalism. For the modernists, the Maoist vision is utopian, a diversion from Marx's method of "historical materialism" which is understood, within modernist Marxism, as having theory and practice guided by historical facts. The modernist framework rejects the notion of defining capitalism, socialism, or the transition to communism without reference to specific historical circumstances. In this version of Marxian theory it makes perfect sense to talk about a Chinese version of transition that comes out of the specific circumstances of Chinese history: *socialism with Chinese characteristics.*

Thus, the modernist version of Marxian theory deployed by Deng and the current leadership is understood by its proponents as truer to the intellectual tradition started by Marx, which is understood as including the development and deepening of capitalism as a necessary condition for modernity, in keeping with the historical facts, and the eventual transition from capitalism to communism. It is important to understand this to gain insight into particular policy choices of the CPC leadership, including labeling decisions to restructure financial institutions and relationships as "socialism," even as these restructurings have fostered capitalist social relationships in the Chinese economy and are widely hailed in the west as the de facto death of Chinese socialism.

It is also important to recognize that the modernist version of Marxian theory is in no way antithetical to state control over the economy. Although in his historical account of the establishment of capitalism in specific cases Marx identified the dispossession of self-employed farmers (peasants) and others whose labor time would become the commodities bought and sold in future labor power markets and further identified the creation of private companies whose management would mobilize the exploitation of these workers for the benefit of capitalists (typically conceptualized as specific individuals, rather than corporate entities), capitalist social relationships do not require the sort of private ownership that prevailed in most of the firms during the period covered by Marx's research per se (a period dominated by partnerships and sole proprietorships and only in the earliest stages of the development of corporate structures, which Marx would perceive as another teleological step along the road to socialism).

Under alternative historical/empirical past and present, as well as future, circumstances, wage laborers have found and do find themselves exploited by firms that are owned by corporate entities (sometimes partially or wholly owned by the state) and/or governmental agencies under the direction of professional managers and boards of directors. There are certainly versions of Marxian theory that allow for these possibilities and there remains a great deal of debate within Chinese Marxism about the significance of these alternative contexts within which capitalist exploitation is exercised, not all of which see this as compatible with socialism (defined as the transition to communism).

The justification for communist party dominance

There is one thing upon which all the various factions within the CPC agree. Both the modernists and the Maoists (and most members of the CPC, regardless of factional alliances) share a class-based justification for communist party dominance of politics in China as a necessary condition for transformation. The CPC is understood to be the sole political force that can represent the aspirations of the working people of China and construct the foundations for a non-exploitative society of the future.[9] While there are, undoubtedly, members and perhaps even factions within the CPC who have their doubts about the real role of the party, certainly cynicism has not been completely banished from the rank and file and there is widespread perception of internal corruption as driving many policy decisions. The moment the party is seen as no longer an instrument of the Chinese working classes is the moment when a serious potential crisis of legitimacy is most likely.

The modernists have reaffirmed their leadership of this vanguard party with the naming of a new 7-member CPC Political Bureau Standing Committee (referred to herein as simply the Politburo), led by new party leader Xi Jinping. Xi, who served as vice president under outgoing leader Hu Jintao, was elected general secretary of the CPC by the 18th Party Congress that was concluded in November of 2012. He became on the position of president (chairman) and head of state in March 2013.

An engineer by training, Xi is considered a protégé of former president Jiang Zemin. Jiang Zemin, the first of the modern generation of engineers to take leadership of the coalition of modernist factions (Hu was also trained as an engineer), is viewed by many as the most influential elder statesman of the CPC, but he is more than simply an elder statesman. Jiang Zemin is arguably both a leader of the modernist factions and a leading conservative voice on political reform, in the sense that he is simultaneously a modernist in ontological framework, pursuing a strategy encouraging technological upgrades and related economic reforms, and at the same time staunchly opposed to any alterations in the political structures that support the CPC monopoly on political power and provide the mechanisms for suppression of rival political institutions. Of the seven members of the new Politburo, five are

---

9 This position is maintained despite the fact that the Party has, in recent years, expanded its membership to include many business leaders and others that, in the past, would have been considered elites, "capitalist roaders," or even capitalists. Whether or not these new party members use or even understand Marxian theory (orthodox or otherwise) is certainly debatable. Rather than being an expression of commitment to the telos of communism, party membership is often an instrument for personal achievement, an entrance ticket into influential circles.

seen as closely tied to Jiang Zemin, with the other two viewed as close to outgoing president Hu. Hu is also considered politically conservative. Thus, while the composition of the new Politburo is solidly within the modernist mold, on economics and culture, with their views on the role of technology dating back to Zhou Enlai's *Four Modernizations* and Deng Xiaoping's *black cat/white cat pragmatism*,[10] and clearly to the left of the self-strengtheners, many of whom opposed cultural transformation, it is likely they will be just as cautious on political reform as past administrations. Perhaps the experiments with village and community elections will be extended, but the CPC monopoly on national policy formulation will likely be maintained and, perhaps, in some ways reinforced. More extensive local reform is not guaranteed, given that the ruling coalition includes some powerful local leaders within the CPC, whose interests would not likely be ignored in future reform efforts.

The link between modernization and financial reforms

On the other hand, the continued focus on modernization augurs well for continuing the current course of relatively rapid restructuring of and dynamic change in the banking and financial services sector in order to attract more capital to fund modernization. The finance-growth nexus was an important aspect of Joseph Schumpeter's theory of capitalism. He understood this finance-growth nexus as critical to technological innovation, economic growth and development. Finance provides for intermediation between savers and productive investors in the economy, but is also critical to improving the effectiveness of capitalist management processes via various procedures by financial institution management for evaluating corporate performance and

---

10 Deng Xiaoping once famously remarked that it does not matter if a cat is black or white, as long as it catches mice. In other words, social and material technology should be chosen on the basis of effectiveness at meeting objectives, not on ideological grounds. This technocratic approach to social evolution includes decisions on the constitution of the underlying economic relationships (e.g. class processes) within the society. It is not by chance that the modernist-Marxists have chosen three consecutive leaders trained as engineers to serve as president and general secretary.

mediating corporate relationships. From Schumpeter's standpoint, a capitalist economy could not function optimally in the absence of a well functioning financial sector and innovation would suffer. More recent empirical work in economic development has supported Schumpeter's thesis. In particular, Robert King and Ross Levine (1993) carried out a direct test of Schumpeter's thesis using data on 80 countries over the period from 1960-1989 and found that financial development is positively correlated with real per capita GDP growth, real capital accumulation, and higher productivity. Furthermore, continued restructuring and expansion of finance are critical to modernization, since modernization is not possible without the material benefits of economic growth and modernization is part of the substance of economic development.

New material technologies and new processes are being introduced within domestic financial institutions, as well as imported into China by foreign financial institutions. These innovations satisfy modernization both in terms of the technological definition, more advanced technologies are being deployed, and in terms of expectations of replicating the social arrangements of a "modern" bank or asset management company or insurance company, particularly the reorganization of these institutions into "modern corporations."

More advanced financial technologies and practices can lead to more efficient use of capital, in terms of higher realized returns on finance capital. This is, in part, because utilizing advanced technologies and practices, such as computerized systems for processing and analyzing data and more sophisticated finance models, may result in improved capital allocation to productive enterprises. Better evaluation of corporate portfolios of investments in plant, equipment, patents, and other assets, combined with the capture of a greater quantum of finance capital by better run, modernized financial firms, provides more capital to those firms most likely to upgrade technologies and practices, such as export-oriented firms competing for customers within global markets. In this sense, modernization breeds more modernization and to the extent modernization makes for more efficient forms of production, it creates value.[11]

Creating value: The five stages in the adoption of innovation

The creation of a larger quantum of value is critical to meeting the other objectives of the Party-state, such as funding modernization of the military and the larger state bureaucracy. The five stages preceding implementation of new projects and embodying modernization (in the form of the innovation of advanced technologies) are as follows:

1. Permeability stage – where institutional relationships are structured in a manner that incentivizes innovation of technologies and practices that achieve desired results, particularly positive additions to social wealth.
2. Intelligence stage – where information on available technologies and practices is gathered in preparation for innovation.
3. Evaluation stage – where quantitative analysis of the likely impact on cash flows and risk of new investments is carried out in preparation for the capital budgeting process.
4. Capital budgeting stage – where specific investments are approved, including innovation of new technologies and practices.
5. Capital financing stage – where funding is secured from internal sources or external financial institutions and/or markets.

Structural reforms have attempted to improve the processes represented by each of these stages, such that more value creation is achieved, as well as improving the realization of other objectives of the Party-state. The first (permeability) stage was directly

---

11 The adoption of modern/advanced technologies, both material and process technologies, may not only generate value by means of more efficient use of inputs (higher productivity) but may also facilitate the employment of previously unemployed resources. New technologies can provide avenues for exploiting existing human and material resources in ways unavailable under older technologies. Whether via the productivity effect or expansion of productive activities into new areas, modernization can be a source of value expansion. Expanded value creates more potential resources for future modernization.

impacted by the rise of the modernists to leadership within the CPC, because the modernists were focused on innovation and promoted individuals and put into place mechanisms supportive of innovation. Thus, the political reconstitution of the CPC after Mao has been one of the conditions for innovation and modernization. Reorganization of state enterprises and dismantlement of the communes also served this purpose, particularly when coupled with expansion in market exchange relationships. Market exchange relationships gave primacy to executing sales and executing sales required satisfying the needs and wants of buyers in the market places, both domestic and abroad. Satisfying demand in markets provides incentives for innovation and modernization. The greater the incentives to innovate, the more permeable are enterprises to new technologies.

The promotion of joint venture relationships with foreign firms is one strategy for gathering intelligence, stage two. Better understanding of technologies and practices, as well as market intelligence, can be obtained by exposure to foreign firms deploying such technologies and practices and operating in a wide range of markets. Gathering intelligence abroad, by professional managers, diplomats, intellectuals, and students provides yet another means for accessing and diffusing this knowledge. Firms operating under more competitive conditions are vulnerable to market share losses if their management has access to less or inferior information than competitors or fails to act in a way that makes good use of available information. Thus, competition serves as a stimulus to seek out information and to improve operational efficiency and effectiveness.

When firms are subject to hard budget constraints (where losses can have negative consequences for management, including the potential for bankruptcy), it becomes critical that evaluative technologies (stage 3) be deployed to improve decision making, particularly decisions about the deployment of scarce capital (stage 4). Such evaluative technologies have become relatively common among corporations based in the OECD nations. The most common evaluative technology used for valuing individual investment projects is the net present value equation as shown in equation (1):

$$(1) \quad NPV = \sum_{t=0}^{n} \frac{CF_t}{(1+k)^t} \, ,$$

where the lifespan of a project is defined in individual time periods, t, usually measured as individual years (t sequentially takes on the values from 0 in the present or the beginning moment of the project to n, the project termination time period in the future). Net cash flows for particular time periods are defined as CF_t. Capital costs are indicated by k in the denominator.[12]

NPV and the problem of growth in the pre-reform era

The net present value (NPV) methodology can be generalized to evaluate investment projects in non-market situations. In the pre-reform era, a significant quantum of value was generated by direct (or corvee) labor, which is not valued in cash terms. Nevertheless, the products and services created by direct labor have equivalents that are valued in markets. It is possible, then, to place a quantitative value on in-kind products and services in calculating the NPV for investment projects where a substantial portion of the output is in-kind, such as was often the case during the pre-reform era. Similarly, some portion of the required return to the state (which for state owned enterprise investments was the entirety of the k during the pre-reform era) took the form of direct labor contributions to the state. The overall value of k during the pre-reform era would have been very high, given the requirements of reproducing the state bureaucracy, of which state owned and controlled enterprises and communes were integral parts. On the other hand, the subsumption of productive enterprises into the state bureaucracy circumvented the need for external capital financing. The stage five process was completely internalized within the state bureaucracy and therefore capital costs (the portion of generated value that was remitted to the state) were politically determined.

The net present value generated by all the productive enterprises

---

12   Capital costs include cash flow distributions to the state as equity owner/ supplier of capital.

in the society can be conceptualized as the sum of NPVs for all investment projects, where enterprises and communes are understood as individual collections of investment projects:

$$(2)\quad \Delta W = \sum NPV_i - \sum NSC_i,$$

where ΔW represents the sum of social wealth generated by all investment projects in the economy (whether within enterprises or other agencies), NPV_i represents the specific additions to social wealth by each ith project, as accounted for by internal accounting within the associated firm or commune, and NSC_i represent the specific additions to net social costs (externalities) generated by each ith project.

Economic growth is an outcome of the aggregated sum of value added from implemented projects whose realized ΔW is positive, thus adding to social wealth over time. The quantum of social wealth indicated in equation (2) would have been relatively lower in the pre-reform era than in the post-reform period as a result of a variety of factors, including the depressed productivity of workers operating in an environment where there was very little incentive to work intensively and similarly low levels of incentive for management to innovate more efficient, i.e. productivity-enhancing, technologies or practices.

These factors would have led to relatively low output value generated and relatively low NPVs. The absence of hard currency would also limit opportunities for innovation because a large subset of technologies are only available in hard currency denominated prices. Thus, the lack of access to technologies that might increase worker productivity and make possible a wider range of outputs would also depress output.

The net social benefits/costs of projects would include not only the aggregated value realized within specific firms but also the aggregated value generated external to the firm. For example, if value creating activities within the firm includes/requires training or other educational processes that produce a better educated labor force and the knowledge embodied in this education improves the ability of trained workers to carry out other social functions beyond the workplace, such as becoming better able to manage household budgets or analyze and decide on more optimal consumption and portfolio investment choices, or becoming better parents, then this improved intellectual capacity may benefit the society in ways that are not recorded on the financial statements of the firm. Better educated workers may even make political processes work better, even in societies with relatively weak democratic institutions. It is also possible that workplace stresses could negatively impact all of the above external (to the firm) social and familial processes, generating negative externalities. Similarly, when the activities of a firm result in the poisoning of the air in communities, the social costs of this *negative externality* impacts social wealth, even though no value reduction is recorded on the financial statements of the firm. Firms are always generating positive and negative externalities. It is impossible for a firm to engage in activities that do not impact the external world.

In the Mao-era environment of 1949-1976, particularly after 1958, the Party-state increased the relative degree to which the state was responsible for meeting a wide range of social needs via state-owned and controlled enterprises and the rural communes. These activities generated value, just as certainly as the production of goods and services that were sold on markets generate value. Thus, a significant percentage of the value generated by state enterprises was in the form of various in-kind value and positive externalities. It is possible that the overall value created by these enterprises, including the communes, if valued in market terms, might have resulted in the overall activities of these enterprises being NPV positive. However, it is clear that the Party-state was not extracting sufficient surplus value from these enterprises to satisfy the objective of modernization. The politically-determined required return of the state was not being met. Enterprises were simply not providing the state with the value to acquire advanced technologies that raised the effectiveness and efficiency at which energy was captured and converted into new products and services, particularly products and services with a high degree of embedded engineering. China continued to lag behind the OECD universe of nations, and, in particular, Japan.

As indicated earlier, relatively low NPVs, measured in terms of internally realized values and cost expenditures, were also a product of the high cost of maintaining the governmental-enterprise-banking bureaucracy, making the required return to the state from so-called communes and state run enterprises relatively high at the same time that enterprise/commune expenses were inflated by internal social welfare obligations. Relatively high required returns to the state qua owner/capital provider and relatively high expense outlays were not compensated by high productivity levels. The pre-reform system was locked into using inferior technologies, low levels of innovation, and related low rates of productivity. The system simply could not generate sufficient capital to fund modernization which might have helped in solving the problem of insufficient surplus value to meet systemic obligations. The system needed to either raise the net cash flows in the numerator of project NPVs and/or lower the required returns in the denominator. While much has been written regarding the role of improved incentives in raising value (primarily by boosting productivity and increasing cash flows in the numerator) during the reform-era, some of the increase in value could have come simply from reducing required returns to the state, as the bureaucracy was reduced in size and scope, as well as reducing expenses related to internally provided social welfare, resulting in higher net cash flows for state enterprises.

In other words, to the extent boosting productivity and raising net cash flows were a function of adopting more advanced material technologies and production processes, i.e. modernization, is the extent to which expanding value depended upon modernization. However, modernization was not possible without first expanding value to make available the necessary capital. Expanding capital budgets required the initial boost in available capital as a source of funding. This interaction of lower cost of capital accumulation and modernization has played a role in the development of capitalist economies in a wide range of locales and is an example of Gunnar Myrdal's concept of *positive circular and cumulative causation* and is illustrated in the following diagram:

Figure 1.1. Modernization as positive circular and cumulative causation

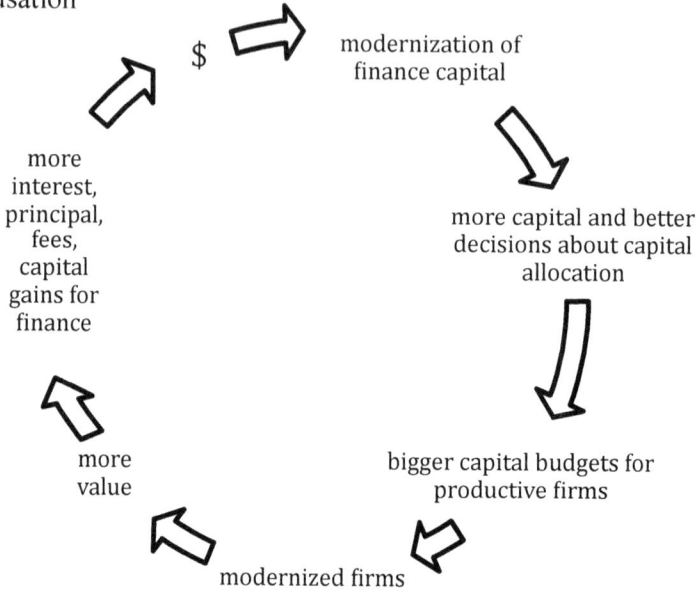

Why financial reforms will reinforce the vanguard role of the Party

In recognition of this positive dynamic, it is a virtual guarantee that the modernists will encourage continued expansion in and improvement of the financial sector as a condition for new modes of capital accumulation and value creation. This is necessary for economic development.[13] For the modernists, development serves as a sign of their successful stewardship of the Party and the Party's successful stewardship of the nation (utilizing the tools

---

13 Economic development is to be distinguished from economic growth, where the former is defined as an expansion in the productive potential of the society and the latter as simply an increase in the real output from one time period to another (with no necessity that productive potential has been positively altered). Economic growth can occur in a society where unemployed or underemployed resources are more efficiently exploited, while economic development requires more fundamental transformation in the technological gestalt of the society. Some economists, such as Paul Krugman, have argued that better use of underemployed (mostly rural) workers explains much of East Asian, including Chinese, growth.

of a modernist Marxian strategy that is understood as unique to China, in contrast to the other communist party-led states of the past or present). In this sense development is a sign of the success of "socialism with Chinese characteristics" because it validates the vanguard role of the modernist-led CPC in taking China forward to a non-exploitative society.[14]

Towards these objectives, the modernists plan to adopt further reforms designed to generate more efficient financial intermediation for channeling capital to state owned enterprises (SOEs) and other firms. A modernized financial sector would also provide a broader range of financial products for addressing return and risk requirements of firms, households, and state agencies. However, reforms are unlikely to diminish the influence of Party-state officials within that same financial structure, particularly among the state owned banks. The pervasive influence of these officials in bank offices shapes decisions regarding capital flows, even as budget constraints become harder and more sophisticated evaluative techniques are applied to loans and other financial products and contracts.

There are a number of reasons to assume that the politically conservative backgrounds of the new leadership points in the direction of a continuation of the Hu administration's relatively slow pace of overall economic reform, particularly a reluctance to reduce existing close ties between the Party-state and SOEs. For one thing, why change a process of experimentation and gradualism that is working so well. There are many other reasons to expect that dramatic ("big bang") reforms are just as unlikely as under previous administrations. It is the widespread perception, both

---

14 This definition of socialism as a society in transition to a non-exploitative society (defined as communism) has a long history within Marxian discourse. It is the most prevalent definition within that literature and contrasts to other popular uses of the term "socialism." This Marxian definition of socialism is, in fact, a particular example of modernist logic: socialism is perceived as a society in which tangible and intangible technologies and social relationships have advanced beyond more primitive types of society but have not yet achieved a level of modernity that would allow the existence of a new form of society called communism (where exploitative economic processes, such as capitalism, feudalism, and slavery ceased to exist, except as historical categories).

in China and abroad, that excessive deregulation is one of the root causes of the U.S. initiated 2007-2009 economic crisis, as well as other recent economic crises. This is because markets are excellent signaling mechanisms, but these signals are not necessarily equilibrating, as is assumed in the standard neoclassical textbook presentation on supply and demand relationships. Markets can send negative signals that result in exacerbating a trend towards destabilization, particularly when those signals are driven by fear. The "capitalist center" came very close to a serious destabilization pursuing the so-called Washington Consensus of market liberalization/deregulation. If there is one thing the CPC leadership fears above all else, it is the potentially destabilizing effects of moving too fast in changing existing economic and political structures in China.

The modernist leadership also perceives advantages to maintaining a system within which the Party-state retains direct economic power via SOEs and state owned banks and other financial institutions over an expanding but still relatively subsumed private sector, part of which are foreign invested firms and much of which has ties to foreign firms and markets. Western financial crises have only highlighted the complexity of finding the right set of reforms to solve very specific institutional and incentive problems and that no dogmatic, ideologically driven solution or solutions is necessarily the right path. This is the legacy of Deng Xiaoping's black cat/white cat pragmatism. Neither Mao nor Milton Friedman is likely to carry much weight in debates on the choices made by the Xi administration going forward. It therefore seems unlikely that the new administration would risk tipping the balance too far in either the direction of reversing reforms and returning to an all-powerful bureaucratic system, or speeding up reforms that dramatically weakens existing bureaucratic power, leading to the closing of existing channels of Party-state influence within financial and non-financial enterprises. This does not mean restructuring will cease, since there is a recognition that restructuring serves as a critical element in changing incentives towards innovation and modernization.

A counter to the argument that the new administration will

continue the Hu administration's political conservatism and cautious approach to deepening economic reforms would be that Xi Jinping's political biography goes beyond his relationship with Jiang Zemin and other modernists with strongly conservative political credentials. Xi had leadership roles in some of the more progressive regions, such as Fujian and Zhejiang Provinces, as well as in Shanghai, arguably the center of progressive politics and certainly a key breeding ground for modernist ideas. Xi has consistently supported the modernist agenda while serving in these regions. Local leaders in Fujian and Zhejiang with links to Xi are clearly reformers and modernists, whose view of the optimal role of the state appears to be as coordinator of public services, rather than as direct controller over enterprise decision-making. Fujian and Zhejiang have strong and rapidly expanding private sectors thanks, in no small part, to Xi and his allies. He also has close personal ties to leaders of political factions centered in Guangdong Province, which is home to an economy that is already predominantly private with a relatively weak state sector. Guangdong is one of the centers of modernist liberalism, where by liberalism is meant an economic philosophy favoring relative corporate independence from government regulation or direct control. Guangdong and Shanghai (which also has a strong private sector) are arguably the sites of the greatest concentration of liberal thinkers in China, as well as the two areas with the highest per capita incomes. Shanghai, southern Jiangsu Province, and Guangdong Province have traditionally had the strongest influence within the modernist factions. Xi may have been signaling a new wave of liberalization by his recent political tour of Guangdong and Shenzhen, echoing Deng Xiaoping's "Southern Excursion" twenty years ago, which signaled the continuation and extension of reforms into more areas of the Chinese economy, including the banking sector. It is possible to read these tea leaves as indicating that liberalism (or a liberal version of modernist Marxism) will be the predominant influence upon the Xi administration.

Whether or not the Xi administration will be more conservative or more liberal than the Hu administration, which is usually noted as having strengthened the state sector of the economy during its ten years in power,[15] it is likely to continue the previous administration's extremely cautious experimentation with political reforms (e.g. the village and community elections model might be expanded) to minimize the risk that the CPC will lose control. The purpose of political reforms is to reduce social unrest by providing citizens with an alternative to demonstrations and other forms of direct action. Elections provide the citizenry with a more passive means of influencing policy options, expressing dissatisfaction with (or support for) existing policies and practices, and similarly expressing preferences for political leaders. Such passive means of gauging public opinion allows for a reduction in costly police actions, including surveillance, as the primary tool for social control. As with many other elements in the reform process, political reforms will be deemed successful if and only if they can achieve their objectives with an improvement in efficiency (lower costs borne by the state to achieve the same objectives). In this sense, political reforms may be an important element in "socialist modernization" under the Xi administration, but nothing quite so dramatic as widescale democraticization is likely.

On the other hand, emergent Chinese capitalism has clearly changed the decision making dynamics within a wide range of social institutions, including the CPC. Corporate structures, SOEs, local government owned corporations, private corporations, and a wide range of other private and pseudo-public-private corporate bodies have evolved, embedded themselves into various social structures through cash and non-cash nexuses, and found ways to shape and reshape the rules of the economic, cultural, and political games. Xi is coming into leadership in this context and appears to have a keen awareness of the limitations that these emergent structures impose.

---

15   As is often the case, reality is a bit more complicated than popularly held beliefs. During the Hu administration, the state sector continued to shrink as a percentage of GDP and employment. This was facilitated by a range of state policies, including opening up many financial institutions to the service of small and medium sized private enterprises.

The link between modernization and reinvestment led growth in the Chinese economy

Xi recognizes, as does the rest of the new leadership, that the CPC has become particularly dependent upon satisfying one central objective: modernization. Modernization is both the core of transforming China's economy and the most compelling metaphor of enlightened CPC rule. And to continue along the path of modernization requires continued rapid economic growth. Thus, the key question is whether or not this new leadership can continue to implement policies that maintain the unusually rapid economic growth that has been the hallmark of modernist rule and has increasingly become the foundation for CPC legitimacy as the monopoly holder of state political power within China. Current reinvestment rates in the economy are unusually high, at around fifty percent of GDP. The growth rate of the economy can be described by the product of this reinvestment rate and the economy-wide return on investment, as depicted in equation three below:

$$(3) \quad \Delta GDP_1/GDP_0 = (RR)(ROI),$$

where ΔGDP_1 represents the change in GDP from period 0 to period 1 and GDP_0 represents the previous year, year 0, GDP, RR represents the economy-wide reinvestment rate, and ROI represents the economy-wide return on investment. Note that there are two ways we can incorporate foreign direct investment into this calculation. 1) add an additional term that calculates the return to the domestic economy from FDI, or 2) recognize FDI as an addition to domestic investment, such that it raises the reinvestment rate, and recognize that the return on investment may be slightly lower due to incorporating FDI in the RR number because some of the ROI generated by FDI is repatriated to the home country of the foreign firms doing the investment. I have chosen to simplify by taking the latter approach

For the Chinese economy to sustain a growth rate of ten percent, with reinvestment at fifty percent, would require an average economy-wide return on investment of twenty percent. If the reinvestment rate falls, as is expected, since the current rate is extraordinarily high, then the average return on investment would need to increase. Of course, even the Chinese government does not target double digit growth rates going forward, so it would be possible for the reinvestment rate to fall somewhat, so long as the ROI does not fall, and meet a more modest target of, say, 7.5% growth in GDP, which is the current target set by the State Council. However, a more dramatic fall in the reinvestment rate would, once again, require an upward adjustment to economy-wide returns on investment to even meet the more modest 7.5% target. Any reasonable estimate of future reinvestment rates would place the level well below the fifty percent level and require significant upward adjustment to ROI to maintain the sort of growth rates that many analysts believe are necessary to maintain social stability. However, continuous increases in ROI depend upon firms and the state making investments that generate higher returns over time. This can be achieved by further improvements to productive efficiencies, which is one of the objectives of modernization, but is hardly guaranteed. Global competition among capitalist corporations and aggressive moves by various nation-states in support of home corporations are likely to keep pressure on Chinese firms to raise ROI in an environment where such increases become more difficult over time. And the competitive struggle is not simply between the low cost manufacturers. New technologies are rapidly being deployed that promise lower production costs for manufacturing in the United States and other higher wage economies, particularly the digitization of manufacturing and three-dimensional printing/fabricating.

Many analysts anticipate a sharp fall in Chinese reinvestment rates from current levels but are, at the same time, skeptical of the possibility of mitigating the fall in reinvestment rates by significant increases in ROI, given current economic structures and the aforementioned global economic environment. The current relatively high ROI for the Chinese economy can be understood as largely a function of a particular moment in the evolution of the global capitalist economy and the emergence of

Chinese capitalism, epitomized by low labor costs,[16] a relatively well developed infrastructure, emergent capitalist consumption markets in China and related changes to consumer preferences that has led to a boom in various types of consumption spending, including conspicuous consumption, and a drop in the cost of data transmission and inventory controls due to digitization and advances in telecommunications. Future changes in ROI in the Chinese economy depends upon continued low wage + benefit conditions, future technological advances, and the continual diffusion of existing technologies to other low wage nations, which would impact China's competitiveness in attracting future FDI and in generating exports. The anticipated trends in these factors are not assumed to be supportive of China maintaining its current edge in the production sphere.

State capitalism vs. "free market" capitalism

For these and other reasons there is a veritable cottage industry in crisis theories that problematize the CPC's ability to maintain the current growth trajectory, going back to the very earliest period of the reforms. These theories are mostly grounded in the neoliberal/ neoclassical faith in unregulated markets as leading to socially optimal results and a related belief that crisis will ultimately come out of the heavy involvement of the Chinese government in the economy, either because government involvement results in inefficiencies to an otherwise efficient market economy and/ or because the innate corruption of state officials is believed to destroy more value than any positive governmental actions can create. Either way, the perception is that heavy state intervention necessarily leads to lower ROI and eventually to an economic downturn/crisis.

In other words, most of those who have propagated crisis

---

16   High returns on investments in the subcontracting industry are particularly sensitive to a system of patriarchy wherein young rural women, enculturated to feudal obedience and providing cash distributions back to home families in the villages, are subject to very low wages, extraordinarily high productivity demands, and low overall benefits.

theories about China are really arguing in favor of an idealized notion of an efficient market (sans state regulation) and against the concept of an effective state-centered version of capitalism, even though the historical record does not support such a thesis. State intervention has been a pervasive element in capitalist development in the United States, Europe, Asia, and elsewhere. It is difficult to find any example of successful capitalist development in the absence of extensive state intervention, at least for significant periods in the early development of capitalism. Even Hong Kong, often touted as a case of the ideal "free market" capitalism is epitomized by extensive state intervention in the economy by the British colonial administration, particularly during the 1960s when the fears of "Maoist" or "Red" China retaking the "Crown Colony" reached an apex. Nevertheless, for the neoliberal critics of the so-called Beijing Consensus, the only way to avoid a crisis is for the Chinese Party-state to rapidly reduce its role in the economy by privatizing and deregulating their way into a more liberalized version of capitalism.

This book does not share the premise of an efficient market or the related critique of the state-centered capitalism that has allowed China to rise from a relative economic backwater into an economic power whose fate increasingly appears to be so linked to that of the global economy that any major economic crisis in China would likely have serious negative impacts throughout the capitalist world. The state centered nature of China's transition to capitalism has been instrumental in driving up returns on national investment at the same time that it is largely responsible for the unusually high levels of reinvestment. It is difficult to imagine how China's extraordinary transformation could have occurred in the absence of the central role of the state in this process. Indeed, as we analyze the relationship between the role of the state in the economy and an extended period of abnormally high rates of economic growth, it will appear likely that it is precisely the state-centered nature of Chinese capitalism that explains the unusually long period of rapid economic growth (and unprecedented absolute magnitude of value creation) without a major domestic economic crisis or even a mild recession having broken the growth path at any point during this period.

Crisis theory and the problematization of continued economic growth

Nevertheless, the ability to continue along the current growth path without a major crisis may not be as easy as the past thirty years of rapid growth would make one believe, no matter what the relative pace of liberalization, although it is quite possible that certain types of liberalization could generate *more* instability and more pathways for crisis. The recent economic crisis of 2007-2009 has certainly undermined the idea that the generally more liberalized version of capitalism (sometimes described as the Anglo-American model of capitalism, although neither the United Kingdom nor the United States has followed the neoliberal blueprint for more than a fraction of its developmental history) is superior to China's state-centered version. Nevertheless, the recent crisis has generated some serious economic headwinds for the Chinese economy. As the U.S. and Europe struggle to reorganize and reform their versions of capitalism to restore conditions for capital accumulation, these headwinds could become more intense, even as the immediate effects of the recent crisis wane. Indeed, the crisis may prove, in typical Schumpeterian fashion, to be a catalyst for more rapid technological changes in the so-called core capitalist nations that ultimately problematizes China's low wage model for rapid growth and development. Advances in digitization, computer assisted design and manufacturing (CAD & CAM), robotics, and three-dimensional printing are among the multitude of factors driving a sea change in manufacturing processes that may prove detrimental to Chinese competitiveness.

But perhaps more importantly, the economic and psychological conditions generated by rapid economic growth can, in and of themselves, give rise to excesses and systemic problems. These excesses are manifest in pervasive expectations of higher than sustainable rates of profit growth. Because capital budgets are a function, in part, of profit growth expectations, then relatively optimistic expectations result in inflated capital budgets and eventually in overinvestment. Inflated capital budgets also generate increasing commitments of cash flows to cover capital costs. The nature of overinvestment is such that anticipated rates of return on capital are likely to be unmet, resulting in an upward adjustment to risk estimates and future required returns on capital. Higher future capital costs would exert downward pressure on aggregate investments, shrink capital budgets, and slow economic growth.

Facing a downward adjustment to employment and value growth, the Chinese government could try to mitigate the problem by using public funds and influence over SOE capital budgets to boost the reinvestment rate, while simultaneously adopting public policies designed to raise economy-wide ROI. The State Council could approve further increases in infrastructure spending, a new round of deregulation of industry to reduce unit costs of production, or push financial institutions to provide capital to SOEs and other enterprises at lower rates, e.g. bank lending rates could fall. However, the deeper the downward adjustment to capital budgets, the more costly this intervention is likely to be.

No less of a problem is the increasing demand for natural resources and energy consumption required to operate projects funded by these expanded capital investments, which poses a problem of both supply and price stability: as capital budgets expand, shortages or bottlenecks of natural resources may arise and, even before these shortages present themselves, the stress of demand rising at a faster rate than supply is likely to cause significant natural resource price increases. Because shortages or bottlenecks are potential sources of discontinuous price shocks and firm cash flows are interconnected, they represent a source of systemic risk. These price shocks can impact the demand for a wide range of goods and services, result in cash flow problems for firms, and slow the growth in employment and output. In this case it is more difficult for the state to manage the problem with demand-side actions because increased infrastructure spending or other efforts to boost demand might only worsen inflationary effects and further constrain other sources of demand, with additional negative impacts on the income statements of a wide range of firms, including SOEs. Cash flow problems within SOEs, in particular, may negatively impact loan servicing and impact the balance sheets of the state banks. The Chinese leadership is concerned about these and other negative consequences of inflation, particularly given the historical memory of inflation and corruption under the Nationalist leadership prior to the 1949 Revolution. Thus, the CPC leadership, and particularly the People's Bank of China (PBOC) has always been vigilant in fighting to dampen inflationary expectations anytime they appear to be rising.

The importance of capital budgets in mitigating risks

To date, the engineers atop the Chinese political hierarchy have done an outstanding job of managing the various pushes and pulls that accompany rapid economic growth and wrenching social transformation, avoiding any prolonged period of inflation or even a short period of economic decline. An important aspect of this extraordinary macroeconomic management has been the ability to use state banks, SOEs, and infrastructure spending to guide the economy through crisis periods and the aforementioned bottlenecks and pricing pressures. However, as enterprise autonomy expands, it becomes increasingly important that capital budgets be constructed on the basis of improved forecasts of future market conditions. If capital budgets inadequately account for future shifts in market demand, supply constraints, or other developments (by either overestimating future cash inflows and/or underestimating the magnitude of cash outflows related to increases in input costs), then directors, senior executives, shareholders, lenders, and other agents dependent upon firm cash flows may be disappointed and contractual obligations may not be fulfilled. And there is certainly no reason to assume that capital budgets would account for either the impact of overinvestment (since the source of the overinvestment is the same expectations driving the capital budgeting processes at various firms) or potential bottlenecks, given the tendency towards optimistic forecasts in an environment of sustained rapid economic growth and the history of state intervention to solve systemic problems.

On the other hand, firms can take actions to mitigate some of these risks. For example, firm management can take actions to mitigate inflation risks by engaging in hedging. Hedging activities are facilitated by the growth of financial derivatives in China, another source of revenues for financial firms and an area requiring new types of prudential regulation by agencies of the state. The growth in markets for futures and other derivatives, as well as increasingly sophisticated financial management practices within SOEs and other firms are an indication that firm managements are not passive in confronting the dark side of uncertainty and risk. To the extent firms are unsuccessful at managing demand-side or supply-side (inflationary) shocks, capital costs may not be recovered, including distributions of value to the state qua shareowner. At the extreme, bankruptcies may occur and a cascade effect of unmet contractual obligations could generate systemic problems.

As we've already seen, wealth is created in society when positive NPV projects are selected and implemented or, more broadly, projects are selected in society that result in a combination of private NPV and public social benefits that are positive in the aggregate ($\Delta W > 0$). Investment projects cover capital costs, add value to enterprises, and should be included in capital budgets if and only if *NPV* exceeds zero. The potential to also generate positive social benefits (versus negative social costs) is always more problematic, since there is very little incentive for enterprise managers to focus on the larger issue of externalities, but if $\sum NPV_i > \sum NSC_i$ and $\Delta W > 0$, then the society is, from an economic standpoint, better off. It is the role of the state to create incentives for firms to invest in positive NPV projects while minimizing net social costs, NSC. The extraordinarily poor air quality in Chinese cities and the severe water problems throughout the country are indications that the state has failed, to date, to create the proper set of such incentives with respect to the NSC portion of that equation. Indeed, these problems are so severe that some people may question whether $\sum NPV_i > \sum NSC_i$, even with the extraordinary rate of economic growth. However, the magnitude of economic wealth and the overall benefits that have come with that wealth would seem to indicate that, at least over the past thirty years of growth, the balance has fallen clearly on the positive side of the balance sheet. Nevertheless, the negative externalities may not simply be additive and continued accumulation of pollution could have catastrophic effects in the future, if actions to mitigate the problems are not implemented.

The central problem faced by political leaders, firm managers, and each and every conscious homo sapien is the same. We do not know what the future will bring but we must, nevertheless, make decisions. These decisions shape the future, transform the uncertainties of yesterday into the reality of the moment and the uncertainties of the days to come. The ability to maintain the necessary growth rates of output and employment in the Chinese economy upon which social stability depends is predicated on making correct decisions about a wide variety of policy variables. These policy variables shape countless NPV and NSC outcomes, both inside and outside of China. However, note that most or all of the relevant net cash flows in the numerator of the NPV equation occur in the future and are therefore, more or less, uncertain. The same is true for the magnitude of externalities generated in economic activities.

Risk is the potential for realized results varying significantly from expected results. In particular, for firms and the state the risk is that future revenues (or the value generated from revenues) will diverge in a negative direction from the estimated mean revenues or net values. Since capital costs are assumed to vary proportionately with risk, and risk is a measure of the potential volatility of these uncertain net cash flows, then future capital costs, which are, in part, a risk variable are also uncertain. The denominator term, k, represents the required return of capital providers, including the state, and is assumed to rise with risk. However, when the state is a major provider of capital, it is possible that, for political reasons, k could fall as risk rises. The Chinese state retains extraordinary influence over k, relative to the determination of capital costs in most capitalist economies. This is undoubtedly one of the reasons the CPC leadership has retained a significant degree of control over the banking system and, despite World Trade Organization (WTO) obligations, has taken measures to protect the state-owned domestic banking giants from competition from the powerful transnational banks of the United States and Europe. The ability to manipulate k and shape capital flows are powerful tools for macroeconomic management.

The Party-state is, therefore, a significant presence in all the capital budgeting decisions in China, whether or not the managers making these decisions are doing so within SOEs or private firms. The estimation of the component elements in NPV must necessarily be based on some combination of forward contractual obligations, political mandates dictating future cash flows and capital costs, and analytical models grounded in theoretical assumptions about cause and effect upon firm cash flows. There is no singular theoretical logic linking changed social and ecological conditions with future cash flows and required returns (which are often embodied in pro forma financial statements or similar summary statements of predicted variable values) but it is clear that estimates of future NPV is strongly influenced by what Keynes might have described as herd characteristics. If it is commonly believed that growth will be strong going forward, then most corporate managers will adjust their models to fit this preconception. The predicted values in the numerator and denominator of the NPV equation are dependent, therefore, on prevalent expectations, as well as upon the quality of quantitative information, including past data gathered from a variety of sources. The coherence (with reality) of the theoretical models deployed by corporate executives can only be assessed, if at all, after the fact. The rate of economic growth for the Chinese economy is determined, in part, by reinvestment of net cash flows and capital raised from financial markets and other sources, which are functions of the variables estimated in these models.

The risk of agency problems and corruption

Extended periods of growth require continual generation of sufficient cash flows to meet contractual obligations and sufficient capital to fund positive NPV projects such that the product of the reinvestment rate and return on investment are relatively high. The Party-state plays a very direct role in generating sufficient funds for the capital budgeting plans needed to generate a high reinvestment rate but must rely on firm management to produce high returns on investment. Higher quality management can generate faster growth for any existing level of reinvestment. Modernization of management practices within SOEs remains, therefore, an important objective for Party-state officials.

Nevertheless, agency problems remain pervasive within SOEs, state-owned banks, the Party-state bureaucracy, and, particularly, at local government levels. Corruption continues to result in negative NPV investment decisions and the pirating of resources such that existing projects operate at suboptimal levels, resulting in lower ROI than might be the case with less corruption. These are factors that may or may not be taken into consideration in estimating NPVs and determining capital budgets. Most likely these factors are not incorporated into the models used to estimate NPVs. Thus, in addition to all the other uncertainties about future variable values determined by market activities and production conditions, these exercises in estimating the future and theorizing the relationships among variables also omit key determinants like the level and impact of corruption. Thus, models of future NPVs are rife with the possibility for errors, sometimes quite egregious errors when the underlying assumptions (and/or the data inputs) are grossly incorrect.[17] As I've already indicated, it is my belief that at some point in the not-too-distant future, it will be apparent that a large share of the capital budgeting decisions related to recent investments in the Chinese economy were far too optimistic.

Why the Chinese economy is headed for a correction

I believe this will be the case precisely because most senior executives and directors are operating under the unrealistic

---

[17] The actual NPV of current investments is not known until such projects have terminated. This is the reason long-lived projects should be subject to periodic reevaluation. If the original assumptions upon which the project was deemed NPV positive have proven to be false upon inspection of existing results or changed underlying conditions (such that future results are likely to diverge from previously projected results), a new estimate of NPV should be calculated. If the new NPV is negative and project termination does not result in an even more negative NPV, then the project should be terminated. However, it is precisely such reevaluations and resultant project terminations that may ultimately trigger an economic downturn when past NPV calculations are recognized to have been overly optimistic.

assumption that abnormal rates of economic growth will be sustained over longer periods than is possible[18], which is partly the result of a myopic focus on periods that are too short-term and/ or too restricted in geographic terms to recognize the potential for nonlinear deviations from recent trends.[19] This belief in the persistence of abnormal rates of growth is directly (and non-linearly) correlated to the length of time over which such abnormal rates of growth have persisted in the immediate past. China's economy has been growing at such abnormally high rates for over three decades, an unprecedented period of export expansion and rapid economic growth, particularly for such a populous country. The conditions making this unusual growth pattern possible, such as relatively low wage rates coupled with high rates of worker productivity and productivity growth, a relatively stable banking sector, despite a significant percentage of non-performing loans, and the aggressive movement of capital in the form of FDI from the OECD nations and the overseas Chinese diaspora, are all being impacted and altered by the very nature of successful growth. And then there are the other factors, such as ecological conditions, that were highlighted earlier. The development of the capitalist economy in China, the simple mathematics of trying to maintain high growth rates with a much larger overall economy, in GDP terms, and changes to a wide range of social and economic factors mean that recent historical growth rates of the Chinese economy cannot be relied upon as an estimate of future growth.

Nevertheless, capital budgets will not contract simply because of a potentiality. Decision makers in corporate suites are just as

---

18 The counter argument is that near double-digit growth rates have already persisted far longer than anyone could have anticipated and exceeded all previous long-term growth periods of any nation-state. Therefore, we are in uncharted waters and there is no reason to assume that past experiences hold any relevance. To the extent this counter argument is pervasively accepted in the investment community is the extent to which I believe the evidence is all the stronger that overestimations are occurring and building up within the Chinese economy.

19 For instance, recognizing that there may be similarities between the developmental path taken by other countries undergoing a transition from feudalism to capitalism, even if such paths occurred in the past, may be helpful in identifying potential "bumps in the road" for the Chinese economy.

prone to riding the wave of growth as are stock market portfolio investors. As long as China is perceived as the place to invest or, more generally, to do business, corporate executives will be inclined towards more favorable assessments of the NPV of projects in China and the approval of larger capital budgets for such investments. It is not surprising, then, that the country is experiencing an investment boom. However, if I am correct in assuming that this investment boom is based on unrealistic expectations for future net cash flows for many, if not most, current investment projects and perhaps an underestimation of risk, then the resultant investment excesses are likely to give rise to some of the very economic conditions that ultimately lead to economic instability and crisis. It would not be the first time an investment boom ends in a bust, although given the long period of this boom and the magnitude of the annual gains it has generated, the bust is likely to be quite spectacular.

The best indicator of problems will be profit or cash flow growth rates at the firm level or GDP growth rates for the economy overall. Most analysts focus on profit growth rates, so it is possible that the first signs of trouble will come from key firms missing profit growth rates, although the ability to manipulate accounting profits makes this an unreliable indicator. Perhaps GDP growth rates will be a better signal, although by the time it is apparent that GDP growth rates disappoint, it might be a bit late in the game. Nevertheless, once profit rate growth inevitably disappoints and the suppliers of capital realize returns that are less than their required returns (and considerably less than expected returns), there is the potential for an investment panic. In the absence of mitigating actions by the Party-state, such as massive increases in infrastructure spending (which is already quite substantial) or other interventions to generate either cash flow support for the numerator or reductions in the cost of capital in the denominator of the NPV equation, corporate policy makers are likely to be forced to make massive cuts in capital budgets. If the Xi administration should decide to further liberalize the SOEs by further hardening budget constraints, the effect could be a genuine Schumpeterian moment of creative destruction.

The resultant drop in overall investment spending would, through the multiplier effect, cut the rate of growth of job creation well below the expectations of China's citizenry and undermine the legitimacy of the Party-state. This problem would be further exacerbated by firms with hard budget constraints, whether SOEs or private firms, getting into serious economic trouble and being unable to pay loans or other existing contractual obligations. When one firm gets into trouble and is unable to pay suppliers, lenders, or even employees, then the problem quickly spreads and the economic woes become shared pain. The cash flow nexuses linking failed corporations to other corporations, as well as to households and the state, is the primary reason that economic downturns can turn from bad to worse very quickly.

As yet, the problems in China have not been of a magnitude to create such an interruption to the reproduction and expansion of corporate structures and related contractual obligations. Many people don't expect to ever see a massive economic crisis hit China or they think it so far in the future as to be of no immediate consequence to their economic plans. However, this faith may have less to do with the underlying economic dynamics than with the role of the state as guardian of the economy and emergency source of cash flows for banks and at least a subset of SOEs. The state has proven to be a very adept protector of the stability of China's economy through recent global economic crises, so why not expect it to continue to do so?

An important condition for the Chinese Party-state to continue to stabilize the economy as growth proceeds is the ability to simultaneously maintain the competitiveness of Chinese firms in the global capitalist economy, which allows continued accumulation of hard currency reserves for use by firms and the state in acquiring advanced technologies, and to boost aggregate demand during times of economic crisis. The former condition is already weakening as wage + benefit demands intensify in key sectors of the economy. The competitiveness condition is also impacted by a relatively high level of corruption among public officials and corporate managers. The continued rapid growth in aggregate demand, particularly from exports, is problematic, as it has depended critically upon a huge current account surplus with the United States, which is a source of political dissatisfaction within the U.S. In addition, there are technological reasons to assume the continued reproduction of this large trade surplus with the United States may weaken and Chinese competitiveness become problematic going forward. Robotic manufacturing and the digitization of physical products (CAD and CAM driven three dimensional printing) will eventually displace low wage labor contract manufacturing as the primary means of securing low cost products. As robotic manufacturing and the digitization of physical products becomes more cost effective, subcontracting with low cost manufacturers in China will become less pervasive, costing countries dependent upon such manufacturing sizeable foreign exchange earnings. The clock is ticking.

In the meantime, it is not difficult to make a case that the Chinese economy is already in the early stages of a socio-economic-ecological crisis, albeit a fragmented crisis simultaneously epitomized by continued rapid economic growth and a series of severe disequilibria located at various nodes (economic, ecological, and political) in Chinese society, some of which are a direct consequence of the unevenness of the growth path. This growth path has become dependent upon sustaining an unusually high level of investments in physical structures, including massive infrastructure spending by various levels of government,[20] an ongoing boom in housing construction, and the construction of new power plants capable of generating the energy necessary for continued growth. These factors are driven by ever rising levels of capital budgets, foreign direct investment (FDI), and aggregate demand, including export growth. Expanding capital budgets, aggregate demand, and exports are not guaranteed, nor is it a given that the Party-state can maintain this growth no matter what else happens domestically or internationally.

Nevertheless, because rapid economic growth is widely perceived to be a critical condition for social stability, it is understood to be politically imperative that the Party-state sustain the current growth path. Although the official unemployment rate is slightly above 4%, large numbers of unemployed are not counted for various reasons, including rural migrants unable to find work in the cities and the vast sea of underemployed workers. It is estimated that the actual unemployment rate is in excess of 11%. If rapid economic growth falters, the unemployment rate could skyrocket. Under such conditions, it might be difficult to restrain the dissatisfied from taking to the streets in open opposition to CPC rule. Indeed, some estimates place current protests at over 100,000 in the past year, although most of these protests target local governments.

However, because the abnormal (from a global or historical perspective) growth rate of the economy is being driven by an investment-construction boom then sustaining it requires an accelerating growth in the quantity of capital,[21] continued growth in worker productivity that outpaces relatively stable wages and benefits (to guarantee firms the net cash flow to meet capital costs), particularly within the export sector, and rising consumption of

---

20 The current five-year plan calls for an extraordinary $3 trillion in infrastructure spending.

21 This implies that the second derivative of the rate of change of capital over time must be positive.

energy and water supplies in a nation with a relative scarcity of both. Because capital is scarce, the Chinese government is aggressively seeking reforms that will dramatically boost the growth rate of finance capital, particularly through financial market restructuring and opening up of the financial sector to foreign firms, innovation, prudential regulation, and other reforms that will attract capital, whether domestic or foreign in origin.

By using various policy instruments, the Chinese government is also encouraging technological innovations designed to further raise worker productivity. This can be depicted in the average variable cost equation below:

$$(3)\ PDY = TQ/LH,$$

where *PDY* is productivity, *TQ* is total quantity of product output, and *LH* is the number of labor hours employed.

Technological improvements that raise TQ more than LH result in higher productivity. Improvements in productivity, all other factors ignored for the moment, improves competitiveness. However, productivity is just one aspect of competitiveness. If productivity rises and labor costs rise proportionately, then there is no improvement in the cost efficiency of manufacturing. Thus, while the Chinese government is encouraging the adoption of technologies that raise *PDY*, it is also acting to hold down the growth in wages in manufacturing by suppressing independent labor unions that might bargain for more rapid rises in wages and benefits. Thus, what matters in measuring the competitiveness of Chinese manufacturers is unit labor costs, as depicted below:

$$(4)\ ULC = (WB*LH)/(P*TQ),$$

where *ULC* is unit labor costs, P is average unit price, *TQ* is total quantity of product output, *WB* is the composite wage + benefit paid to manufacturing workers per hour, and *LH* is the number of labor hours employed.

The Party-state has put in a place a structure that is designed to moderate increases in *ULC* over time, particularly in the export sector. However, this is not so easy, given the rapid growth in the export sector and manufacturing more generally. During the early stages of expansion and reform, the demand for labor was relatively easily satisfied due to the migration of rural laborers to the cities and redundancies in SOEs. Recently, labor shortages have begun to appear in areas where export oriented firms are concentrated, such as Guangdong Province, resulting in upward pressures on WB. If these pressures are strong enough to cause WB to rise faster than PDY, Chinese cost competitiveness in the global industrial supply chain may suffer and inflationary pressures may increase. On the other hand, if the Party-state is unable to accommodate demands for higher wages and benefits of ordinary workers, party legitimacy may be threatened. To make matters all the more complicated, the political leadership clearly recognizes the need to bolster domestic markets. This requires income growth and, particularly, growth in the incomes of the masses of working people. Thus, higher WB may be a necessity for meeting this policy objective, even as it makes the competitiveness objective more problematic.

These contradictions are not easy to resolve. It is widely recognized, both inside and outside of China, that the current trajectory and composition of Chinese economic growth is unsustainable without major technological breakthroughs or unforeseen political-economic solutions. These solutions must come from a coordinated effort by Chinese government authorities, national and local, and corporate leaders working in concert. For example, Chinese government must continue to invest heavily in the infrastructure necessary for a knowledge-based economy and domestic corporations must invest heavily in research and development, as well as in more modern factories and better trained personnel. This is much easier to envision than to implement, particularly since the global economic environment is always in motion. Technological advances in the OECD nations are likely to make the Party-state's efforts all the more difficult. In particular, aforementioned advances in robotization and digitization, including innovation of new computer assisted manufacturing and three-dimensional copying devices, will challenge China's role as "sweatshop of the world" by providing new types of mechanized factories operating at very low overall unit costs of production and very high productivity from skeleton labor crews.

Thus, it becomes clear that most of the conceivable solutions to maintaining China's continued rapid economic growth involve substantial outlays of capital and well-managed, strategic deployment of that capital. However, one of the indicators of economic disequilibria in China is the already existing abnormally high level of investment as a share of aggregate demand relative to personal consumption spending.[22] Gross fixed capital formation has steadily increased as a percentage of GDP since the Mao-era but has accelerated in the past two decades.[23] The formation of capital expands the magnitude of potential output of the economy. However, the value embodied in this expanded output cannot be realized without selling it: buyers must be found or inventories and costs will accumulate threatening the survival of firms. However, this heavy reliance on fixed investments generates an investment-consumption gap which grows over time, particularly given the aforementioned gap between productivity growth rates (*PGR*) and wage + benefits growth rates (*WBGR*): *PGR* > *WBGR*, ultimately leading to overproduction or under consumption (depending on one's point of view) – output is rising at a faster rate than worker incomes such that workers are in no position to buy enough output to eliminate unwanted inventories. This leads to a continued reliance on export growth.

The problem of overinvestment or under-consumption typically self-corrects in competitive private market capitalist societies via a period of what Joseph Schumpeter described as creative destruction (bankruptcies of the less competitive firms with the worse inventory and cost accumulations and restructuring of unwieldy conglomerates, where similar inventory and cost accumulations have occurred, into smaller, more efficient operations). This period of creative destruction is more typically referred to as a recession (or depression, if the correction is

---

22 This imbalance is also reflected in the extraordinarily high savings rate, now approximately 50% of GDP.

23 See World Bank national accounts data.

particularly violent). China has avoided this problem only because export growth has been sufficient to make up for the shift from *PGR >WBGR to WBGR>PGR,* pressuring returns on investment. In other words, foreign buyers have been making up the difference and keeping Chinese firms from building up unwanted inventories and providing the means for generating the revenues necessary to pay capital costs. However, it is unlikely foreign buyers will continue to make up the gap if the current rate of growth of investment continues.

A potential longer term solution to this problem would be to take advantage of the faster *WBGR* growth rates, such that the domestic market could grow at a sufficient rate to provide an alternative channel for revenue growth of domestic firms currently dependent upon export sales growth, since there is obviously a limit to the degree to which export sales growth can be sustained. And this limit is not purely economic. Political tensions typically grow more acute as any nation grows its share of another nation's domestic product markets, particularly when the exporting nation is viewed as a political competitor with the importing nation. Nevertheless, as long as China's economic growth rate is dependent upon incremental increases in exports, the solution of reversing the productivity-wages/benefits gap, such that *WBGR > PGR*, poses its own problems by making Chinese exporters less competitive in global markets, potentially hurting the accumulation of foreign exchange reserves that is playing a critical role in the acquisition of advanced technologies from foreign sources with hard currency earnings. Nevertheless, there is broad room for expanding domestic consumption in a country with more than four times the population of the United States but only one-third of the consumption spending. If domestic consumption can grow fast enough, it could more than compensate for any decline in export growth.

In addition to the problems of overinvestment arising out of a sustained investment boom, there is the aforementioned problem of acceleration in the consumption of energy and water, as well as exacerbating already critical levels of air pollution, all of which could get worse if consumption spending accelerates. Under current conditions, the rate of investment and the rates of energy and water consumption are each racing ahead on an unsustainable growth path, particularly given the excessive consumption of water generated by industrial, power plant, and construction projects, which represent a large percentage of Chinese investments. Rapid growth in consumer spending would generate pressure to further boost industrial production, power plant construction and utilization rates, and the building of infrastructure, malls, housing, and a wide range of facilities.

Thus, China faces multiple paths to destabilization: 1) overinvestment/under-consumption may result in destabilization originating in sharp adjustments to capital budgets when expected profit/cash flow growth inevitably disappoints, leading to downward shocks to demand for inputs and labor time, and 2) energy/water shortages may destabilize China's ecological system with negative economic and social consequences.[24] Either of these paths could generate a negative process of circular and cumulative effects that threaten the existing social order.[25]

---

24 The water shortage problem comes from multiple sources. China starts out water poor in per capita terms and this is made worse by erosion, pollution from industrial and agricultural sources, and poor watershed management. Climate change may add to these problems.

25 These are not the only possible catalysts for a social crisis. China is a much more heterogenous society in cultural terms than is often recognized. In many ways, China is still an imperial artifact comprised of many different cultures. In addition to the officially recognized minority nationalities, representing approximately 100 million people, the so-called Han population is itself a construct. For example, the Cantonese speaking population of the southeast is culturally distinct from the native Mandarin speaking population to their north, as is the former Manchurian speaking population of the far northeast. The idea that these various languages are merely dialects of a common Chinese language is one of the myths upon which the notion of a unified Han race has been constructed. However, the decentralization of power that has been a price the reformers had to pay to build a governing coalition has strengthened local institutional structures (and local identity) and weakened national institutional structures, to an extent. The potential for centrifugal forces to result in political fragmentation is still present, despite years of trying to minimize these cultural influences, partly by creating the idea of minority nationalities and juxtaposing those minorities to a constructed notion of a Han majority. This social construction has been somewhat successful, but it is too early to know if the idea of Han unity would hold in the face of a large scale social crisis in China.

To make matters all the more problematic, the ecological crisis may occur whether or not the Chinese government can solve the overinvestment problem. As already indicated, the impending energy and water shortage, as well as air pollution levels, could get worse with continued rapid economic growth, whether or not incremental growth shifts towards domestic consumption or continues with the current mix favoring export growth. China's new "middle class" will likely continue to accumulate automobiles and add to world leading levels of air pollution in cities like Beijing, Shanghai, and Guangzhou, even if growth slows. Absent some mitigating technological or social restructuring that alters existing patterns of energy consumption, water usage, and transportation, the probability of significant negative impacts, at the least, are quite high.

One of the most distressing potential ecological problems would not likely be mitigated even by an economic slowdown. Such a slowdown is unlikely, in and of itself, to stop the seemingly inexorable decline in *potable water* due to pollution from existing factories, farms, and other sources of toxic runoff and the present rate at which fresh water is being consumed. A large fraction of Chinese citizens are already consuming water that is of questionable quality and a significant number are drinking water that experts would consider unfit for human consumption, resulting in negative health and mortality outcomes. Absent investment in technologies to clean up polluted fresh water sources, reduce new pollution, and lower rates of consumption, the problem will get worse simply as a result of inertia.[26]

The modernist leadership, in keeping with their ideology of progress via technological advance, hope to solve these problems by creating a modern, well-functioning capital market that will finance projects, domestic and foreign, that 1) result in abnormally high worker productivity growth rates and worker wage + benefit

---

26 Wang Jusi was already writing about these problems as early as 1989. Wang Jusi, "Water Pollution and Water Shortage Problems in China," *Journal of Applied Ecology* (1989), 26, pp. 851-857. According to the World Bank, China has approximately 300 million people with no access to potable water, resulting in 66,000 deaths a year.

growth rates, but with the former rates exceeding the latter such that Chinese firms continue to generate the wealth to maintain investment growth, 2) allow for growth in worker incomes sufficient to build a more sustainable domestic consumption base that avoids the under-consumption problem without significantly harming the global competitiveness of Chinese firms (since productivity is growing faster than worker compensation in the form of $W + B$), and, 3) find profitable technological solutions to the energy and water problems. In other words, one of the keys to sustainable economic growth and development is a well-functioning capital market. A well-functioning capital market is one that is capable of 1) generating capital in an efficient and effective manner, and 2) properly valuing investment projects in terms of projections of future cash flows and underlying risk.

China's leadership is engaged in a far reaching search for these new sources of long-term capital for investment, both domestic and foreign, to fund continued industrialization and modernization of infrastructure. Long-term capital is also a condition for funding agriculture, overseas land, and new energy exploration inside China and in other parts of the globe, such as Africa. Funding and subsidizing cutting edge alternative technology projects and building state of the art water purification facilities is another objective of the State Council and will require substantial capital investment. The question remains, will these new investments come online in time to solve the investment-energy-ecological crisis before it becomes destabilizing for the Chinese economy and eventually for the global economy? Failure to solve this crisis could lead to negative outcomes far more serious than were experienced in the more narrowly economics-centered crises of 1997-1998 which started in Thailand and 2007-2009 which started in the United States.

Thus, the Chinese government's role in dampening the effects of disequilibria cannot be restricted to infrastructure spending and other forms of economic stimulus. The government must play an active role in developing a modern financial system capable of providing the capital needed to solve multiple problems simultaneously and to do so in a way that generates the required returns of investors. This financial system must have a global reach because, even with the massive growth in wealth in China, there is simply not sufficient capital in China alone to sustain long-run growth and solve these problems.

This is partly due to the contradictory effects of the long-run growth path itself. Sustaining high rates of growth over time eventually becomes more and more costly for a number of reasons, including upward pressure on $W + B$ as the supply of "surplus" labor coming from the countryside is eventually exhausted. The exhaustion of underemployed rural migrants does not only come about as a result of demographics. As local incomes grow in rural communities, partly due to money transfers from relatives working in the cities and partly because of other economic processes, the attractiveness of migrating to the city may become less. As has been witnessed in recent years, sometimes the flow of migrant workers from certain villages will slow because of repeated reports of maltreatment at urban plants. More opportunities in rural villages coupled with such reports could lead to a drop in the number of migrants. In addition, the discriminatory practices that allow firms to hire rural migrants at relatively low rates of wages and with very few benefits, but with high rates of productivity (because the migrants have fewer employment options, they simply work much harder per hour, and over longer hours, often without being fully compensated) has eroded over time.

The financial system serves a disciplinary function within capitalist economies, incentivizing management to generate value: firm management is encouraged to solve the productivity-wage dilemma in a manner that does not significantly raise overall firm specific risks without simultaneously providing investors with requisite higher rates of return. The financial system further serves the transition to capitalism in China by providing the capital necessary for fulfillment of ambitious long-run modernization/ growth projects, but it also provides mechanisms for policing firm management behavior to reduce agency costs.

Agency costs occur when management takes actions in their own personal interest but at the expense of the value of the firm, such as sexually exploiting workers (which may significantly raise worker turnover rates, search, and training costs), theft of company property, or empire building by expanding the size of the firm to provide management with more prestige but with greater underlying costs than can be justified by additional sales (assuming there are any). Because agency costs generate a negative drain on value, it is possible for such costs to be high enough as to significantly erode the positive value creating properties of the economic system, resulting in economic stagnation or worse. The Chinese government certainly wants the financial system to take some of the burden of policing SOE management and placing downward pressure on agency costs, but the financial system is no less important in providing a similar function with private firms. The more capital markets are necessary for future firm financing, whether with SOEs or private firms, the more leverage financial firms will gain over the practices of these other corporations.

Nevertheless, the continued active government intervention in financial intermediation has served to short circuit Schumpeterian creative destruction by keeping otherwise insolvent firms afloat. Some of these potentially insolvent firms are involved in developing and implementing advanced technological solutions to the energy and water problems mentioned earlier. The economic reforms begun in the late 1970s and then accelerating throughout the 1980s and particularly in the 1990s after Deng Xiaoping's Southern Excursion have been reducing the degree to which these protections are built into the Chinese economy. This being said, it seems likely that, at least for the near term, creative destruction will continue to be contained by governmental interventions, particularly with respect to "backbone" industries that are involved in critical areas of the economy, including the provision of energy and water supplies. The various levels of the government (national and local) continue to be actively involved in expanding the size of the economy, as well as in stabilizing macroeconomic imbalances.

Nevertheless, the ability to contain the effects of disequilibria may become more difficult over time, partly due to the way the reform process has opened up the Chinese economy to a more complex network of increasingly unstable financial flows both internally and between China and other nations, and partly because the material inputs needed to sustain existing growth rates may simply not be acquirable at anything resembling a reasonable cost. Among the more critical material needs is the raw materials for energy generation. China's energy consumption is on an exponential curve in a world where energy supplies are expanding at a non-exponential rate. According to China Daily, energy consumption is expected to double by 2020. Water consumption by industry is expected to nearly double by 2020. As energy supplies lag behind growing demand, global prices are bound to rise substantially. And as industry uses more and more water, as well as continues to pollute large volumes of "fresh" water with industrial waste (or what economists call negative externalities), related health problems for Chinese citizens are bound to become more widespread and the potential for social unrest greater.

It will take a lot of capital to solve these problems, assuming solutions are to be found, either by domestic firms investing in state-of-the-art technologies or by foreign transnationals investing directly in China's energy or water sectors (to the extent this is made possible by the Chinese authorities) or selling energy or water purification technologies to Chinese firms. Either approach is likely to involve huge movements of capital, the source of which are well-functioning financial firms acting as intermediaries and funded by cash flows originating in households and firms with substantial savings. China's economy has, over the past three plus decades produced abnormal income growth with high rates of savings and investment, but is this sustainable?

A variety of interacting variables determine the cash flows generated by domestic and transnational corporations: foreign exchange currency flows, revenues flowing into national governments, and the prices of a wide range of securities, including equities, bonds, futures and other derivative contracts. For example, the sales revenues that constitute the top line growth variable for transnational corporations become less predictable in an environment of intensified competition over global markets, exponentially increasing technological innovations, stressed global commodity markets, and rapidly changing consumer tastes. Just ask the management of companies like Nokia and Research in Motion (RIMM), not so long ago considered the giants in the cellular phone space, but now reeling from the entry of Apple, Inc. with its innovative iPhone. Despite its success at executing a version of creative destruction of the older cell phones, Apple's management should not rest any easier. The same accelerating process of technological innovation that has served Apple so well could eventually prove as problematic for that company as it has for Nokia and RIMM. Indeed, Korea's Samsung, having successfully pushed its way into other electronics markets with innovative products in the past, is an obvious challenger in the cell phone and tablet space with its Galaxy products. Thus, rapid technological change is a two-edged sword for corporations involved in the global marketplace (and very few firms are shielded from this global marketplace).

A key objective of Chinese officials is to create an economy that is highly competitive and breeds corporate success stories like Apple and Samsung. And there are clear signs of China developing such success stories. For example, Huawei has become one of the leading global telecommunications equipment providers, tripling its market share over the past decade and challenging old stalwarts like Cisco Systems with both innovative design and low unit costs. Chinese officials recognize that a condition for Huawei and other domestic Chinese firms to be successful is linked to the Chinese economy becoming more tightly integrated with the global economy, in terms of both the diffusion of technologies (a necessary condition if China is to breed cutting edge innovations, the real core drivers for Apples and Samsungs) and related financial flows (which are necessary to secure access to those technologies, as well as to finance continued rapid investment spending, more generally). The financial flows between China and other nations are influenced, among other factors, by highly contentious exchange rate and trade policies, fierce international competition for subcontracting relationships with powerful transnational corporations, and more liberalized capital flows, as well as growing pressures on an increasingly stressed global market for natural resources.

However, even with extraordinarily rapid economic growth, related aggressive investment strategies, and state bank lending policies pushed by the Chinese government, a wide array of social and environmental problems have arisen. These problems include, but are not limited to, a rapid rise in income and wealth inequality, serious agency and corruption problems whereby corporate and government officials take actions to benefit themselves and kin at the expense of their firms and the tax paying public, a growing unemployment and underemployment problem, and a deterioration in the quality of potable water (in a country that is already in the bottom third of nations in per capita access to potable water). The impact of acquiescing to external pressures to revalue the yuan would only add to the unemployment problems, as the rate of growth of labor-intensive, relatively low wage subcontracting and, more generally, manufacturing slows (which is already in evidence).[27]

Given the well-known lagged relationship between income and investment and multiplier effects, any slowdown in income growth, due to rising unemployment and related pressures on the wages and benefits received by the employed, would likely impact future investment spending, which would, in turn, generate more investment cut backs, layoffs, and downward pressures on labor compensation, creating a process of negative circular and cumulative causation.[28] Agency costs and corruption are recognized

---

27 Official unemployment is below 5%. However, this measure excludes large numbers of rural migrants in the cities who are out of work and would, if counted, raise the unemployment rate into double digits. There is a potential tipping point when exchange rate policy changes generate a faster contraction in the rate of growth of exports, which, along with the problems of overinvestment (the high rate of investment and exports have been key drivers of both growth and employment creation) results in a rapid rise in unintended inventory and slower investment growth or even disinvestment.

28 The Keynesian concept of the multiplier can be understood as a mathematical representation of Myrdal's cumulative effects of changes in spending upon national income and, indirectly, employment. Indeed, Myrdal's formulation owes a debt to his teacher, Knut Wicksell, who predated Keynes in pointing out multiplier effects.

The multiplier is a basic concept in macroeconomics. An increase of $1 in spending would, given multiplier effects, raise income by more than $1 and a cut in spending of $1 would lower national income by more than $1. The magnitude of the multiplier effect

by the modernist leadership as eroding both the value created by the economic system and public faith in the Party-state. President Xi Jinping has already stepped up efforts to fight corruption and agency costs and it is likely these efforts will be sustained until there is marked improvement in the situation for two reasons: agency and corruption problems 1) extract vital value from the economic system, and 2) undermine the reputation of the Party-state and threaten its legitimacy. However, the economic structure and long-held cultural norms may make it just as difficult to reduce agency costs and corruption as to solve the other problems.

These economic, political, and cultural problems combined with the aforementioned environmental crisis could threaten social stability. This threat to social stability would be all the more problematic coming in the context of globalization of financial flows which has resulted in more frequent and increasingly severe global economic crises: the two most serious of which have been the Asian economic crisis of 1997-1998 and the recent American economic crisis of 2007-2009.[29]

So far China has provided one of the few islands of stability in the midst of these global crises, with strong growth rates throughout these crisis periods, albeit below the near double digit trend line of the past three decades.[30] Now that China has

---

depends upon various leakages from the national income stream, such as a propensity to spend some fraction of the increase in spending on imported goods and/or to save a fraction of that $1 increase. The key point is to recognize that positive increases in aggregate demand or spending has a multiplied impact on national income and, thus, a bigger effect on employment than might have been anticipated by simply taking the initial spending change into account.

29 The European debt crisis of the current period is most often linked to the American economic crisis, since the latter was rooted in mortgage backed securities and had a very powerful disequilibrating impact on all debt and, more generally, securities markets. However, in a way all crises are linked because one crisis creates conditions conducive to further crises, including changes in expectations of financial market participants. If the European economic crisis is understood as a separate crisis, then the window between major global crises has, in this instance, narrowed in an extreme manner, raising the possibility that yet another crisis may not be long in the making, perhaps even one that originates in China.

30 The rate of GDP growth in China slowed to 7.6% at the highest stress point of the Asian economic crisis but recovered the double digit pace as the crisis diminished

become the second largest economy on the planet, the potential for a Chinese crisis to serve as catalyst for yet another of these wide-scale crises could potentially put the global economic system into far more dangerous waters and make recovery more difficult than in past crises, including the recent 2007-2009 U.S.-centered financial crisis that came close to triggering a 1930s-style global depression.

The disequilibria that indicate early stage crisis conditions sometimes appear as contradictory statistics. For example, at the same time that overall unemployment in China has become problematic, labor shortages have developed among export oriented firms in Guangdong Province dependent upon a continual flow of mostly female laborers from the countryside. The low wages and mistreatment of these rural women, coupled with growth in employment opportunity in rural villages, has begun to diminish the attractiveness of such jobs. Thus, the supply curve for rural, female migrant labor has shifted backwards in Guangdong, pressuring foreign firms and subcontractors to raise wages and improve working conditions. However, higher wages among these export oriented firms (and a revalued yuan) reduce the "competitiveness" of Chinese subcontractors and subsidiaries of foreign transnationals operating within China vis-à-vis similar operations in other low wage countries, such as Viet Nam.

Similarly, pressures on agricultural land have generated a gap between food consumption and production, given existing technologies employed in the agricultural sector, forcing increased reliance on food imports. China's agriculture is simultaneously in a mode of falling arable land in use and rising input costs and output prices (with a potential scissors effect if disgruntled consumers put effective pressure on the central government to restrict growth in food prices and farmers are less effective at agitating for lower input costs). The country has become increasingly reliant upon high cost imported food stuffs, which has lowered food security (which runs counter to the long held objective of food self-sufficiency of the CPC). On the other hand, if food prices rise

---

and Chinese government stimulus actions took hold.

faster than agricultural production unit costs, partly as a result of productivity gains in agriculture, then investments in agricultural production will become more profitable (higher net present values) and larger magnitudes of capital could flow to the agricultural sector.

Agricultural modernization (driven by these capital inflows) is a key objective of Xi Jinping, who has extensive experience with this sector. This is another area where advanced technologies are increasingly perceived by the modernist leadership to be the panacea. Xi believes that scaling up agricultural production in a manner similar to the techniques employed in American agriculture could raise farm outputs per acre sufficiently to, at the least, slow the rising dependency on food imports. However, if this solution is to work, investment in agriculture must experience a sizable increase over current levels. In other words, domestic agriculture is both in a disequilibrium mode (where outputs and inputs are out of sync) and at the same time becoming more attractive as a venue for investments.

Whether in agriculture, industry, or finance, disequilibria are increasingly present. The manifestation of asset bubbles, particularly in housing prices, is an example of disequilibria signaling crisis: the faster housing prices rise and, therefore, deviate from household income growth (is the key factor on demand side of the housing market), the more stress is placed on the economic system and the higher the probability of a sharp, sudden downward revaluation of housing prices, with potential negative consequences on the supply side of the market.

Fortunately the housing bubble, which is most glaring in Shanghai, is not coupled with an excessive amount of leverage in the form of mortgage borrowing or the deployment of related derivative securities, as was the case with the U.S. financial crisis of 2007-2009. China's domestic savings rate continues to be relatively high, providing the financial raw material to fund housing purchases, and reduce systemic default risks. Tight government regulation of the growing mortgage market should continue to provide one of the impulses for the high savings rate and slow the rise in default risks. Thus, the inevitable bursting of the pricing bubble in China's housing market should have a more limited, but nevertheless significant, impact on the overall economy. Certainly a revaluation of housing could generate a sudden fall in housing construction, which has been one of the leading forms of investment and job creation in the Chinese economy. This would have a particularly devastating impact on the incomes of migrant laborers employed in the construction sector.

The crisis of multiple (and multiplying) market disequilibria in China is all the more dangerous for being only partly recognized and largely dismissed, especially by the international corporate community. Rapid income growth is intoxicating and, for many, a sufficient condition for ignoring problems, even when they are recognized as potentially serious. Nevertheless, many of the conditions in China that can be described using the terminology of economic crisis, particularly economic disequilibria, are not all that different from the identifiable catalysts for past crises in other capitalist economies.

There are parallels both to recent economic crises and to crises that occurred during the early stages of a transition from feudalism to capitalism in other countries. The fact that this instance of transition takes the form of a significantly more state centered version of capitalism than has been the norm has been widely noted. What is ignored is the state centered version of feudalism that predated the recent rise of state capitalism. Most observers do not recognize the feudal nature of China's economy during the period from the Great Leap Forward until the modernist restructurings of the 1980s and 1990s because they have been conditioned to think of feudalism as a particular historical moment in certain geographic spaces, rather than as an economic system with characteristics that can come into being at any historical moment in any geographic space, if the proper set of underlying conditions prevail.

This historicity causes them to miss the parallels between a relatively contemporary period in China's history and other feudal societies, of whatever vintage, and the similarities in the transitional dynamics to capitalism. It is perhaps more common to recognize that there is a hybrid nature to China's newfound capitalism, but to put the blame on "communism" rather than carrying out a deeper analysis of economic structures and processes. Most commentators recognize the state-centeredness of the economy, even without seeing the class aspects, but view this as a temporary aberration, a vestige of "communist" politics, a problem in need of a solution. They certainly do not recognize the degree to which the state centered nature of Chinese capitalism is a function of not only the communist party's exclusive control over the state and its pervasive bureaucracy but also a legacy of reproducing a particular type of class structure in both the countryside and the cities: a form of feudal exploitation that depended upon state power for its reproduction.

Ironically, this state-centeredness, no matter its origins, has proved to be simultaneously fundamental to China's extraordinary economic successes and one of the causes of at least a subset of the underlying and intensifying disequilibria that could ultimately prove destabilizing. The state centered nature of China's economy is also just as important to the suppression and relative opaqueness of the underlying conditions of crisis, as state manipulation of and control over information flows. The effectiveness of state institutions in moving value around in the system to solve problems is a bit like a ship with holes in the hull allowing in water but no one notices as long as there is a mechanism (the state) that keeps pumping the water back out (intervening to close cash flow gaps). The people walking around on the deck do not realize there is a fundamental problem with the vessel.[31]

China's ruling Party-state has navigated the Chinese economy through a series of institutional transformations, particularly the transition of a non-capitalist and closed financial structure into one that is open to globalized capital inflows and outflows,

---

31 This role of the state in suppressing crises is not, of course, unique to China. If not for state intervention, the U.S. initiated economic crisis of 2007-2009 would have exploded into a full-scale great depression event with devastating consequences for ordinary Americans and for the system as a whole. Because the state is the only institutional structure capable of large scale systemic intervention in a counter-cyclical manner, if you remove the state from any capitalist economy disaster is an inevitable consequence.

feeding capital to expanding capitalist economic structures. The transformed financial system increasingly serves as vehicle for the expansion of corporate debt and consumer credit markets that are important conditions for further expansion of the capitalist economy. However, one of the results of this transformation has been the creation of a series of market and non-market disequilibria that have become more severe over time. These disequilibria are, in part, the product of imbalances carried over from earlier periods, particularly within the banking system. The banking problems arose, to a significant extent, from the feudal fealty-based economy. Fealty-based economic decisions within the extensive Party-state bureaucracy, which included the banks, generated a wide range of systemic problems and related moral hazards that ultimately drained value out of the Chinese economy. These problems have been inherited by the current system.

The modernists' faith in the powers of modernization to solve all problems, coupled with the growth of a new nationalism in China, may present another problem: hubris. Hubris comes out of a renewal of the overconfidence that epitomized the thinking of national elites, including intellectuals, during much of the dynastic history of the "Middle Kingdom" from the Han through the Qing, at least up until 171 years ago when the first Opium War burst the bubble of overconfidence. This hubris is one of the reasons the crisis conditions are downplayed or ignored, making them largely invisible.

The invisibility of the crisis also comes from the masking effects of an extraordinary accumulation and deployment of foreign exchange reserves, greater than any nation has ever amassed. This has come about partly as a result of a dynamic of internal colonization within which rural China has served as supplier of a reserve army of extraordinarily low wage labor for the export sector, generating a large quantum of surplus value which is a key source of foreign exchange earnings. These rural migrant laborers are also crucial to the industrialization and infrastructure/housing building boom in urban China.

Another factor in this accumulation is the unusual degree to which governmental entities, both national and local, are intertwined in the fabric of the economic system and have played a leading role as nexus with the global economy. During the early extension of the Chinese economy into the global arena, this was particularly the case with local government owned township-village enterprises that entered subcontracting relationships with transnational firms. However, the most important institutions extending the reach of the Chinese economy have been state owned enterprises (SOEs). SOEs play a critical role in the industrial and extractive sectors and state owned banks dominate the financial sector.

The Party-state has been able to use its power to shift assets around in the system to block the various pathways by which localized crises explode into systemic crisis. However, the same institutional structure that supports the masking of multiple disequilibria is also constructive of those same disequilibria. The process of shifting around cash flows to avoid systemic crises creates unsustainable dependencies that may ultimately coalesce into just the sort of systemic crisis the Party-state has worked so hard to avoid. One of the most obvious sources of disequilibria that may lead to crisis is the serious widening of income inequality. Widening income inequality has implications for transitioning from an investment and export-led growth strategy to one grounded in domestic consumption growth, a necessary condition for economic growth to be sustained.

Perhaps the most noted potential source of crisis is the financial system, and particularly the state owned banks. State directed cash flows and a U.S. style bailout of the banks have papered over problems stemming from the continuation of fealty-based relationships between various levels of government, banks, and SOEs. The banks cannot forever be bailed out of bad lending decisions by state orchestrated cash flows because the underlying obligations are growing at a pace that requires a concomitant continued growth rate in the overall Chinese economy. On the one hand, the Chinese economy has been growing at this extraordinary rate for much longer than anyone could have predicted and it might seem the heights of folly to predict a significant slowdown. On the other hand, it is unlikely that this "magic" will continue indefinitely and the aforementioned disequilibria provide ample evidence that it will not continue much longer. Thus, invisible or not, the underlying crisis conditions are real and threaten the global economic structure that has evolved in recent years and which has become dependent upon China's rapid economic growth, related role as mega-lender, and as "sweatshop of the world."

Before the rise of the modernist factions within the CPC, it was widely presumed that communist parties were populated by individuals locked in a rigid, absolutist ideology and unwilling to compromise or take a pragmatic course to expanding social wealth and pursuing economic progress. The overlords of the centrally planned economies did little to alter this stereotype, appearing locked into a mode of economic management based on solving the unsolvable: pursuit of a bureaucratically established set of global equilibria that would allocate supply of all manner of commodities to meet an ever changing and enormously vast demand array for products and services (meant to satisfy an even more volatile array of wants and needs) within a massive economic structure connected by complex networks of relationships. The entire matrixes of interconnected political, economic, and cultural processes were overdetermined by this bureaucratic allocation of just about everything. No technology known to the human species was capable of revealing all the necessary inputs or processing the requisite massive amount of data required to solve these problems and generate the appropriate outputs or mediate the political pressures that would ultimately undermine even the most astute planners and planning processes. Not to mention the ever present possibilities for human intervention to undermine the plan, including formation of an underground economy for trading goods and services outside of the plan.

In 1978, two years after the death of Mao Zedong, the CPC not only abandoned any connection to the Stalinist orthodoxy that had shaped these central planning policies in much of the so-called communist bloc, particularly the Soviet Union and the CMEA nations, but also rejected the Maoist ideology that had arguably served as the primary alternative to Stalinism.[32]

---

32 It can be argued that Yugoslavia's now largely forgotten version of market

Maoist ideology was a particular source of internecine conflict within the CPC because it had served as the driving force in the *Great Proletarian Cultural Revolution*, a movement designed to undermine the bureaucratic structure upon which the CPC governed. After a relatively short power struggle between factions within the CPC, the party came under the control of leaders who favored resurrecting a set of policies dating before Stalin's rise to power in the USSR. These policies, established under the leadership of Vladimir Lenin, were collectively referred to as the *New Economic Policy* (NEP): the wedding of state ownership to market driven allocation and allowing a mixed economy of self-employment, capitalism, and collectivism. Economic growth replaced class struggle (at least in the terms defined by Mao) as the primary focus of the CPC and the state it controlled, setting in motion a process of transformation that would go much further than any "China watcher" or comparative systems specialist could or did predict.

The success of these policy shifts is well recognized, if not well understood, and is reflected in the achievement of abnormally high rates of economic growth over the past three decades. Chris Bramall (2000) is one of a select few recognizing the critical role of the old centralized planning system in producing conditions that facilitated rapid economic growth and the contemporary transition to capitalism. The plasticity of Mao-era infrastructure and production systems has proven to be far greater than could have been anticipated a priori and the move from serving one economic structure to serving a radically different one has proven far easier and more efficient as a means for wealth creation than even the modernist reformers might have hoped.

The transition to capitalism has fostered a process of rapidly changing institutional structures that have reinforced the new social relationships, forging new cash nexuses binding together the Party-state, firms, banks, and households in a network of interdependence mediated by market transactions. This is the

---

socialism was equally compelling for the minority within the communist movement seeking an alternative to Stalinism.

basis for a new phase of capitalist development within which the relatively effective and efficient financialization of the Chinese economy has occurred, deepening capitalist relationships and providing the means for enhanced capital accumulation.

Capital accumulation is catalyst for future transformations but the existing infrastructure is a necessary if not sufficient condition for these transformations. In terms of the role of the old centralized planning structure in the development of financial institutions, relationships, and instruments, one can see this in the way institutions set up in the old system have worked so effectively to provide necessary data production and analysis for the new system.

Financial institutions, in particular, depend upon the existence and constant updating of data on economic variables and related demographic and social variables. Finance, to be an effective tool for enabling value creation, requires relatively deep data and the means to analyze that data to identify past correlations that may continue to hold true and therefore influence levels of risk. The central planning system and the expansive data oriented bureaucracy it generated created just such a condition, producing a large number of statistically literate (and often data obsessed) individuals and social institutions capable of processing, storing, and disseminating data. The so-called socialist bloc has never suffered from a shortage of "quants." Thus, banks, insurance companies, private equity firms, and other financial institutions have access to the data and analytically trained staff necessary to evaluate and monitor financial contracts and to innovate new financial instruments when necessary.

The successful transition to capitalism was also facilitated by heavy investments in transport, storage, and other forms of physical infrastructure from 1949 to 1978. If any lesson is to be learned from China's rapid economic development during the transition to capitalism, certainly one such lesson is that the successful transformation of a poor country into one that is noticeably better off requires building a strong foundation upon which incentives may be applied to effectively make use of that foundation.

A close corollary to the building up of the physical infrastructure was the creation of a bureaucratic infrastructure capable of organizing and mobilizing the Chinese work force. The existence of a highly disciplined work force was another important condition for the successful transition to capitalism. Market reforms without a strong infrastructure, well developed data systems, including sufficiently trained personnel to analyze data, and a well-organized, disciplined, and mobilized work force, are likely to be far less successful and perhaps even make matters worse.

As for the proof of China's success, one can look to a wide range of empirical evidence. In 2007, China passed the United States to become the world's second leading export nation behind Germany. By 2011, China was the world's leading exporter, surpassing the European Union and the U.S. (CIA World Factbook 2008, 2012). In 2007, China also passed the U.S. to become the world's leading emitter of carbon dioxide. See Table 3.1.

More recently China has become the second largest economy in the world when measured in purchasing power parity GDP and many analysts anticipate that China will eventually pass the U.S. in nominal GDP. See Table 3.2.

Table 3.1.: Total Carbon Dioxide Emissions from the Consumption of Energy (Mil. Metric Tons)

	2006	2007	2008	2009	2010
U.S.	5914.5024	6015.75348	5835.37834	5427.06527	5610.10826
China	5817.1435	6184.09582	6721.43382	7204.88549	8320.96269

Source: U.S. Energy Information Administration (EIA), International Energy Statistics database.

Table 3.2. Top 10 Economies in GDP, PPP (2010)

1. United States
2. China
3. Japan
4. India
5. Germany
6. Russian Federation
7. United Kingdom
8. France
9. Brazil
10. Italy

Source: World Development Indicators Database, World Bank

In a post-Soviet world where capital flows are increasingly unbounded by political barriers, China has surpassed the United States to become the top recipient of foreign direct investment (FDI) (UNCTAD 2012). The dynamic feedback between accelerating investment expenditures, including the aforementioned FDI, rising domestic incomes, and expanding profitability for firms operating within China (a catalyst for further investment spending) has generated unusually large rates of GDP growth for an extended period of time. The growth rate of GDP has averaged 10% per annum for the past thirty years (World Bank 2012). See Fig. 3.1. Over the longer period from the beginning of the reforms in 1978 to 2011, growth has averaged 9.8% (Lau and Li 2012). In economic terms, China's near double digit growth rate over this length of time has been unprecedented, as has been the dramatic reduction in poverty with the percentage of Chinese citizens living below US$ 1 per day (the bare bones poverty rate) falling from 63% to 9% over the past thirty years (Meyer 2011).

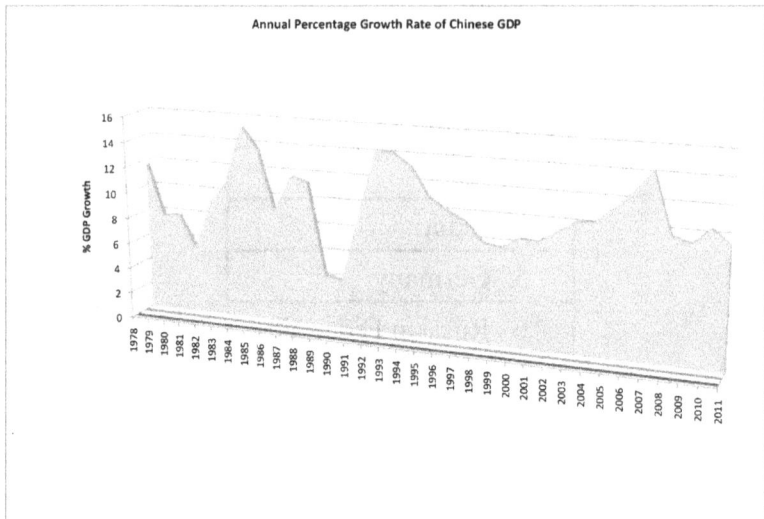

Fig. 3.1. Annual Percentage Growth Rate of Chinese GDP

Source: World Bank national accounts data, and OECD National Accounts data files. Annual percentage growth rate of GDP at market prices based on constant local currency. Aggregates are based on constant 2000 U.S. dollars. GDP is the sum of gross value added by all resident producers in the economy plus any product taxes and minus any subsidies not included in the value of the products. It is calculated without making deductions for depreciation of fabricated assets or for depletion and degradation of natural resources.

The absolute magnitude of value creation over this time span is also unprecedented and has altered global economic, political, and cultural configurations, as well as environmental conditions (as epitomized by the aforementioned carbon dioxide emissions, which are increasing at an exponential rate), in complex ways that social and natural scientists are only beginning to grasp. It is quite likely that the overdetermined impacts of these changes on global political, economic, cultural, and environmental processes will be far more powerful and foster more dramatic changes to living conditions around the world than anyone except those in the hard sciences, particularly climatologists, can currently fathom.

The economic growth numbers coming out of China have been so large that some have questioned their validity, charging the CPC with fudging the statistics in a manner reminiscent of the Maoist era. However, use of coincident indicators of economic growth generally confirms the notion of double digit or near double digit growth for much of the past thirty years, albeit with some short periods where a sharp divergence between reported GDP growth rates and at least one of these indicators, energy usage rates, appears (Rawski 2001). However, even this proxy variable must be seen as confirming the long-term growth trend as China's energy consumption growth has been so rapid that the nation has now surpassed the United States as the world's leading energy consumer (USEIA 2012). See Fig 3.2 below. For a breakdown of the various sources of China's energy usage, see Fig. 3.3

Fig. 3.2: China vs. US Energy Consumption (Energy use (kt of oil equivalent), in millions)

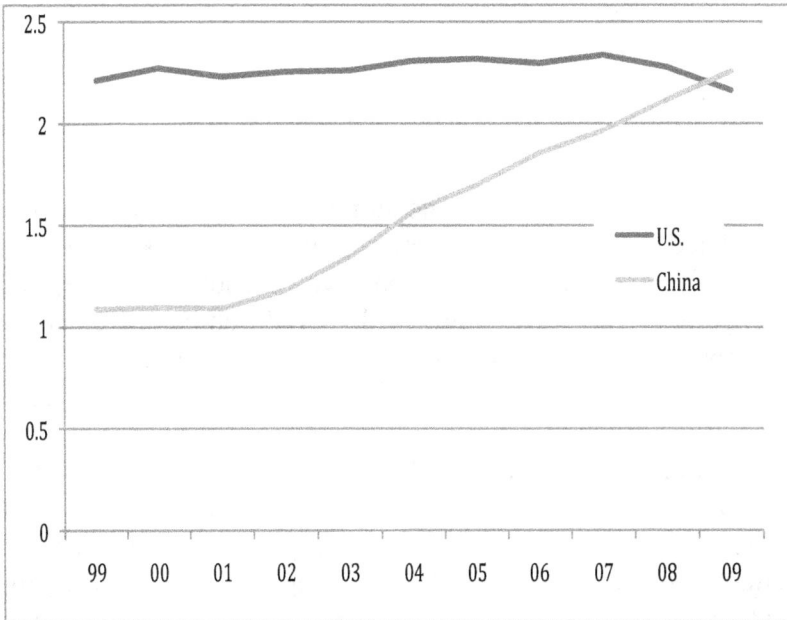

Source: World Bank
Note: Energy use refers to use of primary energy before transformation to other end-use fuels, which is equal to indigenous production plus imports and stock changes, minus exports and fuels supplied to ships and aircraft engaged in international transport.

Figure 3.3.

Total energy consumption in China by type, 2009

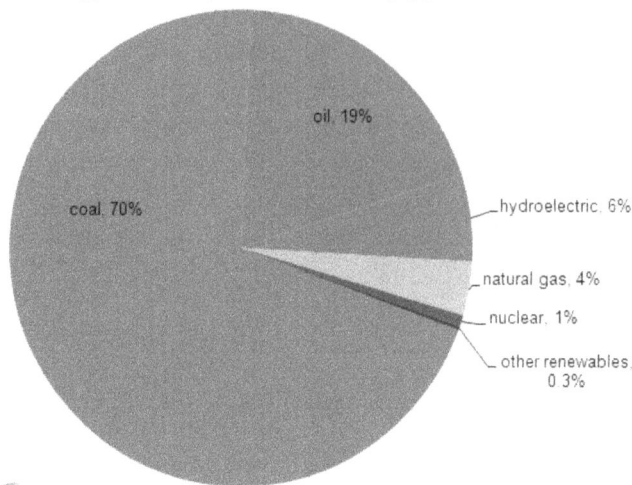

eia Source U.S. Energy Information Administration, *International Statistics*

Thus, to the extent aggregate output and income are positively correlated to energy consumption (with energy a key input to production and energy usage a positive function of income), the energy proxy serves to confirm the GDP numbers. Ironically, the rapid growth in carbon dioxide emissions may be seen as yet another confirming statistical artifact demonstrating China's rapid economic growth.

Overall, the empiricist case for rapid economic growth is easy to make. The living standards of Chinese citizens have improved quite visibly and dramatically, not simply statistically. This is reflected in the rapid and, at least along the eastern seaboard, widening diffusion of advanced infrastructure, production and consumer technologies: new housing complexes with modern appliances, well stocked supermarkets and big box stores displaying products from around the world, modern water treatment facilities and state-of-the-art airports, multi-level shopping centers, freeways, subway systems, bullet trains, and ultra modern sports arenas glistening new and architecturally bold in many cities.

Rapid urbanization is transforming the Chinese landscape, in some places coexisting with structures from the distant past and in other places completely obliterating any sign of China's long historical continuity. When I first visited China in 1983 it was still a largely rural country and even in the cities the technologies employed in infrastructure, production and consumption were many years, if not decades, behind those typically employed in many other cities around the world, even in some so-called Third World cities. The pace of life in China was relatively slow and attitudes relatively parochial. Most people traveled by foot or on bicycles. This same casual pace seen in the streets could be observed in various work places, including factories (except in the case of prison labor, which was not only common but celebrated by the authorities, who arranged a tour of one of these facilities for me during the 1983 visit, seemingly oblivious to the fact that they were exposing a case of slave labor). To see how rapidly China is urbanizing, see figure 3.4.

Fig. 3.4

China: Degree of urbanization from 2001 to 2011

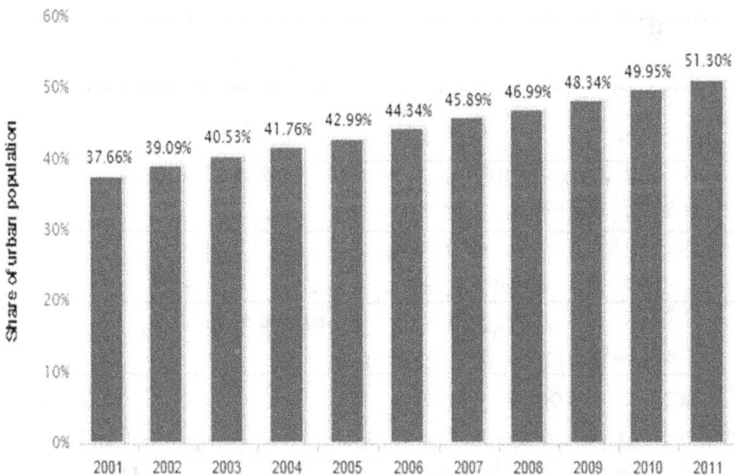

Source: National Bureau of Statistics of China

Urbanization is another dimension of China's modernization. Modernization is clearly not just an economic phenomenon. It is also cultural, changing the way citizens in China perceive themselves and their country. It also changes the way foreigners view China. The Party-state recognizes this and has promoted the construction of artifacts of modernity. Thus, architecture provides the most visually striking empirical evidence of China's modernization, if not the underlying fundamental changes in social relationships.

In the 1980s, the architecture of Shanghai, China's most important economic nexus, then and now, would have been a bit aged but recognizable to a time traveler from the 1920s, particularly the Bund. Our time traveler might have a memory of the foreign traders, sailors, and other agents of European empires, operating outside the jurisdiction of Chinese law thanks to unequal treaties. The most prominent sign of our 1920s time traveler being "out of time" in her trip to the 1980s would have been the blue Mao suits everyone was wearing, symbolic of the Maoist-led ruling party's desire to control every aspect of social life and to level all surface distinctions between classes.

Shanghai today, on the other hand, would be largely unrecognizable to either a 1920s time traveler or one from the 1980s, for that matter. The 1980s time traveler would find that even the once ubiquitous bicycles have mostly disappeared. China has become the world's largest market for automobiles to the delight of many Western automobile companies, particularly General Motors, which has seen its Buick models rise to unprecedented popularity (at least outside of pre-1980s United States). During a recent visit to Shanghai, in 2011, I saw more Buicks than I'd seen in any American city in recent memory.

There are less positive signs of modernity, such as the increasing complexity of human manufactured particles in the air we breathe. Coextensive with the rise of the automobile and modern factories, as well as the explosion in power plants (mostly coal fired), has come a rapid deterioration in air quality. See Fig. 3.5.

Fig. 3.5. PM10, country level (micrograms per cubic meter)

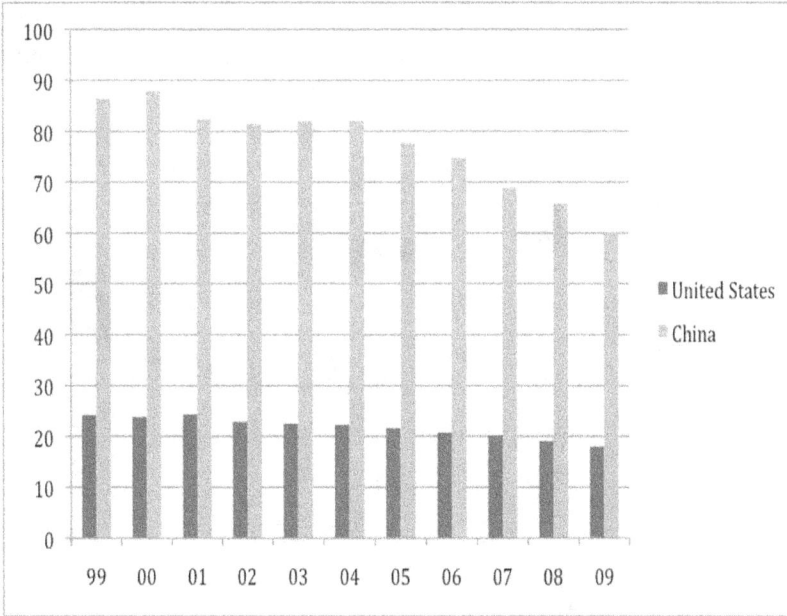

Source: World Bank
Note: Particulate matter concentrations refer to fine suspended particulates less than 10 microns in diameter (PM10) that are capable of penetrating deep into the respiratory tract and causing significant health damage. Data for countries and aggregates for regions and income groups are urban-population weighted PM10 levels in residential areas of cities with more than 100,000 residents. The estimates represent the average annual exposure level of the average urban resident to outdoor particulate matter. The state of a country's technology and pollution controls is an important determinant of particulate matter concentrations.

The taste and smell of the air would be completely unrecognizable to our time travelers, who might also be somewhat dismayed at the limited visibility and the assault upon their lungs. China's cities now have bragging rights to some of the world's worst air quality and pollution of China's waterways is particularly problematic in a country that ranks in the bottom third of countries in potable water per capita. The potential for pollution to trigger social crises is another problem for the Party-state leadership to resolve.

Our time traveler would also confront a radically more connected society, as telecommunications in China, as in many other parts of the world, has gone through a revolutionary transformation. It seems like everyone now has at least one cell phone, increasingly a "smart phone," and internet access is widespread (See Table 3.3 below).

Table 3.3: Internet users by province, 2011

Province	Internet users (10,000)	Penetration rate (%)	Growth rate (%)	Penetration rank	Internet user growth rate rank
Beijing	1379	70.3	13.2	1	9
Shanghai	1525	66.2	23.1	2	1
Guangdong	6300	60.4	18.3	3	2
Fujian	2102	57	13.7	4	8
Zhejiang	3052	56.1	9.5	5	23
Tianjin	719	55.6	10.9	6	17
Liaoning	2092	47.8	9.2	7	25
Jiangsu	3685	46.8	11.5	8	15
Xinjiang	882	40.4	7.7	9	28
Shanxi	1405	39.3	12.4	10	10
Hainan	338	38.9	11.4	11	16
Shaanxi	1429	38.3	10.3	12	22
Shandong	3625	37.8	8.8	13	26
Hubei	2129	37.2	11.9	14	11
Chongqing	1068	37	7.9	15	27
Qinghai	208	36.9	10.4	16	20
Hebei	2597	36.1	18.2	17	3
Jilin	966	35.2	9.5	18	24
Inner Mongolia	854	34.6	14.4	19	6
Ningxia	207	32.8	18.2	20	4
Heilongjiang	1206	31.5	7.0	21	29
Xizang	90	29.9	10.8	22	19
Hunan	1936	29.5	10.8	23	18

Province	Internet users (10,000)	Penetration rate (%)	Growth rate (%)	Penetration rank	Internet User Growth Rate Rank
Guangxi	1353	29.4	10.4	24	21
Sichuan	2229	27.7	11.6	25	14
Henan	2582	27.5	6.8	26	31
Gansu	700	27.4	6.9	27	30
Anhui	1585	26.6	13.9	28	7
Yunnan	1140	24.8	11.7	29	13
Jiangxi	1088	24.4	14.5	30	5
Guizhou	840	24.2	11.9	31	12
Nationwide	51310	38.3	12.2	N/A	N/A

Source: CNNIC

China now has more internet users than any other country, including the United States. Online markets are growing in importance, with domestic corporations, like Alibaba.com and Baidu, already positioned to be major players in Cyberspace. Table 3.3 breaks down internet usage by city and provides the growth rates of internet usage. Young entrepreneurs are starting up new firms operating within Cyberspace or generating products, such as apps, dependent upon Cyberspace at an increasing rate. It is possible that China's rapid deployment and expansion of internet related technologies and services will turn out to be one of the more transformative aspects of the drive to modernity.

As for the Mao suits, they are now gone, replaced with the latest fashions, although one might anticipate a time when they might return as *haute couture* among the well-to-do. China has a rapidly growing subset of these well-to-do, as is becoming increasingly evident in the tourist circuits. It is now commonplace to see signs in Mandarin in some of the top international tourist spots, as China's nouveau riche cruise the globe for luxury goods and the "good life."

The overall conclusion is simple – the orchestrated transition to capitalism has transformed the world's most populous nation into one of the fastest growing economies, turning an economic backwater into the crucible of an increasingly globalized, decentered, and environmentally challenged capitalism. The opening up of China to foreign exploitation has been an incredible boon to a wide range of firms, both inside and outside of China. China's modernization is driven by relatively low wage + benefit packages of workers and relatively high productivity leading to low unit labor costs and relatively high operating margins.

The cost advantages of locating nodes in international production networks in China include the presence of an efficient infrastructure for moving products outside of the country and on to other nodes in the supply chains of transnational companies. Relatively low wage + benefit rates, high productivity, and compliant labor relations are all factors generating relatively low unit labor costs for production in China and relatively high ROI for firms operating there. Transnational companies (their management and shareholders) have benefited from China's transition in the form of boosted revenues, earnings, and cash flow. This is precisely why China now leads the world in production of manufactured products. Chinese markets for goods and services, as well as Chinese labor power markets, are increasingly important to the growth strategies of transnational firms.

However, there are some clouds on the horizon. Upward pressure on wage costs has become an issue for some firms; especially subcontractors working with transnationals, as incremental increases in labor supply have not kept up with incremental increases in labor demand. Wage cost pressures have intensified in some regions as worker militancy has intensified despite the absence of independent labor unions and the close cooperation between local government officials and manufacturers.

Wage cost pressures may add to inflationary pressures that have already become problematic, particularly in food prices and for other consumer goods. Figure 3.6 shows the official rate of inflation in consumer prices from 1999 to 2011. As can be seen in Figure 3.6, the trend since 1999 has been towards slightly higher inflation over time, except for the dramatic deflationary effects of the U.S. centered financial crisis.

Figure 3.6: China Consumer Price Inflation from 1999-2011

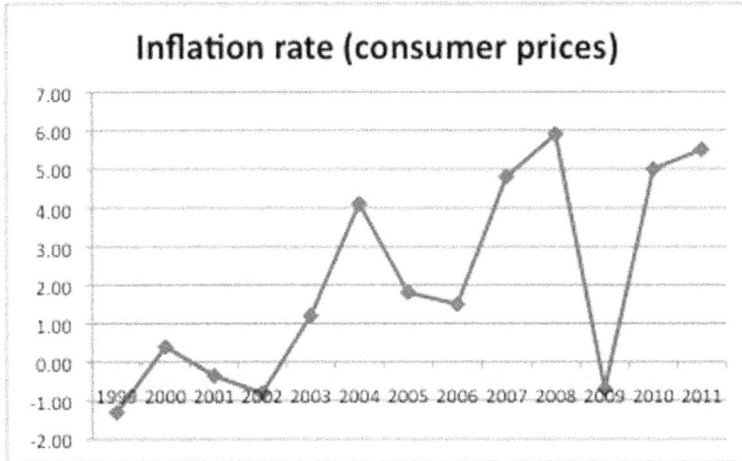

Inflation rate (consumer prices)

Source: CIA World Factbook

It is commonly perceived that the official rate understates the actual rate of inflation, particularly the rate of consumer price increases. Some citizens have become quite vocal in their displeasure at the rising prices of consumer necessities, particularly food. The decentralization of the economy makes it difficult for the central government to act as decisively against inflation as has been the case in the past. The more the economy is shaped by independent private firms and more autonomous SOEs, the more inflationary potential exists in the economy.

However, this is one of costs of creating a system that is more innovative, since the same autonomy that allows for independent price setting also allows for more creative interventions in product and service markets. Nevertheless, inflation does present a wide range of risks, not the least of which is social instability. Add to this that inflation could harm the competitiveness of domestic exporters in an environment where global economic growth has become problematic and other low wage countries, like neighboring Viet Nam, are vying for OEM contracts and it is clear that pressures on Chinese exports and continued growth in the subcontracting sector may be intensifying.

The rate of growth, the absolute magnitude of value added to the Chinese economy, and the unexpectedness of this extraordinary growth are all reasons to be amazed by what has been achieved since the early 1980s. Development specialists are particularly interested in China because the country appears to have found the holy grail for transforming a poor, mostly agricultural nation into a more well-to-do, industrial, and dynamic fast growing nation. China appears to be in the early stages of a series of sweeping technological and sociological leaps that could make its economy the largest in the world in a couple of decades. It even appears possible that China could eventually leapfrog over the United States to become global leader in technological innovation and invention. Thus, this may be the growth story that changes the modal path for other national governments of relatively income poor nations seeking similar economic development successes, even if on a smaller, more modest scale.

But economic growth is always an uneven process, one that generates paradoxes, disequilibria, and even crises along the path to economic development. Economic growth is the result of new value being created in the society, in the form of products and services valued more than the resources consumed in making them. When properly functioning, financial institutions and instruments provide conditions for such value creation in society. Financial institutions provide a financial intermediation function to firms, households, and other economic entities. The resources firms secure with funding provided by financial institutions include technological inputs (in the form of hardware and software) for productive purposes. Financial firms may also provide funds for unproductive consumption (which, nevertheless, enhances aggregate demand and provides the market for the finished goods and services that are the source of firm cash flows and societal value creation).

Well-functioning financial institutions, by deploying technologies for evaluating the net present value of investments and carrying out due diligence prior to lending, improve a society's allocation of resources. The raw materials, technology, and labor services of a wide range of managers and productive laborers, embodied in the capital budgets of business entities, are secured primarily by cash distributions, where the necessary cash is secured either through internal or external sources. In most circumstances, particularly where fractional banking prevails (providing banks the power to create money via demand deposits), financial institutions serve as the primary external source for cash distributions to secure productive investments. In China, state owned banks have traditionally been the primary source of funding for SOEs.

Financial institutions providing this cash nexus for productive activities are linked by contracts to non-financial firms within which value is produced and to households whose savings provide the capital that financial institutions deploy. In China, households traditionally had few options for generating a return on savings and were mostly limited to opening savings accounts at state owned banks. These banks used the deposited funds as financial capital but provided households with relatively small remuneration in the form of deposit interest determined by rates controlled by the state.

Whether it is the relationship between banks (or other financial institutions) and firms or between banks (or other financial institutions) and households, financial contracts create mutual obligations, sometimes in the form of periodic and conditional cash payments. However, financial contracts are often about far more than cash obligations. They can stipulate conditions that influence enterprise planning and choices of technologies deployed.

As with all contracts, financial contracts are mediated, when necessary, by government agencies, including courts and regulators. In China, the banks and the mediators have traditionally been parts of the same governmental bureaucracy.

It is a bit as if one or both teams (as when state owned banks lend to SOEs) in a competitive contest are employed by the same organization as the referees.

The payments embodied in financial contracts are always dependent upon economic transactions whose occurrence is not determined by any *known* probability distribution. The greater the number of parties involved in the determination of outcomes, the more unpredictable the outcomes. Market reforms expand the number of parties determining a wide range of variables, including sales, prices, and input costs. Despite the complexity of the processes that determine firm cash flows, all existing financial decisions (including loans) are based on someone's estimates of future sales, prices, input costs, and other variable values. The potential for actual cash payments to deviate from contractual or expected cash payments is defined as financial risk (often referred to herein as simply risk).

A wide range of activities necessary to the successful functioning of a capitalist economy are made possible by these contractual relationships and any breakdown in the capital market, as embodied by a failure to satisfy the obligations built into financial contracts may potentially cause a rupture in the value creation process, generating a larger economic and social crisis. The potential for capital market problems to spread to the larger society is the result of the manner in which financial contracts serve as a form of social glue securing productive labor, technology, and resources necessary for value creation and bringing together, via cash flow distributions, disparate parties in an alliance that reinforces existing economic and larger social relationships in the society. The network of relationships and related cash flows linking financial institutions to productive enterprises and markets is depicted in Figure 4.1.

Each of the arrows in Figure 4.1 denotes critical connections in the capitalist economy and potential moments of disequilibria or even outright crises (the potential for a break that threatens the functioning of the economy and generates, at a minimum, significant systemic recovery costs if existing social relationships and institutional structures are to be reproduced).

Figure 4.1. Financial Institutions and the Capitalist Economy

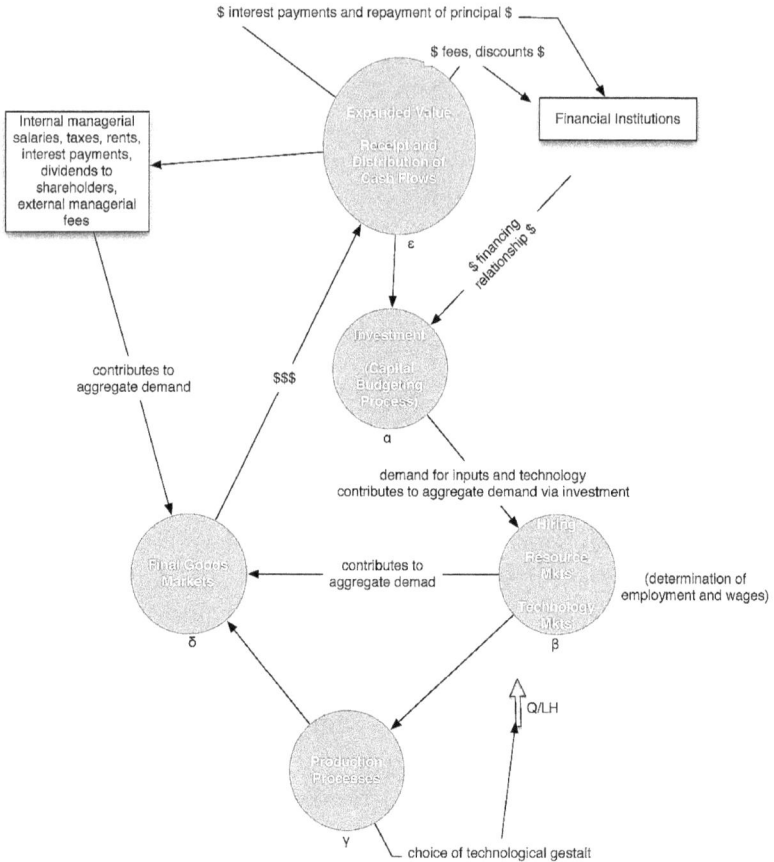

Investment or the capital budgeting process (circle α) generates the corporate demand side of the money capital market and the corporate supply side of the securities markets. China's corporations have become increasingly hungry for capital, creating pressures on the Party-state to reform equity and bond markets domestically and allow SOEs and other domestic firms to access foreign securities markets. In a self-reinforcing process, the growth in capital budgets has reinforced close relationships between SOEs and Party-state officials, at all levels (national, provincial, municipal, town, and village), pushing forward the reform process that has opened up new channels for capital accumulation by SOEs and other firms.

However, as capital budgets expand over time, driving up the demand curve in the capital markets, the ability to secure the necessary capital may become more costly, as demonstrated in Figure 4.2 below:

Figure 4.2: Effect of an Increase in Demand for Capital

CAPITAL MARKETS

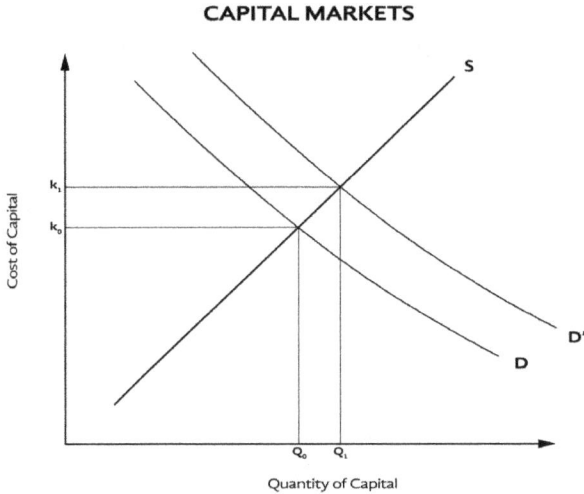

The increase in demand for capital drives up capital costs from k_0 to k_1, as depicted in Figure 4.2. The higher capital costs turn some subset of previously positive net present value investments into negative net present value investments.

Aggregate investments in the economy are, therefore, negatively correlated to capital costs. Wicksell, Keynes, and others have built their macroeconomic analysis upon the capital costs-investments-income nexus: Aggregate investments, which are partly a function of capital costs, act as a key driver of *GDP* growth. These same theorists have also pointed out that *GDP* is also an important determinant of firm sales (higher incomes/GDP indicates growth in the size of markets for output sales). This is the so-called accelerator effect. It is precisely this accelerator effect that is responsible for the strength of China's recent growth, as growth in domestic and foreign direct investment have driven growth in China's GDP and GDP growth in China has stimulated capital budget increases by firms hoping to sell more goods and services in China's booming domestic markets.

The primary counter force has been the continuation of state-centered finance, with state owned banks and other financial institutions still dominating the capital markets. This allows the Chinese government to dampen the impact of rising demand for capital. Another factor that may serve as counter force to rising demand for capital is financial market reforms that have resulted in expanded supply of capital, as depicted in Figure 4.3 below:

Figure 4.3: Simultaneous Increase in the Demand and Supply of Capital

CAPITAL MARKETS

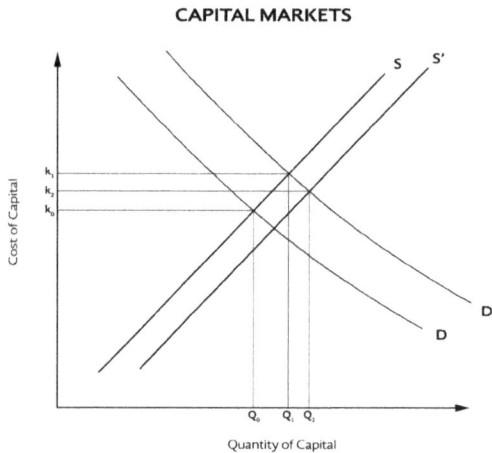

Thus, as demand for capital increases, the increased supply of capital would reduce the impact on capital costs. Instead of a movement from k0 to k1, as in Figure 4.2, it would result in an increase only to k2, which would have a less negative impact on project valuations and therefore result in less negative drag on aggregate investments. This sort of dynamic may be one of the reasons China has not experienced a significant economic decline during the last three plus decades of abnormal GDP growth, despite significant annual increases in the demand for capital. Nevertheless, capital costs have risen to an extent. Bond rates today are much higher than ten years ago. The stock market has signaled higher required returns in the form of equity underperformance.

Financial market reforms have helped to attract new capital to Chinese firms. However, these same reforms have reduced the degree to which the Party-state can exert control over capital markets. In a more deregulated, less state-centered financial context, continual expansion of capital budgets could, in and of itself, eventually generate a decline in future investments.

If Xi Jinping pursues more aggressive financial sector reforms, capital costs may rise faster. Even if he does not do so, future earnings growth disappointments and reevaluation of NPVs, may result in much higher discount rates and much lower expected net cash flows. Excess demand for capital and increased perceived risks could both drive up k in the NPV equation.

There is reason to believe that both excess demand for capital and higher risks are likely to occur with the present rate of investment spending, such that k will increase in the future, whether or not financial reforms deepen. This is because the magnitude of investment growth in China, by domestic and foreign firms, appears to be predicated on optimistic rates of growth in markets and related project cash flows. Indeed, a large fraction of existing project investments may depend upon an *accelerating* rate of growth in GDP. But expectations of accelerating growth in GDP may be bound for disappointment.

On the one hand, the Chinese economy requires ever expanded sources of capital to maintain high rates of GDP growth. On the other hand, the more the Chinese economy is opened to new investment, whether from domestic or foreign sources, the greater the level of competition and the more likely overinvestment will occur, exacerbating this disequilibrium between investment growth and future GDP growth. It may simply not be possible for China to generate the growth in incomes required to meet the sales expectations built into current investment growth rates. The size of the net cash flows in the numerators of many NPV calculations may turn out to be too high and some of these projects may have to be prematurely terminated. Between existing projects with NPVs that are too high and future projects that may be cancelled for the same reason, the impact could mean a sharp drop in future investment (negative growth in investment rather than simply a slowdown in the rate of growth). Thus, an unanticipated lagged negative relationship may exist between current extraordinarily high levels of investment and future levels of investment.[33]

Referring back to Figure 4.1, the movement from α to β results in growth in employment and input purchases but this lagged negative relationship between growth rates and investment would imply an eventual break between α and β constituting a slowdown in employment creation and input purchases. Neoclassical models have always posited some market process by which this break is resolved. However, in the real world of the Chinese economy, the consequences of such a break could be socially destabilizing, resulting in a negative feed-back between α and β as capital budgets shrink in response to negative expectations triggered by social unrest.

Social unrest would raise risk perceptions, driving up k in equation 1, and resulting in cancellation of some previously planned investment projects. Falling investment would then lead to further social unrest. The Party-state could attempt to intervene to slow the fall in investment, including ratcheting up already high levels of infrastructure spending, but the success of such interventions depends upon state revenues, which could be threatened if social unrest appeared to be spiraling out of control, forcing the diversion of state funds to surveillance and security, as well as putting downward pressure on inflows of tax revenues from any related contraction in income taxes.

We will explore other movements in the cycle depicted in Figure 4.1 as we proceed through the text. The key point is to recognize that these movements represent necessary activities and transactions to reproduce and expand the capitalist economy. However, the successful circulations of value within the economy that unites the circles that depict different moments in that economy are not guaranteed. The uncertainty surrounding the reproduction of this economic process is overdetermined by the

---

33 The extent of the lagged relationship, both in terms of how long before the lagged effect kicks in and how powerful the effect is in quantitative terms, depends upon many factors. However, it is clear that the more optimistic the current expectations, the stronger the negative reaction will be in the future, all other things being equal.

particular type and configuration of political, economic, cultural, and environmental processes that are the product of the unique history of the society. This is the challenge faced by the Chinese leadership in their attempt to continue to modernize the society and maintain the pace of rapid economic growth.

The finance-capital budgeting nexus, which has undergone dramatic transformations since the reform process began, is only one aspect of the problem faced by the Chinese government. For much of the history after the 1949 revolution, the central government subsumed the banks within the larger governmental bureaucracy and exerted strict control over cash flows within the financial system and between financial and non-financial entities. The central government largely set the terms of contractual relationships (which were, in many cases, implicit and subject to central government alteration by fiat at any point). Interest rates on deposits and loans were administratively set and kept low. Competition among financial (or non-financial) institutions was non-existent. Households, lacking any alternative means of saving at a positive nominal rate of interest, held most of their savings in the banking system. Capital and currency flows into and out of China were strictly controlled.

A dual currency system existed as one aspect of this control over flows into and out of the country. I experienced this dual currency system first hand when I first visited the country in 1983 and in a later visit in 1985. Dollars were exchanged for foreign exchange certificates with which one could buy products at "friendship" stores, department stores that were far better stocked than those available to ordinary citizens, who, nevertheless, gathered in large numbers to watch the strange foreigners shop. It is noteworthy that these friendship stores were also known for being favored shopping venues for party leaders, so they represented more than just vehicles for separating foreigners from their hard currency. They also came to epitomize the sharp divide between the haves (party leaders) and the have-nots (everyone else). Although the dual currency was eliminated, the underlying moral issue of privileged leaders in a party that professes to serve the working class still plagues the Party-state and is yet another source of potential social unrest, as many citizens find the contradiction between the rhetoric of the party and the fact of inequality difficult to reconcile.

The transformation of the financial regime as part of the overall transition of the Chinese economy, the evolution of financial relationships from the repressed state of the pre-reform era to a more flexible and competitive system, and the abandonment of the dual currency system and rigid capital controls have been carefully guided by the planners in Beijing. In particular, the leadership has only gradually loosened the reins on capital flows, loanable funds, foreign exchange, and the competitive landscape (for example, granting foreign firms limited access to domestic financial markets initially and only expanding that access as part of the negotiated conditions of entering WTO). The government has liberalized interest rates to an extent, giving up some degree of predictability of interest rates and the larger functioning of the financial system (no amount of controls can ever make an economic system entirely predictable) in order to allow for improved resource allocation. The Party-state leadership recognizes that the financial system must be flexible enough to foster greater innovation, efficiency, and value creation in domestic firms, particularly as those firms become increasingly part of a global economic landscape with very different rules of the economic game than existed in the old system.

Nevertheless, the relatively strong role of the Chinese state in directing financial and, to a significant extent, productive sector activities, provides some element of protection from the aforementioned global economic crises and has moderated the effects of the unfolding domestic crisis. However, the reform process has continued in the direction of greater decentralization and growing private control over cash flows, including a broadening and deepening of the role of private financial institutions. This makes the systemic response to shocks at any point in the network of relationships depicted in Figure 4.1 less predictable over time.

Statistical analysis may help policy makers improve their decision making in advance of crises and, perhaps, even provide tools for avoiding crises. For example, there is ample evidence that fiscal and monetary policy instruments can serve to limit the number of crises and shorten the duration of existing crises. However, statistical analysis is not a panacea for two reasons. One of the reasons has already been alluded to – the tendency to overoptimistic expectations during an extended economic boom. During such times, key economic agents who are in a position to approve and implement investment projects may ignore relevant probabilities of negative outcomes. And, secondly, the past is not always prologue. Historical crises may have similar origins and dynamics but the specific events of these crises and their resolutions must be necessarily unique, since they each occur in unique historical time periods.

The overdetermined and, therefore, unique nature of economic (and, in general, social) events is precisely why statistical analysis of past events is always somewhat problematic as a predictor of future events, guaranteeing that stochastic probability distributions (which play the role of certainty equivalents in variants of neoclassical theory) are rarely accurate depictions of social phenomena in future time periods. One way of thinking about stochastic variation is to recognize that real world probability distributions are unstable. The existence of any particular probability distribution of events shaped by human behavior are constantly changing because of being sensitive to all the other social and ecological processes occurring in the society. Since these other social and ecological processes are also in motion, this adds to the uncertainty about underlying probability distributions. Thus, the posited stochastic probability distributions used in decision making must necessarily contain unpredictable errors. This leads to the conclusion that in standard financial decision making models, the potential for unpleasant surprises exists. In other words, there will always be some degree of error (and potentially, the appearance of Nassim Taleb's "black swans"),[34] even when careful statistical analysis is applied.

---

34 Black swans can be viewed as results on the extreme ends of probability distributions or as events not considered at all within standard probability distributions. In this latter view, the very idea that a probability distribution contains 100% of possible events is challenged, calling into question whether a

Unfortunately, the potential for error is likely to be even greater when statistical analysis or the data upon which it depends is poorly constructed or past events are insufficiently considered or completely ignored in valuation, as is the case with hubris or over optimism. After all, just because the past is not necessarily prologue does not mean the past is irrelevant. Nondistributional uncertainty does not completely negate the utility of statistical analysis (or other forms of historically based analyses) in improving decision making. Of course, in reality it is not simply that errors exist in the probability distributions but that in many cases knowable probability distributions for future phenomena in the social sphere simply do not exist.[35]

Human societies are in constant flux and do not simply change in quantitative ways but undergo fundamental systemic transformations in which social relationships and institutions that existed in the past (and may have formed the basis for posited stochastic probability distributions of related quantitative variables) cease to exist and are replaced by new social relationships and institutions with consequences that were often unimaginable in past societies.

As G.L.S. Shackle famously argued, surprise is always possible in a non-determinist world and unanticipated events, such as arise from systemic transformations, may generate conditions that problematize the reproduction of existing social relationships. This is the case when such unanticipated events result in a break in the movement of cash flows and the conditions necessary to satisfy financial contracts fail to materialize. It is not necessary that revolutionary changes in systems occur in order to generate such breaks.

---

statistical model based on past events (or constructed by humans incapable of including all past events that may have significant future corollaries) can ever capture all possible future events relevant to the issue at hand and, if not, whether calculations based on that model might actually result in higher systemic risk by causing market participants to act with more confidence than is justified.

35 A topical example of this is the way climate change may dramatically change all sorts of social and ecological relationships, making correlations that may have seemed predictable during certain historical periods less so in the future.

The activities of financial institutions or the consequences of capital market relationships may generate these unanticipated events, sometimes through malfeasance or misfeasance or simple hubris, and produce breaks in the reciprocal obligations underlying financial contracts. Negative net present value financial decisions, for example, may generate breaks in the value creation process when capital costs are not recovered, e.g. loans are not repaid. These breaks in the value creation process can generate problems for both financial and non-financial institutions, government agencies, and even the society as a whole as the social cash flow nexus unravels. This is one of the sources of risk in the economic system, where by risk we refer specifically to breaks in the value creation and distribution processes and related cash flow nexuses such that reproduction of existing social institutions becomes problematic.

Thus, the development and deepening of increasingly autonomous financial institutions within the overall context of a capitalist economy, as we are witnessing today in the People's Republic of China (PRC) simultaneously provides conditions for economic growth *and* new avenues for economic crises. No probability distribution of variables exists by which to predict future outcomes of the various processes that have been set in motion and are undergoing transformation every day in the PRC, not to mention the impact on these domestic processes of the simultaneous transformation in the global economy, international politics, and the natural environment.

The only certainty is that every action taken today contributes, in some way, to all the relevant variables by which we will measure economic performance tomorrow, including such critical variables for determining cash flows as unit labor costs, cash revenues from operational activities, and cash losses from natural disasters. The reform, restructuring, and establishment of financial institutions and instruments, the expansion of financial relationships both domestically and abroad, and the continued evolution of the Chinese legal and regulatory framework alters the underlying dynamic of China's economy and of the larger global economy, impacting all of the aforementioned variables that determine cash flows received by corporations and other agencies and the cash flow distributions that reproduce and fund changes in the economic and social systems.

The reformers at the top of the Party-state are responding to a range of pressures, including growing demand for finance capital (partly stimulated by the liberalization of financial institutions), but are *primarily* concerned with reproducing conditions for social stability, economic growth, and modernization. The financial sector reforms are linked to economic growth and modernization through the nexus of financial capital, which fuels investment in property, plant, equipment, and research and development of new technologies. To the extent financial capital is supplied by which productive (of net present value) investment may be expanded, growth rates in income and output, expanded networks of cash flow distributions, and modernization of technology may continue at above normal rates.

Alternatively, a failure to further expand and innovate in the financial sector, such that the system fails to generate the supply of finance capital necessary to meet growing capital financing demand, may have negative consequences for these same growth rates, cash flow networks, and modernization, short circuiting the objectives of the Party-state. Thus, it is not a given that growth could be sustained even if capital costs could be contained and markets continue to expand sufficiently to generate the cash flow increases conducive with positive *NPV* calculations. In spite of efficient market theories, in the real world the fact that firms can identify positive *NPV* projects does not guarantee the availability of funding.

Thus, one of the problems faced by newly installed President Xi Jinping and the rest of the next generation of PRC leaders is that economic growth may be reduced by a failure to sufficiently fund positive net present value projects when the necessary financial infrastructure is underdeveloped such that money capital is simply not available for significant numbers of highly valued projects. However, it is not guaranteed that Party-state success at pushing forward with financial market reforms must necessarily have the aforementioned positive effects.

As has been demonstrated in a wide range of capitalist economies and most recently in the United States, it is possible for value destruction to occur when the financial infrastructure is well developed and highly modernized. This is possible because unexpected negative events may arise out of the interactions created by that modern financial infrastructure, precisely because it is more complex and for more prosaic reasons, such as the fact that management of financial institutions are incentivized to take excessive risks (which hardly requires modernization of the financial system as a prerequisite). Financial and non-financial (industrial, extractive, commercial) relationships may be more likely to be disrupted by financial crises when the system is more decentralized, whether or not modern institutional innovations are present. This potential for financial crises is all the more important to economic and social analysts precisely because it is possible that such crises may be triggered by the normal functioning of the capital markets, given relative decentralization and/or "wrong" incentives (incentives that may satisfy the personal objectives of agents operating in the financial system while generating social results that are value destroying (negative externalities)).

Financial crises elevate the risk of larger social crises and social instability that may potentially result in unanticipated and possibly revolutionary changes to the political and/or economic structure of the underlying society. While financial institutions and instruments may serve to reproduce an existing social structure, financial crises may threaten that same social structure. Thus, the promise and the threat of finance always coexist, particularly in those variant forms of capitalist society where productive investment is largely the province of privately controlled enterprises; a variant form of capitalism that many economists and others believe is the likely end result of the current transition in China.

As Chinese policy makers proceed to deepen the web of interconnections among capitalist firms and government agencies within the new capitalist society that has been under construction since the 1980s, the gradual development of capital markets and constituent financial institutions and instruments that serve as solutions to the growing hunger for capital and risk mitigation (or, more likely, risk shifting and sharing) has become increasingly important.

At least in these early days of reform, authorities recognize the effects of these new institutional structures and relationships are less predictable than might be implied by the deterministic relationships in mainstream economic theories, whether neoclassical or Marxian. The interaction of innovations with the matrix of other social and natural processes is overdetermined, therefore unpredictable. Sometimes X is followed by Y and sometimes it is followed by Z. When the X is the formation of financial contracts, Y is positive value added to the society, and Z is value destruction, then it is prudent to proceed to the formation of those contracts with some degree of caution, particularly if Z might be of such a magnitude that it could trigger destabilizing effects within the economy.

The reform minded leadership of the Chinese Party-state have, therefore, recognized the importance of prudential regulation to the proper functioning of financial institutions and to mitigating the potential for large-scale economic and social crises arising out of malfunctioning or improperly (from a social stand point) incentivized financial processes. This has caused the Chinese economic development model to significantly diverge from the neoliberal "Washington Consensus" model that has been promoted by U.S.-based institutions, both corporate and governmental, and is based on a more deterministic set of assumptions about the way economies and societies function.

The uniquely Chinese transition to capitalism combines the following features: 1) the strong state model that was one of the foundational aspects of the so-called socialist bloc and has Chinese roots dating back to the Han Dynasty, and particularly to Emperor Wu; 2) notions of reciprocity and worker discipline shaped within state feudal structures from 1959 until the dismantling of the communes in 1985; 3) Confucian-patriarchal ways of thinking with roots in pre-1949 feudal life, particularly the role of *guanxi* in shaping business relationships; 4) the aforementioned version of modernist Marxism that drives much of current public policies; and 5) a form of post-colonial nationalism (a reaction to the humiliations suffered during the late Qing and the centrifugal forces unleashed by the collapse of imperial rule) that serves as a prime ingredient in identity formation in transitional China.

These features shape the structure and functioning of all of China's current institutions, including financial enterprises. In turn, financial enterprises, via the disciplinary aspects of financial contracts, have served to reinforce these cultural attributes, in many ways acting simultaneously as modernizing force and vehicle for reproducing a conservative status quo. They do this, in part, by restricting access to capital to favored corporations, particularly state-owned enterprises, providing conditions by which favored corporations face relatively lower weighted average cost of capital, and providing ongoing input to senior executives in those corporate structures about the proper way to manage both internal and external contractual relationships, including those with workers.

Thus, the role of financial institutions is not simply economic but is also political and cultural. Most people understand that politics plays a key role in shaping economic conditions in every country. Depending upon the relative strength of state institutions, judicial constraints, existing laws, regulations, and tax policies, political leaders and agencies can make it easier or more difficult for specific firms or business, in general.

In pre-reform China, banks served as political and economic institutions. This legacy continues to influence bank behavior, including the determination of lending policies. To some extent, politics shapes all aspects of the financial system and is a factor in determining the cost of capital for specific corporations. Corporations with political ties to powerful leaders within the Party-state generally face lower cost of capital than firms without such access to political influence.

Cultural theorists have clearly demonstrated that cultural factors also exert significant influence on economic growth and development. In this regard, financial institutions influence the social permeability and diffusion of new ideas, including ideas about the organization of society (the proper structure and functioning of government agencies, markets, household units and kinship groupings, firms, religious institutions, and the proper modes of interactions between them), the social status of occupations, and the morality of particular types of economic relationships. New ideas are the driving force behind innovation. Innovation generates new channels for the creation of value in the society and, in a larger sense, shapes the physical, economic, cultural, and political structures and boundaries of the society. Thus, as the transition to capitalism in China advances, financial institutions will play a critical role in the evolution of new structures and new value creation pathways in the society.

The last quarter century during which the PRC has been transitioning to capitalism has been epitomized by a relentless stream of experimentation and institutional innovations. Reformers have adopted a *strategic options approach* to institutional change. This approach allowed for the innovation of new systems of production in a limited and experimental way, at first, and then these changes were adopted on a large-scale if and only if they proved successful. Success meant that the project in question was value creating (generating a positive net present value stream of additions to social wealth) and/or met other economic and political objectives, often related to long-term value creation. Experimental projects would be assessed by state agencies, often under the direct authority of the State Council. Most of the reform experiments/projects were assessed on the basis of quantitative variables, usually positive net cash flows. These experiments were constructed to allow for the possibility of project termination if it proved value destroying or otherwise ineffective at meeting objectives without ever becoming embedded in the national culture. However, when the Party-state leadership decided to become signatory to the World Trade Organization (WTO), the reform path was altered, with a significant degree of institutional and legal changes locked into place without the flexibility that had come out of the prior strategic options approach to transition.

Nevertheless, WTO was (and, to some extent, still is) seen as a critical component in modernization, particularly since the global agreement provided greater stability for keeping the channels of hard currency cash flows and imported technologies open. Modernization remains arguably the most important goal of the Communist Party of China (CPC), despite the Party-state's official dedication to creating a communist (non-exploitative) society.

This focus on modernization is driven, in part, by the dominant role that nationalism plays in Chinese politics. After all, the CPC or simply "the Party," as well as the Nationalist Party (which fled to Taiwan after losing the civil war in 1949), was influenced in its goals and objectives by a desire to "self-strengthen" (to make China stronger in economic and military terms) and, by doing so, to make possible the recovery of China's lost honor from the humiliation of losing the Opium Wars and being forced subsequently to submit to unequal treaties with European powers and Japan that relegated the Middle Kingdom to the unfamiliar status of a peripheral and largely marginalized nation-state. Technological inferiority was understood by most Chinese intellectuals as the disease at the root of these defeats. Modernization was the cure.

The CPC leadership that coalesced two years after Mao's death charted a path to modernization that began with creating incentives for value creation (generating the requisite wealth to finance modernization) by opening up the economic system to the operation of incentives that had previously been suppressed, such as granting rural producers the right to legally engage in self-employment under the so-called household responsibility system. The alteration in class relationships in rural China quickly expanded to other aspects of the social matrix, replacing relatively meager underground markets with vastly expanded legal markets, altering rural credit relationships and institutions, changing use rights to land and inputs, and transforming political relationships. The success of rural reforms generated a dramatic boost in rural reinvestment rates, which had positive effects on other areas of the Chinese economy, including manufacturing. At the same time that progress was being made in improving economic conditions, the party was also gaining in popularity among the rural population, proving that economic reform could also generate greater social stability and support for the Party-state. Within a relatively short period of time the leadership, having noted the success of the experiment with productive self-employment and relatively free markets, moved to reforms that would promote capitalism, unequal income and wealth distribution ("to get rich is glorious"),[36] and ultimately generate value in the form of accumulated hard currencies that could then be used to purchase advanced technologies from foreign sources. This was in recognition of the fact that developing advanced technologies domestically, even in the face of rising capital investments, would be too slow and problematic, given the dearth of scientific and technical expertise and patents, to serve the modernization goal. China has now accumulated more hard currency (in excess of 3 trillion U.S. dollars) than any country in history. See Figure 5.1.

Figure 5.1. China Foreign Exchange Reserves 1999-2011 (in U.S. $100 million).

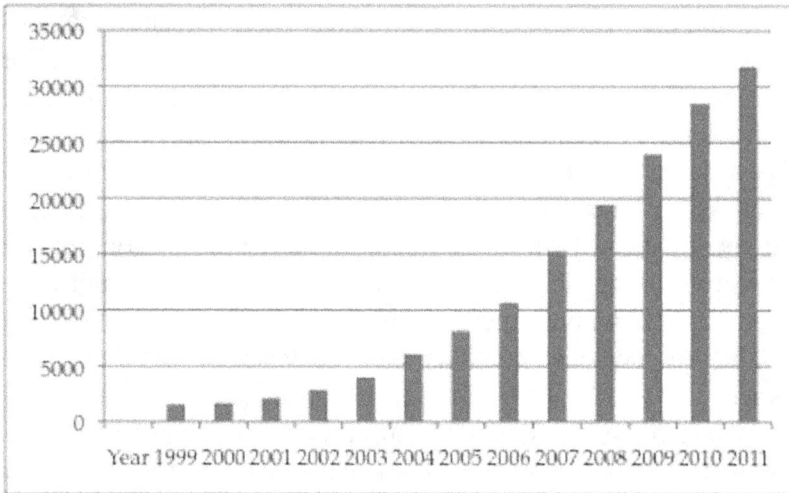

Source: Bank of China, State Administration of Foreign Exchange

---

36 This is supposedly Deng Xiaoping's famous saying that served as a rallying cry for the transition from a system justified on the grounds of egalitarian wealth distribution to one that was justified on the grounds of generating greater material prosperity, even if the fruits of that prosperity accrued unequally to different individuals or households. Deng is supposed to have said this during his 1992 "Southern Excursion" in Guangdong Province. However, there is no record of Deng actually having uttered these words.

This hard currency buys a lot of advanced technology, sometimes by the purchase of the material technics directly, sometimes by the purchase of patents, and sometimes by the purchase of foreign firms that hold patents to desired technology and employ the creative individuals who ultimately invent and innovate these technologies. The accumulation of so much hard currency also gives the Chinese government more degrees of freedom in pursuing its strategic options strategy for economic development. A large horde of funds provides the means for a wider array of economic experiments and exit strategies (since exiting an experiment typically requires some outlay of additional funds).

Thus, although membership in WTO has locked certain structural reforms in place, it has also created new opportunities for using the strategic options approach. Hard currency provides the flexibility to take advantage of uncertainties by allowing for new possibilities for acquiring or enhancing or even abandoning technologies, depending upon the results of experimental projects. The accumulation of hard currency has also provided the means to circumvent some elements of WTO, such as agreements to expand foreign financial firm participation in the Chinese economy, by providing domestic firms with advantages that could not have been possible without these accumulated funds.

The presence of so much hard currency also allows the state to experiment with new forms of infrastructure under circumstances where a hard currency poor country might have only the option of adopting a single approach in large scale without the possibility of experimentation. The Chinese government has been using this approach with advanced transportation technologies, trying such technologies as Maglev trains on an experimental basis with the option of either wide scale adoption or abandonment should the technology be deemed suboptimal. Thus, hard currency reserves reduce systemic risk from adopting new forms of technology, making modernization more attractive. As it is, the Chinese government and associated SOEs have become very experimental in trying out different technologies precisely because of this flexibility accorded by the hard currency accumulation.

The strategic options approach supports the modernization

objective of the Party-state by reducing the risk of adopting new technologies. Once new technologies have proven successful in the experimentation phase, it can be more widely adopted. This has been the case, for instance, with the modernization of China's airports. It started on a small-scale but early successful airport modernizations have since sparked an airport modernization boom, with many new airports having been constructed or under construction. Tourists, foreign business executives seeking subcontractors or other types of business deals, domestic business executives seeking to expand to other cities, and foreign students seeking study abroad opportunities are all likely to be enticed by new airports, as well as other forms of modernized infrastructure. The expansion of airports has, therefore, served to reinforce the positive circular and cumulative causation from reforms, as part of a larger strategy to expand business opportunities and make China's cities more accessible to both domestic and foreign travel and goods transport.

On the one hand, expanded air transport of people and products, both domestically and internationally, forecloses the option of using the land that has been taken for the airport for agriculture or other alternative purposes. This loss of land may pose a problem for food security, given the relative scarcity of arable land. On the other hand, the airports have created new options for local businesses and new opportunities for the accumulation of record amounts of hard currency.

The more hard currency accrues to Chinese firms, the more opportunities for acquiring not only individual assets, including technics in tangible or intangible forms, but also acquiring whole foreign firms, with all their technological and human elements. The market for corporate control that exists in many securities markets represents one of the most efficient institutional settings for adopting a strategic options approach. This is because buying firms in securities markets exhibits strategic options characteristics: firms can be bought *and* sold in securities markets. A corporation that buys and merges another firm into its corporate structure can also sell and divest component elements, including those elements of previously purchased firms deemed

NPV negative or otherwise unattractive. Thus, buying foreign firms has been a particularly attractive proposition for SOEs, as a short cut to modernization and another doorway providing access to foreign markets and intelligence.[37] See Table 5.1 in appendix A.

In order to maintain this important access to foreign markets for corporate control, Chinese authorities recognize that they must gradually open up more Chinese firms to a similar market for corporate control within the PRC as a necessary quid pro quo. Spurred, in part, by WTO agreements, Chinese authorities have been gradually but inexorably expanding this domestic market for corporate control, moving more corporate structures into the set of publicly traded firms and, similarly, expanding the entities that might ultimately take control of such corporations, including foreign corporations, by purchasing controlling interest in securities markets.

Exposure of Chinese firms to these securities markets also provides a mechanism for opening up the restructuring process to outside input from investment bankers and buy side institutions, such as large investment fund companies. The investment bankers have been instrumental in mergers and acquisitions designed, in part, to make the equity of Chinese SOEs more marketable. Similarly, investment bankers have provided advice to SOE executives on cultural means for "selling" the image of their firms to the portfolio investing public. These changes to SOE structures and practices are viewed as another instance of modernization, although it is unclear whether these restructurings and marketing activities actually fit the stricter definition of advanced technologies.

Recently, the China Banking Regulatory Commission (CBRC)

---

37 It is also important to note that the purchase of foreign firms, patents, and other assets helps to diversify the national portfolio of assets held by either the Chinese government directly or held by state owned firms. Presently, the PBOC horde of hard currency assets is heavily weighted in U.S. treasury bonds, exposing the Chinese government to a potentially very large loss when (not if) U.S. treasury bond prices fall, given that there is presently a rather large bond price bubble in the U.S., mostly as a result of a fear driven rush to own treasuries during and after the 2007-2009 financial crisis.

announced a major expansion in this market for corporate control. Banks and most other financial enterprises had been shielded from the possibility of takeover in the market for corporate control, at least in part because authorities view financial functions as pseudo state functions, and because of the key role that financial institutions have played in maintaining central state authority over the allocation of capital and money creation. Money creation, in particular, is viewed as a state responsibility, even if the practical activities that generate expansions or contractions in the money supply, broadly defined, occur mostly within banks and other financial firms, at least some of which are not state owned and most of which act autonomously from central government authorities.

The state has sold significant shares in the state owned banks, although the State Council remains ultimate authority over these banks and controls the appointment process for senior executives. Under the reforms announced by the CBRC, the publicly traded banks and other financial corporations are supposed to become subject to the market for corporate control where private firms would be able to purchase controlling interest in those institutions through a wide range of mechanisms, including private placements of stock and mergers and acquisitions. In mergers and acquisitions activities, both private domestic firms and foreign firms could purchase controlling interest in domestic financial corporations, including banks, in some cases by purchasing shares directly from the central government.

Although this policy has not yet been implemented, the announcement is indication of at least the intention to carry forward a significant expansion in the role of the market in determining control over firms of all types, including banks. This is yet another indication of the extent to which the Party-state is willing to go to secure additional capital and embed a strategic options approach into corporate restructuring and, more generally, capital budgeting decisions. The market for corporate control significantly expands the extent of strategic options and fosters the further transformation of the Chinese economy and society along lines conducive to achieving the broader goals and objectives of the Party-state. This policy comes at a time when powerful transnational banks have been expanding their participation in the Chinese economy, in accord with WTO provisions, and may at some point be interested in acquiring controlling stakes in certain of the big state-owned banks.

In *Chinese Capitalism and the Modernist Vision* (2006), I argued that China's rapid growth was and is, in part, a complex by-product of a contemporary *transition from feudalism to capitalism*. In particular, I argued the transition is from *state* feudalism to *state* capitalism. The adjective "state" is consequential. A central empirical fact of the transition in China (and one that will play a critical role in the analysis embodied in this text) is that a society where the state played a dominant organizing role in the economy is being transformed into a radically different society where the state *continues* to play such a role.

In order to understand the context and future trajectory of Chinese society, it is important to grasp the nature of this transition. In particular, it is critical to recognize that the early period of a transition from feudalism to capitalism, at least to the more decentralized versions of capitalism, typically results in increased returns on invested capital (ROI). This higher ROI, coupled with a boost in reinvestment rates as capitalist enterprises build up the machinery of production and hire wage laborers generates rapid economic growth. One of the reasons for increased ROI is that incentives are put into place for relatively autonomous firms to compete with each other for markets, talent, and resources (rather than territorial jurisdiction, as is typically the case in decentralized variants of feudal economic systems), resulting in more efficient deployment of invested capital. Market competition drives firms to adopt more efficient technologies and practices that lower unit labor costs. Competition also drives firms to seek new markets for outputs in order to generate more cash flow to satisfy capital costs, provide the means to finance expansion and higher managerial compensation, and to acquire more "competition beating" technologies. All of these activities drive firms to make positive NPV capital investments and increase the intensity of existing capital investments. It is, therefore, not so much capitalism that drives capital accumulation, but market competition in the context of capitalism.[38]

Because the feudal system rewarded very different behavior, primarily enterprise management political skills, particularly the ability to satisfy political objectives established higher in the bureaucratic hierarchy and to do so without "rocking the boat," the managers that were more successful in the feudal order were not guaranteed to be so under the new system. The new system rewarded the rapid innovators who made good choices of new technologies and practices such that they lowered unit operating costs below the industry average, providing the basis for reaping above average earnings and using a portion of these earnings as capital for further investments. The equation for above average earnings is as follows:

$$(5) \quad AAE_1 = ((P/UOC_1) - (P/UOC_A)) \times TUS_1,$$

where $UOC_1 < UOC_A$, P represents the competitive unit price for the product, UOC_A represents average unit operating costs for the industry, UOC_1 represents unit operating costs for the advantaged firm, and TUS_1 represents total units sold by the advantaged firm. AAE_1 is the above average gross earnings for the advantaged firm, which provides the basis for the aforementioned advantage.

If such senior executives do not fritter away their advantage through higher than normal bureaucratic expenditures (typically referred to on income statements as sales, general, and administrative expenses or SG&A) or other unproductive costs, then they would be in a position to catapult their firms into a leading position in the new capitalist economy. Thus, while the old system had generated management incentives almost exclusively related to political objectives, the new system shifted the focus heavily towards value creation, even if political objectives might continue to play some role in achieving value creation. Agency

---

38 Monopolistic or oligopolistic forms of capitalism may be less prone to capital accumulation and innovation and more likely to result in economic stagnation.

costs was an issue under both systems.

While bureaucratic politics was a problem that had to be overcome in the transition from feudal to capitalist structures, the feudal era fostered worker discipline – the ability to follow orders within a hierarchical structure – that would prove advantageous in moving to capitalist social relationships. Feudal discipline provides capitalism with relatively docile workers accustomed to being exploited, providing the means for relatively low surveillance costs and, given new incentives, relatively high worker productivity. Docile workers are less likely to protest new capitalist wage labor arrangements than, say, individuals with a long history of self-employment. And they are also more likely to be ready to reshape their work and home lives to fit the demands of a new master. Despite all the rhetoric about socialism, this appears to have been the case with the transition in China.

Nevertheless, capitalism does tend to generate greater unemployment risk than feudal structures, where long-term relationships of bondage to a particular employer is the custom. And workers have not always been happy about this increased unemployment risk, as evidenced by some protests. The more decentralized and deregulated the form of capitalism, the greater the degree of unemployment risk. However, the higher the degree of unemployment risk the weaker the bargaining position of workers, all other things being equal. Thus, higher unemployment risk results in downward pressure on wages, which can be beneficial to firms by both lowering labor costs, a key component of unit operating costs (UOC).

Workers who are at greater risk of unemployment are also likely to put in more effort during work, which is one of the determinants of productivity. Higher productivity means more output per labor hour hired. More output per hour with the wage remaining constant or rising less than the productivity growth rate results in lower UOC. IF UOC falls while output prices remain constant or falls at a slower rate, then gross earnings per unit of output would rise. The rise in gross earnings per unit of output would drive up net cash flows in the numerator of the NPV equation for all related investment projects, whether new or ongoing. Thus, higher unemployment risk under capitalism could directly contribute to improvements in value creation within firms transitioning to capitalism (or created under the new market conditions of capitalism).

The creation of capitalist labor relations are not the only institutional channels through which greater risk is transmitted to the economy. Decentralization of cash flow decision making processes from the bureaucratic structure of state feudalism to relatively autonomous corporate structures may result in more systemic disequilibria. Directors and senior executives at these relatively autonomous firms adopt capital budgets based on their own micro view of relevant markets. They are necessarily operating with only partial knowledge of what other firms are doing, as well as countless changes in market conditions and other factors that ultimately impact whether their investment projects are actually NPV positive. The potential for making mistakes is always present and, during periods of rapid change, can quickly intensify. If mistakes occur within a large enough subset of firms, where investment decisions that were assumed to be NPV positive turn out to be NPV negative, then a systemic crisis can be triggered by downward adjustments in the underlying capital budgets, resulting in a sharp contraction in investment spending.

Overinvestment, which becomes obvious ex post when unexpected downward adjustments are made to investment spending, occurs when capital budgets overestimate either cash flows and/or the risk of investment projects. It is precisely these adjustments to cash flow expectations and/or risk that turn investment projects from NPV positive to NPV negative. Both projections of future cash flows and risk estimates are likely to be overly optimistic after long periods of rapid growth. It appears to be common for senior managers to project current growth rates too far into the future. In this sense, senior managers and the directors who approve their capital budgeting strategies during a long period of rapid economic growth are behaving very much like equity investors in a bull market, becoming increasingly blind to increasing risks.

Thus, in addition to an increase in unemployment risk for

workers, there is an increase in systemic risk of overinvestment during a successful transition to capitalism. Early in such transitions, it is typically easier to reap super profits, as underutilized assets are shifted to more lucrative investment projects. As time goes on, however, this "low hanging fruit" becomes more and more scarce and it becomes increasingly difficult to find projects with relatively high NPVs. However, NPV calculations are based on expectations and those expectations may not adjust quickly enough to avoid the overinvestment problem, which always leads to some form of correction, as surely as a stock investment bubble is always followed by a nasty "correction."

The correction to overinvestment is, if anything, likely to be even nastier. But it will come. And when it does, it will add to the unemployment risk faced by workers, as well as the bankruptcy risk faced by companies. In China, this bankruptcy risk is a relatively new phenomenon and so far wide-scale business failures have been avoided. Perhaps this is precisely why the Hu administration was so reluctant to push for more radical restructuring of the SOE sector, which remains under the protective cloak of the state, at least to an extent. The potential for wide-scale economic failures, the ghost of Joseph Schumpeter, depends on such restructuring. Big SOEs continue to provide a safety cushion for the economy.

This is why speeding up reforms that remove the state's role as protector of many SOEs would likely raise the level of systemic risk, even if it also resulted in more efficient deployment of capital (more positive NPV projects, fewer negative NPV projects). Typically it has only been through the reassertion of central authority in raising aggregate demand and providing the conditions for increased investment spending that overinvestment crises have terminated without resulting in large scale economic disruptions, and sometimes depression conditions. The Chinese government has used its pervasive role in the economy to dampen the impact of recent economic crises and it seems unlikely the Xi Jinping administration would want to weaken the power of the state to carry out such interventions in the future.

The pre-reform "Maoist" system should not, however, be viewed as more conservative than the system that has been developing under the post-Mao reforms. Centralized command planning structures, like the ones dominant within the CMEA nations, were very conservative, inflexible, and slow to innovate the positive results of experimentation, which was generally limited, in any event. Mao did not want to replicate the Stalinist model. That much is clear. Under Mao's leadership, the Party-state was wildly experimental, took excessive risks (the Great Leap Forward is arguably the best example of excessive risk taking) and the results were often catastrophic. Mao wanted to build a new society from the ground up, but the implementation was crude, undemocratic, brutal, and left workers bound to the service of the state, via its central executive authority, the *State Council*.

The State Council served as the first receiver and ultimate distributor of the surplus value embodied in the resources generated and corvee labor performed by commune and urban enterprise workers. The State Council was at the top of the hierarchy, lording over the various other agencies of the state, charged by the communist party with executing its policies, delegating various powers to lower level agencies, and ultimately distributing shares of value to those agencies, firms, and other institutions within the bureaucracy. The State Council was liege lord over both the political and economic world, since most of the economy was incorporated within the state bureaucracy after 1958 and the bureaucracy was a seamless combination of the political and economic. This incorporation of politics and economics within a singular body is a common phenomenon in feudal societies, as is the breakdown of the feudal economy into various fiefdoms (in the Chinese case, this was mostly in the form of communes and urban work units).

It is doubtful that Mao would have consciously sanctioned the establishment of a new state feudalism in China. Mao was not always aware of what was happening in China during the period in which he was paramount leader. He was often told what he wanted to hear and when he toured the country, great effort was made to put on a spectacle for the Chairman. The country he saw, through the narrow window of these displays, was not the country that most people lived their daily lives within. The feudal bureaucratic structure rewarded proper display (the ability to create a proper spectacle of success, whether or not it had any genuine substance) over activities that had a positive impact on actual economic outcomes.

If recreating a feudal structure, albeit one centered on the state, was a failure, then this failure appears to be grounded in the absence of a microeconomic understanding of class, a common malady among orthodox Marxists, as Stephen A. Resnick and Richard D. Wolff, in more diplomatic terms, have pointed out on numerous occasions. Resnick and Wolff view the absence of analysis of microeconomic processes of surplus production and appropriation as a key element in explaining the construction of social structures antithetical to "liberating" working people from oppressive conditions in socialist societies. How can the leaders of such societies construct non-exploitative social structures when they do not have a definition that allows them to see exploitation, especially when they are unable to see exploitation in their own social constructions?

Stalin was blind to the possibility that the state could engage in exploitation, given the assumption that the communist party was simply representing the working people. Mao suffered from the same blindness. He simply did not see the Party-state as capable of exploitation, at least not when he was in command. Perhaps he did recognize the potential for the Party-state to regress to the ills of the older societies or to go down a capitalist road, and therefore to become complicit in exploitation, since this was the excuse behind the Cultural Revolution, but this conceptualization appeared to be based less on a micro analysis of class than on a notion of corruption. Mao simply did not have a conception of feudal class processes that would allow him to recognize that the conditions for feudal exploitation had been met within CPC-ruled China via the social relationships established on the communes and within urban work units.

But if one applies a Resnick-Wolff micro analysis of exploitation, those conditions were met. The Party-state did establish feudalism, defined as an economic system epitomized by a particular type of inflexibility of labor contracts, in particular the inability of feudal direct producers to choose their employer. This feudal system, like past feudal systems, was also one in which state powers and economic powers were integrated into the fabric of economic enterprises.

Thus, in more general theoretical terms, if we accept the notion that there is an economic arrangement which can be defined as feudal, rather than defining feudalism in purely political or cultural terms (with knights in shiny armor as a prerequisite, for example), then there must be variant forms of feudal economic systems, conditioned by alternative political and cultural systems, as is the case with variant forms of capitalism. These variant forms of feudalism may have different internal dynamics, including different tendencies to generate certain types of economic problems, although there may be some problems common to all forms of feudal economic structures and, in the case of transitions to capitalism, these problems may spill over into the capitalist economic structures.

This is certainly the case in China's transition, as we will see. The CPC created a form of state feudalism which had very real impacts on all the structures of Chinese society and on people's behavior. The new society that has been under construction since 1978 is being built with the "bricks" (the social structures and cultural habits) of that state feudal society. It is, therefore, important to recognize the nature of China's transition from feudalism in order to understand how rapid economic growth was generated, why we are witnessing certain types of problems associated with that growth, such as specific types of corrupt behavior from officials, and to be aware of the *change in stability conditions* for underlying economic structures in transition. This has implications for the probabilities of experiencing crisis conditions in future time periods.

To reiterate, in economic terms, feudalism exists when workers are bound to the service of a specific lord (where this concept of lord is associated with exclusive rights to exploit laborers within a particular domain and can refer to either an individual or an institution) and have little or no choice about complying with the implicit or explicit labor contract that specifies the conditions of this servitude, in part because the enterprise (and the lord over that enterprise) possesses state powers. This was the fact of life for Chinese workers. It does not matter that a "communist party" was in power over the state. Feudal economic relations are not negated because a ruling political party calls itself "communist." The direct producers in the communes and urban work units (danwei) were not workers in a capitalist sense, with the freedom to choose their employer or to choose not to work for any employer, nor were these workers slaves because they did not have the status of chattel (property). Instead, these Chinese workers were bound to the service of the state qua lord, where the executive (lordly) authority of the state was vested in the State Council. The State Council appointed a complex array of managers to oversee their power over these workers. And some subset of managers had the responsibility of assigning jobs to citizens initially and when transfers were allowed, which was rarely. The State Council set the administrative rules for all these management activities. Thus, the State Council ultimately served as the highest (liege) lord over state feudal China. All other managers within the state bureaucratic hierarchy served the State Council.

The relative inflexibility of feudal labor in China mirrored similar inflexibility of labor arrangements in other instances of feudalism, past and present. As is usually the case with feudal economic arrangements, these conditions in China served to stabilize labor costs but simultaneously served as an impediment to improving productivity and lowering unit labor costs, key conditions for generating a positive rate of value expansion.

The integration of economic enterprises within the larger feudal bureaucracy created a condition of relative stability. Enterprises were not subject to failure due to negative NPV decisions. Enterprise managers could and did make negative NPV decisions, and not because of miscalculations of future cash flows or underestimations of risk. Managers made such negative NPV decisions consciously because doing so satisfied the desires of higher level lords in the system, particularly the State Council. In an economic system in which political power relationships prevail, as is the case in feudal economic structures, the criteria for approving investment projects is whether or not those projects make higher level officials happier and, by doing so, improve the status of the officials approving the projects. NPV is purely secondary, if considered at all. This feudal decision-making logic does not go away immediately upon transitioning to a capitalist society. It takes time to change the underlying culture of an institution, a society, or individuals. Behavior modification occurs over time as decision makers are punished for following criteria that may have previously been rewarded and rewarded for following new criteria that are consistent with the functioning of the new social norms.

In the state feudal context, enterprises could be shut down only for political reasons, as ultimately determined by the State Council, ministries under the jurisdiction of the State Council, or local administrators vested with this authority by the State Council. Financial flows between enterprises, between state agencies, and between enterprises and state agencies, were politically determined. Under conditions where state run enterprises were treated in a similar manner to other agencies of the state, as components of the larger bureaucratic structure unified by a single budget and national plan, operating at a value deficit was not, in and of itself, a problem, at least not for the management of the unit generating the deficit. Of course, the moral hazard created by incentivizing state-run enterprises and other state agencies to operate at value deficits in pursuit of political objectives had larger social costs, draining the national economy of resources that might have gone for modernization and higher rates of long-run growth in output and income.

Banks were also component elements in the bureaucracy. Loans from state banks to enterprises were often treated as akin to grants. The implicit cost of capital could even be negative under these circumstances, as the state subsidized capital investments. All loans were policy loans: loans designed to meet political policy objectives of the State Council, the Ministry of Finance, or local leaders with sufficient clout to get their objectives pressed upon the banks. Without positive value growth and related capital accumulation in the form of investments in infrastructure, property, plant, and equipment, enterprise management was often placed in a position of being unable to service these policy loans. This was not a problem for enterprise management as long as political ties to higher authorities guaranteed their status and the reproduction of their enterprises. The larger consequence of this feudal arrangement was that China, as a whole, was doomed to fall further and further behind those nations that were generating value growth at a faster pace and reinvesting to expand the productive capacity of their economies.

If feudal structures are such poor vehicles for value creation, then why did some feudal societies last for relatively long periods of time? The answer has to do with the stability of rigid, hierarchical structures where uncertainty in economic relationships and related value flows is significantly reduced. The feudal structure substitutes for the innate instability/disequilibria of decentralized relationships between relatively autonomous, decentralized, and non-state economic agents, whether under self-employment-based economies or decentralized versions of capitalism, with the relative stability imposed by authoritarian/ command control over economic relationships by a limited number of actors.

In China, the State Council was at the apex of a pyramid of authoritarian control. The Party-state hierarchy headed by the State Council commanded a network of tightly controlled domains within which exploitation occurred, creating the value that allowed for the disjuncture between the freedom and livelihoods of party leaders, particularly those living in Zhongnanhai, and the rest of the country. This hierarchy was structured by a singular bureaucratic structure of interrelated cash flows and asymmetric and mostly implicit contracts between state controlled entities, including workers who were denied the right to choose whether or not to enter into an employment relationship with state run enterprises. As sub-units within the feudal hierarchy, managers within these enterprises exercised state powers over the workers, including the right to control worker movement within China (and, in the rare case where it was even possible, outside of China, as well) and to allocate special privileges or bonus goods. The Party-state constituted a network of superordinate and subordinate agencies that ultimately survived on the value extracted from workers in the various rural and urban enterprises subsumed within a single bureaucratic structure.

The extraordinary management powers wielded by enterprise and commune managers and the high cost of maintaining a bureaucratic network of agents subservient to a hierarchy of "lords" would not be surprising to anyone recognizing the feudal nature of this period in China's history. After all, feudal lords are, by definition, politically powerful labor monopsonists and sometimes, though not necessarily, local product monopolists. They typically delegated some of this power to managers, whose primary mission in life often appeared to be the simple reproduction of the power hierarchy within which they and the workers they managed were trapped. In other words, feudal institutions possess relatively strong political and economic power. This power is magnified by the bonded position of workers, the fact that within their domains the workers have no other choice of livelihood than serving the lord.

In order to exert such control, feudal lords must necessarily have the means to restrict the movement of workers. A wide range of instruments and institutions were developed during the state feudal period to restrict worker mobility. One such institutional arrangement was the household registration (houkou) system that labeled a person as agricultural or non-agricultural from birth. While it was highly unlikely that a non-agricultural person would want to register in the countryside, since the system had a clear urban bias and being agricultural meant being assigned to work within a commune, it was the dream of many agricultural persons to someday hold a non-agricultural houkou and be able to live in one of the cities. However, there were very few paths for an agricultural person to escape his or her fate and each of them was difficult to traverse, such as joining the elite People's Liberation Army or passing examinations to study at university. Worker travel was also restricted, partly through use of the houkou system. If a worker wanted to travel to another city (via the state controlled transportation system) then he or she had to get permission from the commune or work unit to which he or she was assigned. This immobility was reinforced by cultivating negative attitudes toward rural people by urban residents, a cultural process I discussed in my 2006 book and compared to the cultural process that social scientists call racism because the conception of the rural person was, fundamentally, as a separate "race" of Chinese citizens. This fragmentation of the Chinese population was just as important as a condition for state feudalism as were notions of loyalty to the dictates of the Party.

The underlying bonded relationship between workers and particular domains, whether communes or work units, has the effect of both restricting freedom (both parties are locked into the relationship unless higher authorities allow some form of divorce and, in the case of the worker, transfer) and reducing certain types of risk. The feudal relationship reduces the risk that the feudal enterprise will have to go into some form of market to seek qualified workers, either initially or subsequent to a worker exiting the firm voluntarily. The firm's managers know the workforce and it is relatively stable over time. The feudal worker also enjoys a relatively low risk of unexpected unemployment under this system.

Furthermore, this arrangement reduces the potential volatility of labor costs for feudal lords, while also reducing income uncertainty for feudal workers (although the actual level of income compensation may leave much to be desired, given the lack of alternatives for workers). However, the same bonded relationship that reduces some risks may raise costs in other ways. Workers with more job security may be inclined to put in less effort, therefore resulting in relatively low levels of productivity. The parcellization of sovereignty at various levels of the bureaucracy provides the means for local managers to abuse their position, creating tensions between workers and the Party-state and undermining the legitimacy of the CPC monopoly on political power.

Furthermore, the same concentration of economic and political power that generates more stability in institutional structures and economic variables also reduces incentives to innovate. Facing less risk than in a more competitive environment, the feudal lord has less pressure to make positive NPV investments, including positive NPV investments in technological research and development that could raise long-run economic growth potential. Feudal investments tend to ignore such factors as product quality and customer service because these are not typically important to meeting political objectives.

Similarly, feudal societies may focus on political investments in infrastructure, property, plant, and equipment with negative NPV results, simply because such investments satisfy political objectives or favor particular political leaders in factional infighting for greater power and status within the Party-state. Such negative NPV investments are wealth destroying, rather than wealth creating, leaving the society worse off, in total income terms, than might be the case if enterprise management (and political leaders) were more focused on making positive NPV investments.

In order to examine the general matrix of the feudal structure of the period from the Great Leap Forward until the reforms dismantled the system from late 1978 through the 1980s, Figure 6.1 provides a basic accounting of a subset of the political, cultural, ecological, and economic processes shaping that system:

Figure 6.1 gives us a better sense of the complexity of the state feudal system in China and also provides us with some indication of the difficulty of making a transition to capitalism from such a system. The problems of that earlier system are not easy to resolve. Certainly one of the most vexing problems of China's state feudal period, at least from the standpoint of the modernist leadership, is the way that system so effectively focused economic decision-making on meeting the political objectives of the State Council, various factions within the CPC, and local leaders, often to the detriment of economic objectives.

Given that the modernists have placed economic objectives, and more specifically value creation that provides funding for modernization, at a higher priority than had previously been the case, it is imperative to overcome the programming of the old system as quickly as possible. The after effects of the feudal investment regime, in the form of inferior legacy investments in manufacturing infrastructure and a large accumulation of non-performing loans in the banking system (and state asset management company) balance sheets, continue to plague the Chinese economy in the contemporary era and may have implications for future economic crises if not properly and sufficiently addressed by public policy.

Figure 6.1: The State Feudal System in Mao-era China: post 1958 until the reform era

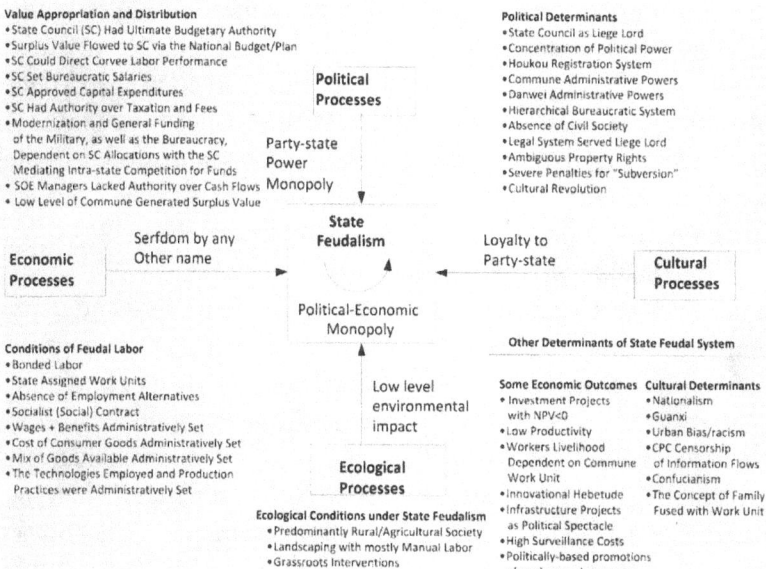

Value Appropriation and Distribution
- State Council (SC) Had Ultimate Budgetary Authority
- Surplus Value Flowed to SC via the National Budget/Plan
- SC Could Direct Corvee Labor Performance
- SC Set Bureaucratic Salaries
- SC Approved Capital Expenditures
- SC Had Authority over Taxation and Fees
- Modernization and General Funding of the Military, as well as the Bureaucracy, Dependent on SC Allocations with the SC Mediating Intra-state Competition for Funds
- SOE Managers Lacked Authority over Cash Flows
- Low Level of Commune Generated Surplus Value

Political Processes

Party-state Power Monopoly

Political Determinants
- State Council as Liege Lord
- Concentration of Political Power
- Houkou Registration System
- Commune Administrative Powers
- Danwei Administrative Powers
- Hierarchical Bureaucratic System
- Absence of Civil Society
- Legal System Served Liege Lord
- Ambiguous Property Rights
- Severe Penalties for "Subversion"
- Cultural Revolution

Serfdom by any Other name

Economic Processes

State Feudalism

Loyalty to Party-state

Cultural Processes

Political-Economic Monopoly

Conditions of Feudal Labor
- Bonded Labor
- State Assigned Work Units
- Absence of Employment Alternatives
- Socialist (Social) Contract
- Wages + Benefits Administratively Set
- Cost of Consumer Goods Administratively Set
- Mix of Goods Available Administratively Set
- The Technologies Employed and Production Practices were Administratively Set

Low level environmental impact

Ecological Processes

Ecological Conditions under State Feudalism
- Predominantly Rural/Agricultural Society
- Landscaping with mostly Manual Labor
- Grassroots Interventions

Other Determinants of State Feudal System

Some Economic Outcomes
- Investment Projects with NPV<0
- Low Productivity
- Workers Livelihood Dependent on Commune Work Unit
- Innovational Hebetude
- Infrastructure Projects as Political Spectacle
- High Surveillance Costs
- Politically-based promotions of workers and managers

Cultural Determinants
- Nationalism
- Guanxi
- Urban Bias/racism
- CPC Censorship of Information Flows
- Confucianism
- The Concept of Family Fused with Work Unit

It is a common characteristic *ab initio* of feudal societies that economic allocation decisions are inordinately shaped by factional alliances and other political determinants. The state feudal era in China was no different. Budgetary decisions of the feudal bureaucracy were constrained by heavy commitments to secure the support of various elements in the social structure, including social welfare spending related to a "socialist" contract between the state and the people that served to legitimate CPC rule and reduce the risk of (feudal) worker unrest. These constraints limited the ability of management in state enterprises and communes to seek improvements to productivity and innovation, as well as their interest in such objectives. Feudal arrangements involved reciprocity. The most fundamental reciprocity (overdetermined by socialist ideology) was the state's provision of secure employment, housing, and other social welfare in exchange for workers doing the labor necessary to generate surplus value for the state. The state (or, more precisely, the State Council) used this surplus value to secure the conditions for reproducing the feudal order, including making distributions to various feudal managerial personnel and the communist party. Thus, Chinese workers enjoyed a high level of social welfare support in exchange for their loyalty to the party and the state it constituted, but they did so at the expense of supporting a vast bureaucratic structure whose focus was on reproducing itself, rather than generating economic growth, which may have resulted in higher overall income for workers' families, and modernization, which could have improved the quality of life for those same workers' families.

It might seem that when the state is the feudal lord and enjoys both monopsony/monopoly economic power and a monopoly over the political power to set and enforce legal rights and obligations, it might not be necessary to provide the level of social welfare observed in Maoist China. Why not just use coercion exclusively? This is the image that comes to mind for most people when they contemplate a feudal society, even if the stereotype was not always or even most of the time correct. One of the reasons China's leadership might not have opted for coercion is that such a tactic is expensive, requiring substantial outlays for supervision and policing. Perhaps a more important reason is that such an approach might have undermined the ideological basis for communist party rule. CPC legitimacy depended, in part, upon reproducing the illusion of a socialist society, where the term "socialist" implied a ruling party committed to serving the best interests of working people.

Given the problem of reduced incentives for innovation under conditions of monopolistic market power, guaranteed sales, and soft budget constraints, the internal dynamics of the feudal economy constrained the growth rate in overall value and made it difficult to raise living standards. Management careers in China were not linked to value creation but, rather, were linked to political patronage relationships. As long as managers satisfied their patrons higher in the bureaucratic structure, they had little to worry about and were more likely to move up the hierarchy. The attitudes cultivated by these patronage relationships may also be a factor in the contemporary problem of corruption among Chinese officials, particularly at the local levels. In many ways, corruption both reflects the breakdown of the old patronage order and a reproduction of economic relationships such as guanxi that was an important cultural and economic aspect of that feudal order.

Where the old feudal relationships had linked the status and economic livelihood of local officials to patrons higher in the state bureaucracy, today local officials often depend more critically upon reciprocal relationships with capitalists who have built factories in the local area with the permission of the officials, who continue to provide "protection" to the enterprise in exchange for an ongoing share of the surplus value generated in that facility. As I pointed out in *Chinese Capitalism and the Modernist Vision*, these local officials also serve more directly as receivers of shares of surplus value in local-government owned enterprises.

Thus, it was not only institutions that were constituted by the feudal structure of pre-reform China, but the cognitive determinants of the behavior of Chinese people. It is this foundation upon which the new capitalist society is being built. However, the old society also created expectations about the social contract between the Party-state and the people. The CPC's legitimacy was and continues to be linked to its ability to improve the lives of ordinary Chinese citizens. This was a major contradiction faced by the CPC leadership under the pre-reform structure. The moral hazard problem that eroded the aggregate value available for distribution as income posed a challenge to the Party-state claim to having superior ability, vis-à-vis their opponents, to create a better society. The CPC-led state needed to provide some sort of dividend to Chinese citizens or risk the possibility of political instability, particularly given the continued presence of an alternative regime, one that claimed legitimacy over all of China, residing on the island of Taiwan. It appeared all the more pressing to give the people something when that alternative regime, calling itself the Republic of China, had the backing of the most powerful nation on the planet.

The primary argument for the CPC's monopolizing political power on the mainland was based on the simple Leninist argument that the vanguard (read communist) party was the critical driver for the inauguration of communism, an economic system that would end all forms of exploitation and foster a better life for workers and their families. The demands of legitimacy and the contest with the Nationalist Party required that the communist party-led state provide fairly extensive social welfare benefits or so the CPC leadership believed until Deng Xiaoping and the other modernist reformers would prove otherwise.

Thus, despite rhetoric from a wide range of CPC leaders in favor of modernization, including both Mao and Zhou Enlai, technological upgrades in agriculture and industry may have been stifled, in part, by this ideologically driven need to finance social welfare spending. However, the bigger problem was the stifling of invention and innovation by the monopolistic structure of the overall economy and the cost of maintaining the local fiefdoms and the national bureaucracy.

In addition, political power monopolization reduced incentives for improving national infrastructure. In particular, it diminished available avenues for pushing innovation in governance systems, including making it very difficult for workers to organize and push for workplace reforms or improved compensation or better environmental conditions (any one of which could have stimulated innovation) with the only mitigating factor being the provision of the aforementioned social welfare in the form of commune and danwei provided goods and services.

More generally, the demands of maintaining a feudal hierarchy may counter any attempts to generate the sort of surplus value growth, distribution, and investment necessary to modernization. To the extent this is the case, despite the fact the leadership of the CPC unconsciously adopted feudal relations of production (certainly Mao articulated a desire to move directly from the old society to communism, without the need of establishing an intervening capitalist economy, much less reverting to a version of feudal economy), this step in the late 1950s, setting up the communes and danwei system, ran counter to their stated objective to modernize Chinese society.

The death of Mao in 1976 created a power vacuum and opened the door for the possibility of changing public policies and reforming institutional structures in pursuit of the until then elusive objective of modernization. By this time, the state feudal system had not only become an obvious economic drag on Chinese development but had also come to be associated with Mao's infamous *Great Proletarian Cultural Revolution,* which had destroyed many lives and careers, created a great deal of animosity towards the party, destabilized the internal political structure of the party, and, more generally, disrupted any semblance of normality in economic or social life. The Mao-era structures, communes and danwei system, were seen by many within the party, particularly at the local levels, as elements in a larger socio-ideological system of which the Cultural Revolution was a symptom.

The push for reforms would unite the various opponents of the Cultural Revolution in a concerted effort to replace that system. Local leaders, who had seen their power diminished as the central government had grown more powerful during the post-1958 period and downright oppressive during the Cultural Revolution period from the mid-1960s to Mao's death, joined with modernist factions within the national leadership, most notably the faction associated with Deng Xiaoping, and leaders within the People's Liberation Army (PLA) who were concerned about losing more military-technological ground to the West, to create a governing coalition that displaced a weak post-Mao caretaker regime, the so-called "whatever faction" of the party, and initiate the reform process (that would eventually lead to a full scale transition to capitalism) in late 1978.

From 1978 to 1985, commune administrators saw their power over workers' lives gradually diminished. In 1985 the transition out of feudalism in rural China was completed as the communes were completely dismantled, shifting control of commune factories to local governments, granting farmers leases to commune lands, and liberating rural workers to the relative freedom of newly created capitalist labor power markets or newly legal spaces for self-employment. A small but significant number of these liberated commune workers became self-employed entrepreneurs, operated their own farms (on the aforementioned leased land) and/or some other type of business for which they had responsibility and the right of controlling their own labor, products and cash flows.

A tripartite market system was developed by which farmers were able to sign onto futures contracts with the state for sale of a portion of their crops at fixed prices, another portion at negotiated prices, and a third portion which they would sell in spot markets at whatever price the market would bear at the time of harvest. The futures contract arrangement between the farmers and the state provided farmers with a degree of income security, lowered their risk, and encouraged innovation. The manner in which the state would become intertwined in the economic process, providing protections that lowered risk, acting as economic agent in other aspects of the process, and ultimately playing the role of business partner would be a model for future reforms.

The triumph of the reformers was measured in increased rural incomes: real per capita income in the countryside rose by an annual average of 6.4% between 1978 and 2003, as compared with a mere 1.7% for 1957-1977 (See Table 6.1 for rural income annual growth); increased quantities and diversity of agricultural goods; and expanded demand and production in rural China for manufactured goods, including consumer durables (such as refrigerators and television sets) produced in the TVEs (Yang 2006).

The boost to rural purchasing power provided much needed growth in domestic demand that was ultimately as beneficial to cash flow growth among urban enterprises as it had been for rural farmers and town-village enterprises. There was widespread agreement that the reforms had been a brilliant strategic success for the Party-state and a powerful configuration of interests formed around the idea of expanding the reforms to other areas of the economy.

Table 6.1: Rural Per Capita Annual Income Growth Rate, by region (in %)

Region	1957-77	1978-2003	1978-84	1985-88	1989-91	1992-96	1997-2003
National	1.7	6.4	14.2	1.9	0.6	7.9	4.2
Coastal		6.8	15.5	2.5	1.7	6.7	4.6
Center		6.1	15.5	-1.2	-0.6	8.8	3.8
West		5.3	13.2	2.5	-0.5	2.8	4.8

Source: China Statistical Yearbook, Yang (2006)

The urban labor system linking all aspects of the workers' life (and their families' lives) to their danwei (work, food, housing, education, health care, and recreation were all provided for in the work unit) was also gradually replaced with capitalist (voluntary) labor power markets. And, again, as in rural areas, a small subset of these workers became self-employed entrepreneurs.

The transition from feudal labor arrangements to capitalism (and some degree of self-employment) dramatically lowered the social welfare obligations of the state, satisfying one of the objectives of the ascendant reformers, who wanted to shift scarce state funds to higher priority uses, such as investments in technological upgrading of manufacturing and extractive industries, building infrastructure, and modernizing the People's Liberation Army (PLA). The greater insecurity of employment in capitalist labor power markets coupled with greater flexibility for management in deploying workers led to a significant rise in productivity, helping to satisfy yet another objective, lowering the unit labor costs of production and raising the surplus value generated in state enterprises. Lower unit labor costs in production were also made possible by the rapid expansion in competitive labor power markets comprised of millions of workers unfamiliar with job insecurity and lacking any effective representation. Lower unit labor costs and greater flexibility to respond to product demand contributed to higher profit rates and free cash flow in state enterprises.

The dismantlement of the communes left county, township, and village governments as primary manifestation of state power in rural China and resulted in the creation of newly autonomous enterprises from the industrial structures of the old commune system. The ownership of these township-village enterprises (TVEs) was shifted from the central government to local governments, who sometimes contracted day-to-day control to private parties (with the local government receiving various rents, dividends, and taxes). This decentralization was an important price that reformers in the central government had to pay to build a governing pro-reform/pro-capitalist coalition within the CPC.

During the early stages of the transition to capitalism, the TVEs were among the fastest growing enterprises in China. Discussions of the TVEs tend to ignore the fact that they were former commune enterprises and, after the dismantlement, remained state-run enterprises. Most of these enterprises were transferred to contracted management, yet remained state-owned enterprises. Thus, even during the early period of the reforms, the rapid economic growth was mostly generated by state enterprises.

Management in traditionally state-run urban enterprises were granted greater autonomy and eventually most of these enterprises were converted to corporate structures where partial state ownership, rather than full state ownership and direct control within the bureaucratic structure of the state, came to prevail. Senior managers exercising greater autonomy and incentivized to improve production efficiency by harder budget constraints and a career path based more on generating free cash flow and less on allegiances to factions within the ruling party, the state, and/or local government circles made use of the flexible labor systems to improve productivity. More competitive market conditions compelled managers to seek ways to improve product quality and customer/client service. Managerial control over product mix resulted in a wider range of product offerings than the old one size fits all approach under the feudal regime.

The reform of agriculture and industry set the path for China's transition to capitalism. It was an experiment that yielded almost immediate positive results, buoying the confidence of the reformers. Transformation of the financial system has been underway just as long, but has proceeded with a great degree of caution.

The first stage of these financial reforms involved the granting of central bank powers to the People's Bank of China (PBOC). The PBOC was moved out from the shadows of the Ministry of Finance (MOF), where it had been subsumed, to take on this role of central bank extraordinaire, at times acting as principal agent of the State Council and at other times as its own power center in restructuring financial relationships and institutions and catalyzing the innovation of new financial instruments. Nevertheless, despite the separation of state enterprises from the bureaucracy, thanks to the power of the PBOC over the state banks and the PBOC's close connection to the State Council, MOF, and broader CPC leadership, senior management in state owned enterprises continued to have privileged access to loans.

Thus, while management changes altered a wide range of practices within state enterprises, including capital budgeting and financing decisions, the tendency of bank loans to follow politically directed paths persisted: government officials retained influence over the distribution of loans to firms, without respect to the relative quality of projects financed. Consequently, state commercial banks, particularly the big four (Bank of China, Industrial and Commercial Bank of China, Agricultural Bank of China, and China Construction Bank), accumulated more non-performing loans (NPLs) on their balance sheets than might have been the case if economic criteria had prevailed over political criteria.

These NPLs have posed a problem for the Chinese leadership, reducing financial liquidity within the banking system and leaving banks more fragile. The central government has attempted to plug these holes in the financial system by creating asset management companies (AMC) to take some of the bad assets off the balance sheets of the banks. However, the continued close ties between the bureaucracy, the PBOC, the state banks, and various types of state enterprises have continued to result in the issuance of bad loans.

Thus, the legacy of feudal-era allegiances (sometimes subsumed within the general concept of *guanxi*) continues to influence financial decisions, including bank loans, bank purchases of government issued bonds at higher than market prices (repressing interest rates), and a web of patronage relationships throughout the corporate structure with concomitant creation of cash flow obligations unrelated to shareholder value maximization. These complex relationships and the obligations they create overdetermine management decisions in a wide range of corporate structures, financial and non-financial, generating decisions that are sometimes net cash flow negative, heightening the risk of cash flow disturbances reverberating throughout the financial structure, creating more avenues for the transmission of risk from one institution to another and raising the potential for financial crises.

CHAPTER 7
THE OPEN DOOR POLICY

The complex risk structure of an economy in transition from state feudalism to state capitalism, as well as new found riches generated by that transition, would be further heightened by arguably the most audacious objective of the reformers: the successful opening up of the Chinese economy to exports, imports, and foreign direct investment. Perhaps more than any other development outside of the military realm, this opening up demonstrated the CPC's readiness to turn the page on the humiliation of the Qing at the hands of the British and other Western powers, which had shattered the long held self-confidence of the "Middle Kingdom" and fostered suspicion of any interaction with foreign business enterprises. Nationalism was one of the strongest shared ideologies of the CPC membership on the mainland and the Nationalist Party membership on Taiwan, so this was no minor matter. The CPC reformers had to recognize the risk of being identified with a return of foreign enterprises to Chinese soil, as well as the risks from opening up cash flow channels to markets outside of China, markets outside of the control of the State Council and the rest of officialdom.

Nevertheless, the "open door" policy was aggressively pursued.[39] It was precisely this open door policy that allowed the newly autonomous senior managers in state enterprises, and eventually managers in privately owned Chinese corporations, to gain access to new forms of technology, both material technics, like new types of machinery, telecommunications and computer systems, and more immaterial, digital manifestations of technological knowledge, such as various types of software or process

---

39   Ironically, the term "open door policy" was originally associated with a policy pushed by certain Western powers, particularly the United States, to keep China open to business interests from all the Western nations, as opposed to India or other colonial domains where British (or other "mother" countries) could monopolize the fruits of an unequal international relationship.

algorithms, such as new methodologies for organizing and managing productive activities within manufacturing, services, extractive industries, financial institutions, etc.

In the transition to capitalism, Chinese firms did not always adopt "best practices," but the pressure of competition from foreign firms, as well as the desire to sell into foreign markets, has dramatically improved a wide array of business practices and made most firms more open to new innovations. Integration of the Chinese economy with a highly competitive global capitalist system has increased the relative complexity of economic processes, creating linkages between economic activities in wide ranging geopolitical environments, making it that much more difficult for the central planners, whose role has diminished but not terminated, to guide the Chinese economy through the hazards of potential economic crises. As with any system, social or mechanical, increased complexity creates more possibilities for malfunctioning, breaks, or disequilibria to occur.

The relatively new capitalist labor power markets in China have also become linked to global markets via expanded production networks centered on foreign transnational firms, creating yet another layer of complexity. These foreign firms are allowed to exploit Chinese labor, both directly (via foreign direct investment) and indirectly (through subcontracting relationships). The addition of millions of new workers (currently estimated at over 800 million) onto global capitalist labor power markets could not help but have a disinflationary effect upon international wages. In other words, global wage growth would likely have been greater if not for the addition of millions of Chinese workers onto international labor power markets.

But perhaps even more important than the direct disinflationary impact of an enlarged supply of laborers in international labor power markets, particularly low skilled manufacturing labor power markets, is an indirect disinflationary effect via the impact on the consumer goods manufacturing sector. Chinese workers produce a large quantum of consumer goods, as is easily evident by inspecting consumer goods at any department store or so-called big box store, such as WalMart. Chinese workers have, both through relatively low wages and relatively high levels of productivity, driven down the cost of a wide array of consumer goods, particularly many of the products in the consumption bundle of ordinary working families in countries like the United States. This downward drift of the overall cost of the consumption bundle of these working families puts downward pressure on the wages of those workers. It becomes possible to satisfy their family budgets with lower wages than might have been the case if it were not for these relatively cheap goods coming out of Chinese manufacturing plants.

This disinflationary effect and more generalized productivity increases have helped to generate higher rates of profit/free cash flow growth for a wide range of firms, raising the market value of and attracting more capital to those firms. The higher profitability resulting from improvements in technology and capitalist labor power market conditions combine with export earnings in hard currencies to provide senior management in Chinese firms, as well as the state agencies involved in building infrastructure, with the wherewithal to broaden and deepen investments in more advanced technologies, most of which are imported or licensed from firms based in more advanced capitalist countries (particularly, firms based in countries that are members of the Organization of Economic Cooperation and Development or OECD).

The impact of these changes to productive technologies and techniques, and the aforementioned increases in worker productivity directly from the transition to capitalist labor power markets, was a large boost to surplus value/free cash flow available to senior management for investment and other distributive purposes. Chinese workers are also benefiting from these conditions, as the demand for workers in the capitalist sector, particularly among exporters, intensifies and wage growth in China races ahead of wage growth in other parts of the world, as depicted in Figure 7.1.

Thus, while China's integration into global production networks may have a disinflationary impact on global labor power markets, it is also driving wage and income growth in the domestic Chinese economy. The ability for Chinese workers to benefit from the reforms in this way is important for legitimizing the Party-state, the overall reform process, and the rise of capitalist relationships in the economy.

Fig. 7.1. Annual Average Global Real Wage Growth, 2006-11

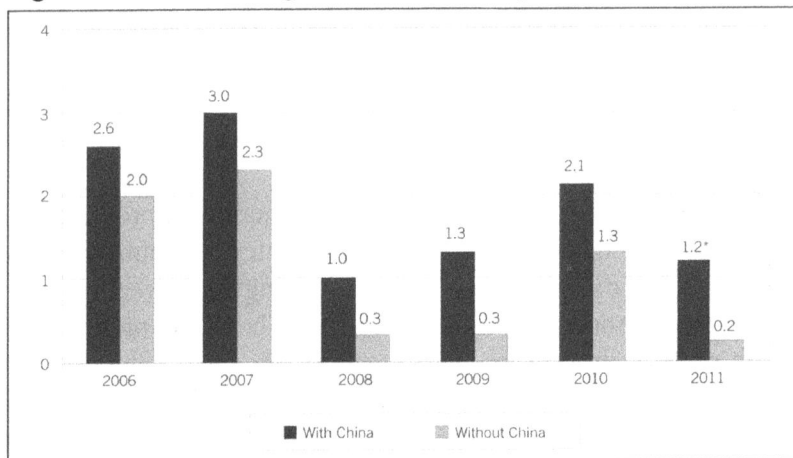

Source: International Labor Organization database

In the long-term, if this gap between wage growth in China and the rest of the world persists, then the competitive advantage of subcontracting low wage labor to China will erode. The Party-state recognizes this and is encouraging Chinese firms, particularly SOEs, to ratchet up investment projects that move Chinese manufacturing up the so-called technological ladder, producing with more advanced production technologies and generating more advanced outputs, which requires more highly trained labor. At the same time, efforts to train more highly skilled labor have been a priority for some time now. All of these activities require increased investments by both firms and the state. The following Table 7.1 shows that China is already becoming a major player in high technology manufacturing, occupying first place in high-tech manufacturing as of 2007, although a sizeable amount of these exports originate in original equipment manufacturing (OEM) contracts with transnational corporations headquartered in OECD nations, who retain patents on the embedded engineering in the products.

China is also the leader in low-tech exports, some of which are produced for foreign transnational firms. As is now widely known, a large percentage of the low-tech products sold in WalMart stores are manufactured in China and serve as key drivers for WalMart's cash flows and earnings.

Table 7.1. Leading Exporters of high-tech, medium-tech, and low-tech products, 2007

High-Tech				Medium-Tech			Low-Tech		
Year 2007 Ranking	Country	Export (USD mil)	Share (%)	Country	Export (USD mil)	Share (%)	Country	Export (USD mil)	Share (%)
1	China	409663	15	Germany	610066	15	China	384474	19
2	United States	311634	12	United States	411103	10	Germany	170388	9
3	Germany	236260	9	Japan	394413	10	Italy	133030	7
4	Hong Kong, China	154828	6	China	280454	7	United States	114216	6
5	Japan	149454	6	Italy	214286	5	Hong Kong, China	95087	5
6	Singapore	141202	5	France	203565	5	France	79670	4
7	S. Korea	123216	5	United Kingdom	150728	4	Belgium	66352	3
8	France	110759	4	S. Korea	149775	4	United Kingdom	60152	3
9	Chinese Taipei	105678	4	Belgium	142932	4	Japan	59785	3
10	Netherlands	103404	4	Canada	122496	3	Netherlands	45874	2

Source: adapted from Woo (2012)

The combination of growing household incomes, household and local government debt, and related expansion in domestic markets for a wide range of goods and services, particularly the exploding growth in the automotive sector, coupled with the decentralization of cash flow control to individual enterprises has driven the rapid expansion in capital budgets. The rapid growth in overall investment, including infrastructure investments by a state that had been freed from a large array of social welfare obligations, improved efficiency from modernization, and political stability has driven double-digit GDP growth in China and served as catalyst for growth throughout East Asia. The benefits to American and European transnational corporations spread the effects even further, contributing significantly to growth in the OECD universe, as well.

China has become the nexus for an international division of labor and a decentered process of manufacturing generating dramatic disinflationary and profit enhancing effects around the world. The rapid growth in Chinese exports to the OECD economies is shown in Table 7.2.

Table 7.2: China's Top Export Destinations, 2010 ($billion)

Rank	Country/ region	Volume	% change over 2009
1	United States	283.3	28.3
2	Hong Kong	218.3	31.3
3	Japan	121.1	23.7
4	South Korea	68.8	28.1
5	Germany	68.0	36.3
6	The Netherlands	49.7	35.5
7	India	40.9	38.0
8	United Kingdom	38.8	24.0
9	Singapore	32.3	7.6
10	Italy	31.1	53.8

Source: uschina.org

The trade surplus with the United States is particularly large and the source of some degree of political tensions between the two nations, as U.S. politicians have taken to charging China's leaders with not playing fair in the export-import game. The charge that China is a currency manipulator, which just means China's leaders use monetary policy instruments to help maintain the dollar-yuan exchange rate within certain parameters, is the most frequent complaint, although the same complaint could certainly be made about monetary policy in other countries, including the United States. The China trade surplus with the United States is depicted in Figure 7.2 below:

Fig. 7.2: China Trade Surplus with U.S., (US$ million nominal basis)

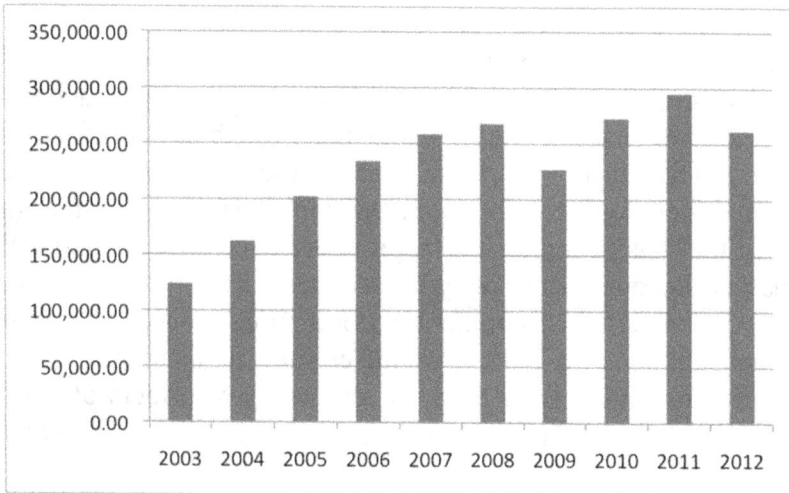

Source: U.S. Census Bureau

China's overall trade surplus, mostly with the U.S., has allowed the PBOC to accumulate massive foreign exchange reserves in excess of three trillion US dollars. The accumulation of foreign exchange reserves by the PBOC has been largely invested in bonds issued by the United States and selected other OECD economies, which has served to moderate interest rates globally, raising the net present value of investment projects around the world and resulting in more overall global investment spending than might otherwise have prevailed. Thus, these policies by the Chinese government, particularly the PBOC, have served to stimulate economic growth in the rest of the world, as well as in the domestic Chinese economy.

Indeed, the impact of Chinese capital flowing into the U.S. bond market can be said to have both added to the housing bubble, by supporting efforts by the Alan Greenspan-led Federal Reserve to keep U.S. interest rates low, and helped in the recovery, by helping the Ben Bernanke-led Federal Reserve drive U.S. rates down to historically low levels in an attempt to stave off a deflationary spiral.

The aforementioned disinflationary effects of Chinese workers joining the global capitalist labor power markets have, generally, fostered price stability and healthy productivity growth. This combination of factors has helped to generate higher net cash flows and profits for a wide range of corporations, particularly transnationals who have been able to take advantage of expanded global production networks and WTO-liberalized product and service markets. The relatively high real growth rates in earnings and cash flow that comes, in part, out of these conditions contribute to macroeconomic stability in the capitalist world system (a term that has become more appropriate over time, as national markets become increasingly interconnected and interdependent and transnational corporations become more embedded in and dependent upon the economies and cultures of a widening array of nations), mitigating many of the negative effects of poor macroeconomic conditions in the European Community and elsewhere.

To reiterate, China's impact on the global economy has been a major stabilizing force in several economic crises, including the 1997-1998 Asian economic crisis that resulted in dramatic restructurings throughout East Asia and generated significant shock waves in economies around the globe, while Chinese authorities managed to continue to produce growth, albeit at a slower pace. Without China's stabilizing effects, in part a product of the state centered nature of the Chinese economy, it is likely this crisis would have been far worse and the contagion effects devastating. The same can be said of the current economic crisis triggered by the U.S. financial sector and now reverberating in the financial markets of Euroland (where macroeconomic weaknesses were magnified by the sharp increase in risk aversion in global sovereign and corporate bond markets).

Nevertheless, the same dynamic that drives down unit labor costs and pushes up profit and cash flow growth rates may also be a key driver in generating greater income inequality. One measure of the degree to which worker compensation lags behind the growth in overall social wealth, which ultimately comes from the higher productivity of that same workforce, is the adjusted labor share of national income, which calculates the percentage of national income going to wage laborers as a whole. Figure 7.3 shows the steep drop in the share of Chinese national income accruing to laborers since 1992.

Figure 7.3. Unadjusted labor income share in China, 1992-2008

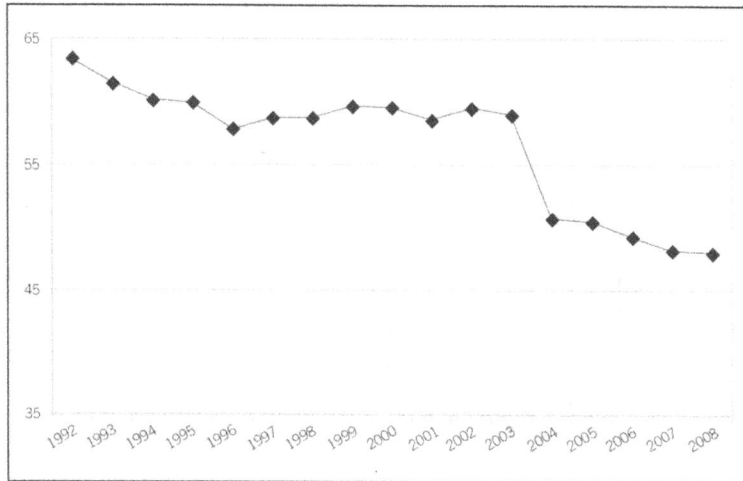

Source: ILO calculations based on data from the China Statistical Yearbooks.

Rising income inequality is a countervailing factor to those generating greater macroeconomic stability, engendering destabilizing effects by producing unstable disequilibria conditions in global markets. Around the world, working people and their families make up the market for countless consumer goods. If these families see their real incomes rising too slowly (or not rising at all), then it becomes problematic to purchase the automobiles, refrigerators, televisions, houses, and other consumer durables that drive the mass consumption side of economic growth. After all, overproduction is simply another way of saying underconsumption. Underconsumption can be addressed by an increase in household borrowing, which is becoming an increasingly important aspect of life in contemporary China.

The culture of consumer credit is still relatively new but spreading fast among new "middle class" consumers. The banking system recognizes the profit potential in consumer credit and it is likely that new innovations will continue to proliferate and credit expansion to serve a leading role in pushing consumption spending rates higher. This process poses its own risks, however. Spontaneous household debt accumulation is not easy to control and can generate systemic risks related to income instability and poor forward planning. These household debt issues are not the only problems in an economic environment of transition and financial transformation. China is also experiencing a significant expansion in local government debt financing that is almost as anarchic as the rise in consumer credit and certainly poses similar issues of potential disequilibria. While the central government has consistently and significantly increased its revenue year over year, this is not always the case with local governments where political factions sometimes push through project financing in cases where future cash inflows to pay for the projects are less than certain. As we shall see later in the text, these increasingly disequilibrating forces make it more difficult to predict the risks (in the form of stochastic evaluations of future cash flows) associated with a wide array of investments, both real and portfolio, and is particularly problematic for valuing derivative instruments or crafting hedging strategies. Increased uncertainty about future cash flows alters expectations of senior management and directors such that investment becomes more volatile (reflected in cautious sentiment about future demand for capital goods) and greater volatility in investments (including a higher probability of disinvestments) is, in and of itself, a risk factor for economic crises.

Thus, the entry of China into the world capitalist system has simultaneously had positive effects on the mean value of a troika of key financial variables: revenue, earnings, and cash flow growth rates. This expansion of the capitalist world system has simultaneously generated more uncertainty in a wide range of factors, by introducing Chinese firms, workers, and consumers into an already complex global economic game, as well as by forging new connections between these Chinese agents and those outside of China, in both advanced capitalist nations and in so-called peripheral nations which are often critical resources suppliers. This uncertainty is reflected in higher rates of variability of market outcomes, on both the demand and supply sides. While higher mean values of income statement variables have the effect of raising the valuation of investments, higher variability, by increasing discount rates/risk, has the opposite effect. This tug of war between positive income statement effects and higher variability/risk to cash flows can be seen in the booming Chinese automobile market where foreign automobile companies have been particularly successful at gaining market share and increasing value, while the lion's share of the risk in the auto market appears to have been absorbed by Chinese domestic automobile manufacturers who have found it difficult to gain market share and yet are subject to the full effects of foreign competition on sales and pricing. In other words, the value of Chinese automobile manufacturers has suffered, even as the Chinese automobile market has been booming.

The development of Chinese capitalism has clearly generated transformative effects on capitalism worldwide and any economic disturbance in China is likely to reverberate throughout the global economic landscape. The aforementioned higher mean rates of revenue, earnings, and cash flow growth generated by the expansion in China's entry into the capitalist world system has been a factor driving the stock market valuations of transnational firms higher and generating "Goldilocks" conditions of growth with low inflation in many OECD countries.

This story has unfolded in a climate of increasingly frequent economic crises, including some very major ones, such as the Mexican economic crisis of 1994-1995, the Asian economic crisis of 1997-1998, the American economic crisis of 2007-2008, and the current economic crisis in the European Union (E.U.), which may be viewed as an extension of the earlier American economic crisis. This latter crisis threatens to rip apart the E.U. and cripple global capitalism, particularly given the way the American economic crisis has undermined confidence in the financial systems of numerous OECD countries. China's effect on global capitalism, providing necessary liquidity, keeping downward pressure on global wages and upward pressure on resource commodity prices, and opening up a relatively new and rapidly growing market for a wide range of products and services is all the more important as a stabilizing force under current crisis conditions.

Given these conditions, it would be potentially devastating for China to enter into an economic crisis before the aftereffects of the American and E.U. economic crises have completely calmed and sufficient healing of the economic and financial infrastructure has taken place. The overdetermined effects of combining a Chinese economic crisis to the aftereffects of the American-Euro crisis are disquieting, at the least. It is, therefore, imperative that we gain a better understanding of both the cracks in China's economic foundation carried over from the feudal-era and those generated more recently by the process of extraordinarily rapid, yet uneven, economic growth, as well as the potential strengths of China's state-centered version of capitalism (coupled with the rhetoric of "socialism" coming out of the ruling party) that may or may not protect this new economic superpower from following down the road of economic crisis that has plagued every other capitalist nation.

The global impacts of the transition of the Chinese economy to capitalism from a form of state feudalism are, quite clearly complex, and very much a work in progress. These impacts, both domestically and globally, are further complicated by the Party-state's continued dominant role in managing the Chinese economy and as the largest equity owner in the society. This persistent dominant role for the state and the CPC in Chinese society continues to be exercised by the same State Council that dominated the feudal bureaucracy and the wide array of lesser state agencies and functionaries operating with the force of law and under the direction of a set of less than fully transparent economic *and* political goals and objectives set by the CPC. As China has become increasingly important to global economic growth and stability, the CPC has gained in global political clout, particularly as a factor in macroeconomic stability. This was epitomized recently by the parade of European dignitaries and banking executives to Beijing seeking financial help for a European Union straining against disintegration.

However, as China has become more important in global economics and politics, the lack of transparency about the decision algorithms and confusion regarding the underlying theoretical framework(s) employed by the CPC leadership, the State Council, the People's Bank of China (PBOC), and other state bodies has become all the more stressful for policy makers and economic analysts outside of China.

One of the sources of confusion is Marxian theory, which continues to rest at the ideological core of the CPC. Most Western policy makers and analysts operate on the basis of a caricature of Marxian theory, at best, devoid of any deeper understanding of either Marxian theory, in general, or the particular Marxian theories that have been at the center of debates within the CPC. Therefore, they completely miss the influence of these debates upon policy making in China. Most economists simply ignore the question altogether, being ill equipped to do otherwise. In part, the response of political leaders has been to try to jawbone the Chinese authorities into becoming more like the OECD countries in policy terms, particularly as regards exchange rate and trade policies.

However, the leadership in China continues to be influenced by Marxian analysis (with its focus on the fundamental importance of rates of exploitation, class processes, forces of production/ technologies, and transition) and has remained keenly focused on the dynamic and unstable process of transitioning to capitalism. Unlike their counterparts in the West, these policy makers start with the Marxian assumption of disequilibrium and continuous change as normal characteristics of an economy. Thus, their ongoing concern with managing stability and economic growth in the context of such forces results in much greater caution with adjusting key macroeconomic variables, such as exchange rates, than Western counterparts would like to see.

The increasingly serious economic crises in the West have only reinforced this reliance upon Marxian theory and its ontological focus on instability in combination with sophisticated analysis of empirical data on past performance of the domestic Chinese economy, foreign economies, particularly those that have gone through past transitions to capitalism, and the global economy (a methodology consistent with the Marxian concept of historical materialism). Thus, the *state capitalist* nature of new China is unlikely to change anytime soon.

The leadership in China views markets as instruments for achieving certain ends, but also recognizes markets as a source of instability, requiring varying degrees of external control from governmental agencies. It is critical to recognize that Chinese authorities will, therefore, continue to retain an unusual degree of control over a wide range of macroeconomic variables, such as exchange rates, vis-à-vis other more decentralized forms of capitalism, relaxing these controls if and only if social stability conditions are believed to allow for such relaxation *and* it is deemed in the long-term interest of China (and/or the CPC). Any relaxation of such controls, such as the recent decision to widen the trading band for the yuan should be recognized as contingent, rather than permanent. On the other hand, the emergent autonomous capitalist culture of households, corporations, and other private businesses creates stresses on these systems of control, pushing the social dynamic in less predictable directions as various institutions are organized to meet internal objectives.

CHAPTER 8
SOEs AND STATE BANKS: ENGINES OF ECONOMIC GROWTH?

In this chapter we explore some of the key institutional structures and networks shaping rapid economic growth in transitional China. These institutional structures and networks have contributed to a context of relative macroeconomic stability and political inertia: state agencies with regulatory powers that are unusually strong for a contemporary capitalist economy and a powerful central bank with powers held over from the central planning era coordinate financial institutions, including the big four state-owned commercial banks, and large scale industrial corporate structures within which the lion's share of productive investment in the society is planned and implemented. These institutions are linked in a cash flow nexus that has simultaneously produced conditions for the existence and reproduction of relatively high annual GDP growth rates, relatively low rates of inflation, and low variability in rates of employment over time.

The financial players within this institutional network include that subset of state agencies and functionaries with authority over (and within) banks, particularly the State Council (which, as has already been indicated, has a much broader mandate than financial flows but is, nevertheless, the most important single recipient and source of such flows), the People's Bank of China (PBOC, China's central bank, formerly part of the Ministry of Finance), the aforementioned state-owned commercial banks, and other state controlled and/or owned financial institutions, such as the China Investment Corporation (CIC), a sovereign wealth fund providing a vehicle through which the Chinese government accumulates and diversifies its holdings of foreign non-governmental assets, and the nonfinancial firms connected to the financial system.

The State Council plays a critical role in shaping and implementing broad fiscal policies, coordinating regulatory policies, and exercising ownership rights over that subset of SOEs where the central (as opposed to provincial or local) government holds the shares. The PBOC and commercial banks play a key role in determining macroeconomic flows through the supply of loanable funds and, more generally, the manipulation of the money supply and the provision of foreign exchange. These macroeconomic flows and the provision of loanable funds are key determinants in capital budgeting and financing decisions and related project valuation of both SOEs and private enterprises.

The list of key economic players would also include industrial, commercial, extractive, and conglomerated corporate structures that were formerly component elements in the state bureaucracy and within which the state currently retains significant (and often controlling) ownership of equity shares (these non-financial *central government owned* firms and conglomerates are referred to herein as SOEs, distinguishing them from their former status within the bureaucratic structure as *state-run enterprises* or SREs), but whose senior management and directors enjoy a significant degree of decision making autonomy.

It would be naïve to assume that the presence of state ownership, particularly controlling interest, has no impact upon capital budgeting, financing, and other corporate policy and executive decisions. A large subset of state firms is owned, in part or whole, by local governments, municipalities, and provinces (and sometimes the role of government officials goes beyond ownership rights to serving in a capacity akin to directors, including controlling the appropriation and distribution of free cash flows generated by such enterprises). These firms are often pushed to invest in projects that serve the narrow interests of local political leaders. I've chosen not to focus on that subset of SOEs in this text (although I devote a full chapter to such enterprises in *Chinese Capitalism and the Modernist Vision*), which does not imply that these firms are insignificant, quite the contrary. In any event, for those firms associated with the central government and not designated as *backbone industries*, the State Council has made it clear that it is up to management and directors to develop strategic plans for positive net cash flow generation and growth or face the risk of bankruptcy.

SOEs are connected to both the State Council via the state

ownership relationship and to state-owned banks via the capital provision/debt and distribution nexus. State-owned banks provide loans that constitute a significant share of the capital driving the construction of plants and other facilities, purchases of technology, and the mobilization of labor forces. The flow of funds into the SOEs has been growing continuously over the reform period and the availability of hard currency has also been on an upward trajectory, allowing state conglomerates to modernize facilities and improve productivity, often in spite of having poor track records for profitability and loan repayment.

However, in a manner reminiscent of U.S. automobile companies and other large-scale firms in the West who have received bail-outs and other forms of state support, the SOEs have been able to take advantage of the state's largesse to generate more positive cash flow over time. Today most of the SOEs are relatively healthy and are, as a group, a powerful element in the economy. Indeed, SOEs have become a major contributor to overall economic growth, through both direct and indirect effects, and are in the vanguard of expanding Chinese capital to foreign markets. Receipt of state support and subsidies does come at a price, however. The State Council has retained considerable influence over SOEs and the state banks. Thus, the *State Council-state finance-SOE nexus* is one of the driving forces behind the rapid economic growth in and the relative macroeconomic stability of the Chinese economy.

Operating margins, net profits, and free cash flow of SOEs have been steadily improving since the late 1990s when a large percentage of SOEs were bleeding red ink and in danger of insolvency. During the early period of the reforms, particularly after the industrial reforms of the 1980s led to increased transparency, exposing the alarming level of non-performing loans in the system, many economists and others expressed concern about whether SOEs could survive in a more competitive environment. However, exposure of the problems in the SOE sector may have actually strengthened those factions within the CPC committed to reform and since 1998 SOEs have gone through restructuring, including divestitures and spin-offs, designed to improve operating efficiency and to protect "good assets" by placing them into corporate structures unburdened by some of the negative obligations associated with "bad assets." Managers in SOEs were incentivized to implement new production techniques and improve product offerings and they used their network of relationships with government officials to secure subsidies, market advantages, and access to better technologies. The result has been double digit rates of profitability growth and concomitant growth in productive investments in a large fraction of SOEs, enough so to produce double digit growth rates for the SOE sector overall.

High rates of productive investment by SOEs, particularly in new production technologies, has driven increases in productivity, while the continuous expansion in the competitive labor power market has moderated wage increases, leading to lower unit labor costs and growth in profitability. Firms have recently experienced a tightening in labor power markets, putting upward pressure on the wage bill (wages plus the cost of benefits), reflecting labor power market disequilibria in some areas of the country, particularly those where original equipment manufacturing and other forms of subcontracting firms are concentrated, making at least one element in the rapid economic growth story more problematic. We will return to this point as we explore the potential for a more explicit and dangerous future economic crisis.

Repression of interest rates by the PBOC, state subsidies for energy consumption, and other favorable conditions made possible by a cooperative State Council have supported SOEs becoming more competitive, even as more foreign firms enter the Chinese economy and the non-foreign private sector expands rapidly. Rising exports by SOEs, foreign-invested firms, and non-foreign private firms have resulted in an accumulation of foreign exchange reserves in the PBOC greater than any country has ever experienced. By the first quarter of 2012, the PBOC had accumulated $US 3.3 trillion in foreign exchange reserves. China is second only to the U.S. Federal Reserve as purchaser of U.S. treasury bonds with 73% of the non-Fed purchases of such bonds. Historically low interest rates in the U.S. could not be sustainable without the continued support of PBOC purchases. Thus, the PBOC supports dovish/expansionary Fed policy of repressing U.S. interest rates. This provides support for the U.S. real estate market and related derivatives. The aggressiveness of this strategy is testament to the continued impact of the derivative driven crisis that started in 2007 and the difficulty of working through all the bad contracts that come out of that crisis.

The PBOC accumulation of foreign exchange reserves and the cooperative attitude of state banks make it relatively easy for domestic Chinese firms, particularly the SOEs, to acquire advanced technologies outside of China and use these technologies to further drive productivity growth and changes to product mix, moving up the so-called technological ladder from less to more sophisticated products.

The presence of these reserves makes it possible for domestic Chinese firms to secure the conditions to continue to generate abnormal growth in revenues and to distribute a portion of those revenues to the Chinese state, which is also involved in a modernization drive. The State Council will collect 28% more revenue in 2013 than in 2012, providing substantial cash flow for new and ongoing projects. The accumulating reserves, abnormal growth, and visible modernization of the Chinese economy all contribute to more positive expectations on the part of a wide range of investors. George Soros would see this as an example of positive reflexivity. Similarly, Sigmund Freud and the French philosopher Louis Althusser would describe it as an example of the positive effects of overdetermination.[40]

---

40 This social scientific use of the term overdetermination, as the assumption that all phenomena have some type of significance in shaping all other types of phenomena, is not to be confused with the related mathematical concept of overdetermination. One should also note that the interpretation of overdetermination used herein is not the same as that posited by some other social analysts who argue that it means the same as multiple causation. The concept of "multiple causation" is a different ontological position than overdetermination. To say that a vector of causes, X, shapes a phenomena, Y, is not the same as saying that all phenomena (X being inclusive of everything) shapes every Y. In the latter formulation, there are no insignificant phenomena.

And the Nobel Prize winning Swedish economist Gunnar Myrdal would have described it as an example of virtuous *circular and cumulative causation.*

The state plays a critical part in this transformation, investing in infrastructure, intelligence, and in projects that raise the profile of China in the global community, such as the Beijing Olympics and the Shanghai World's Fair. These public investments complement SOE investments in new technologies and modern production facilities, as well as private investments in state of the art malls, apartment complexes, and other facilities.

Foreign firms recognize positive net present value opportunities in the new China and increase their investment there. Portfolio investors scoop up Chinese IPOs. Chinese consumers spend more on both domestically produced and imported goods, further expanding domestic markets and making China appear all the more attractive to foreign firms. The formerly ailing SOEs benefit with increased cash flows and profits, validating the reformers strategy and strengthening their factional position within the CPC.

From 1998 to 2008, profit growth in the SOE sector was over 35%. Over this time, expectations of high rates of cash flow and profit growth became the norm for a wide range of actors, including Chinese officials, SOE managers, portfolio investors inside and outside of China, and foreign multinational managers and directors. Similarly abnormally high growth rates were recorded in the non-state sector. Expectations for high rates of future growth have provided an incentive to further increase investment spending, even to accelerate the rate of growth of investments (turning the second derivative of a constantly changing investment function positive), stimulating even greater growth in GDP, adding to the aforementioned virtuous circular and cumulative causation.

This virtuous causation cycle has a dark side, however. It has been accompanied by a concomitant growth in income inequality, as the distribution of generated cash flows has hardly been egalitarian. Because the disequilibrating effects of this growing income inequality are being masked by the state-centered model of extraordinarily high rates of investment and state directed infrastructure spending (a sort of "permanent" stimulus program), a sort of complacency has set in among policy makers in China, foreign managers and academic observers abroad, and most problematically, by bankers, both domestic and foreign. However, one should note from past experience with economic booms and busts in other economies that high expectations are easily shattered, once the anticipated high rates of growth are broken (a virtual inevitability, if history is any guide), potentially with very negative consequences on private investment spending, as well as other economic variables. When investors expect the stars, the moon may not be enough.

Thus, the expectations that have engendered the virtuous cycle represent a double-edged sword, since any disappointment in those expectations could trigger a significant reassessment that results in sharp downward adjustments to valuations of assets and a down shift in the levels of investment and consequently aggregate demand and income. And the rising level of income inequality could, in and of itself, precipitate an economic crisis, as has happened in other capitalist economies. Income inequality skews markets for final products and services toward more imported luxury goods, relatively high priced housing, and other amenities whose overall impact on domestic employment and income are relatively limited, while simultaneously shifting spending away from affordable housing and domestically produced consumption goods for the masses which tends to have a bigger multiplier effect on the economy. Boomtime spending also tends to stimulate excessive borrowing, adding to a commodity fetishism driven change in consumption behavior, even stimulating frenetic waves of consumption in relatively frivolous goods and services that do little to foster a more productive society. Boomtime spending is also prone to driving up inflation rates, further stimulating excess spending and debt.

China's long-term economic boom has frequently generated periods with inflation rates exceeding the upper bound of the leadership's target rates. Inflation has tended to hit ordinary working people particularly hard, lowering real incomes, even as the nouveau riche see their asset-based wealth and related incomes rising sharply along with national GDP. A healthy rate of growth in mass consumption which is exhibited by rapidly expanding retail establishments catering to China's "middle classes," as well as coastal working classes, and real income for ordinary working households may be critical to macroeconomic stability, creating employment growth and conditions conducive to improvements in overall quality of life.

On the other hand, continually shifting income to the wealthier segments of the population, coupled with overinvestment, may result in disequilibrium conditions in the manufacturing sector, and a subset of service sectors and real estate markets. Whether or not adjustments to expectations and aggregate demand can be made quickly and effectively enough to stave off crisis conditions remains to be seen.

In the world of neoclassical economics, adjustments to stable equilibria are depicted as instantaneous, but in the real world no such adjustments are forthcoming, instantaneous or otherwise. Once an economy has been shaped by particular disequilibria, that economy and the path it follows are forever changed from what might have been if underlying macroeconomic variables had been different (such as satisfying the elusive equilibrium conditions set forth in neoclassical parables).

As George Soros has frequently pointed out, in the real world of markets equilibria do not exist and there is no obvious movement towards such equilibria, nor are the solution sets for interactions of economic processes convex or bounded or even appropriately modeled in Euclidean space. Instead, economic transactions must, necessarily, occur outside of equilibria (under conditions of irreversibility), in disequilibrium conditions that are the norm, and with solutions that are not always predictable or even within the set of anticipated possible solutions. This is precisely what we mean by uncertainty (as opposed to the certainty equivalents of mathematically more sophisticated versions of neoclassical theory). Sometimes disequilibria can spin out of control, absent appropriate (or lucky) intervention from governments, whose structure and political powers allow for counter-cyclical (or counter crisis) behavior without threatening its continued existence (which often cannot be said of corporate structures, especially commercial banking or other financial firms). Perhaps this is where China has an advantage by being governed by a strong state with unusual economic and political authority, providing even greater powers to act counter-crisis.

It is important to recognize that the entire state bureaucracy remains supportive of SOEs and particular ministers within the State Council may continue to act as patrons for specific SOEs. Rural enterprises, the descendants of the TVEs, are likely to have similar relationships with local government officials. In other words, despite the transition to capitalism, feudal-era patronage continues to play a role in the cost of and access to resources and regulatory treatment of SOEs and some locally-based corporations, protecting them from some of the effects of market competition. As indicated earlier, state run firms (which would evolve into SOEs in the cities and TVEs in the countryside) had a privileged position within the old feudal structure and were able to draw on state funds to finance both productive investments and unproductive social welfare expenditures. The latter has been largely jettisoned, reducing the cash flow obligations of the SOEs (and the TVEs have been completely transformed such that social welfare obligations are completely non-existent in that sphere and some of these firms have been completely privatized). However, some of the feudal-era advantages have been retained, at least to an extent.

For example, a subset of SOEs (in so-called backbone industries) operate with monopolistic or oligopolistic market power, allowing them to extract a rent in their sales of commodities or other critical inputs. These firms have higher revenues than would be the case under more competitive conditions. The higher revenues provide firm directors and management with the means to secure conditions for maintaining their monopolistic or oligopolistic position, as well as the means to support their patrons in the political struggles for ranking within the CPC, reinforcing existing power imbalances.

During the 1990s, as the SOEs struggled to survive the shock of facing more competitive conditions and gradually hardening budget constraints, the State Council played a key role in keeping many of these conglomerates afloat through various subsidies, discriminatory enforcement of regulations, and sharing of market and technology-related intelligence. To the extent the State Council continues to shield many of these firms from the full effects of competition, it provides the basis for higher rates of profitability than might otherwise be the case. These hidden subsidies allow SOEs to finance a higher level of investments than would be possible with lower, more competitive, profit rates. The subsequent higher level of investment demand adds to GDP and, perhaps, reduces the variability in the rate of growth of GDP over time (although it could be argued that the favored position for SOEs negatively impacts private investment, by lowering the net present value of private investments in SOE dominated markets, and perhaps this effect lowers the long-run growth rate for GDP). In any event, the CPC may ultimately benefit from the sustained investment of the SOE sector through a legitimacy effect: higher GDP and macroeconomic stability (less variability in income and employment) legitimizes CPC rule.

The higher levels of and lower volatility in cash flows and profit rates of SOEs, as a result of close ties to public officials and consequent privileged access to resources and biased regulatory treatment, influence risk assessments and, therefore, valuations of SOEs by portfolio investors and bankers. Since a large number of SOEs are now publicly traded, some portion of the market valuation may be the result of this privileged treatment, resulting in SOEs raising higher sums from the initial public offering, although it is also possible that the portfolio investors who participate in early stage fund raising may be savvy enough to discount this condition because it may be perceived as only temporary such that SOE management and directors are unable to valorize their special relationships to the government or even suffer a reduction in initial funding as a result of such relationships (if funders perceive state influence in the SOEs as a potential risk factor).

The issues outlined above are related to the level of investment of SOEs and former TVEs, as well as private corporations, and the impact of that investment upon economic growth rates and the potential for steep downward adjustments in growth rates, i.e. economic crises. In his *General Theory of Employment, Interest, and Money*, Keynes recognized investment as the most volatile component of GDP and the component most likely to precipitate business cycle recessions or expansions as changes in expectations stimulate changes in investment spending which then alters aggregate demand.

Aggregate demand changes alter the context within which firms generate revenues, such that these changes can then exacerbate the drift downward (or upward) in a self-reinforcing process. The more volatile the changes in investment spending, the greater the multiplier effect and the more likely the drift downward (or upward) will become a massive movement in aggregate demand, income, and employment. As we've already seen, the Chinese government has successfully reduced the overall volatility of investment, smoothing the business cycle, partly by retaining a large degree of direct or indirect influence over capital budgeting within the SOEs and the state banking sector. The high degree of state influence over the banking sector extends and enhances the state's channels of influence over all aspects of the economy, including private investment, consumer spending and housing growth rates.

To the extent Keynes was correct that investment is the most volatile component of aggregate demand (primarily due to the underlying volatility of directors and senior managers' expectations about future cash flows), and regression analysis of lagged correlations of the components of GDP supports this conclusion, then stability of investment growth should translate as greater macroeconomic stability. Indeed, in the *General Theory*, Keynes argued for government to play a much larger role in the determination of investment than is common in contemporary capitalist societies in order to achieve such stability.

In this sense, the Chinese government can, arguably, be viewed as following a Keynesian macroeconomic management strategy more closely than leaders of most capitalist nations.

The question remains to be answered, however, whether this strategy can continue to generate growth with relatively low levels of demand/income volatility and, by doing so, avert the financial/economic crises that are so common to less state-centered, more deregulated forms of capitalism.

The variant form of capitalism that has been developed in the PRC is in many ways sharply divergent from the form that has prevailed in the OECD universe of nations, although similar to variants that served as vehicles for rapid economic growth in the so-called East Asian tigers during the latter half of the twentieth century. Democracy, a judiciary relatively autonomous from either the executive or legislative branches of government but governed by the rule of law, a free press, and independent labor unions are present in only a subset of capitalist societies, providing the basis for what is sometimes described as liberal democratic variants of capitalism, and has only relatively recently come to prevail among the so-called Asian tigers. Nevertheless, most of the more successful capitalist societies have adopted this variant and it would be logical to assume that there are advantages to adopting these institutions which contribute to such successes.

For some time it was believed that long-term, sustainable economic growth required the development and deepening of democratic political institutions. Democracy provides citizens with a means to shape the economic rules of the game, to constrain the behavior of corporations and other superorganic institutions, and to compel the state to adopt progressive and countercyclical policies to soften the impact of natural and human-made disasters, including economic recessions and/or to take actions that mitigate some of the negative consequences of such disasters, including the negative consequences of economic downturns or larger scale economic crises.

Thus, democratic societies have built in mechanisms for addressing rising unemployment, income inequality, pollution and other externalities, and other side effects of capitalism, moderating the extent to which economic downturns or other negative outcomes are tolerated without government intervention. It is through these democratic processes that the state and larger social structure is legitimized and opposition, including attempts to overthrow the existing order, is minimized.

Relative judicial autonomy governed by the rule of law is a key factor in establishing predictable rules of the economic game in capitalist societies. Because capitalist relationships depend upon contracts, this condition may significantly improve the functioning of a capitalist economy, lowering transaction and administrative costs, reducing risk, and encouraging expanded investment. However, it is questionable whether any capitalist nation can claim to have a judiciary strictly governed by the rule of law, meaning that judges must apply laws in accordance with legal intent and without prejudice. In fact, the greater is judicial autonomy, the more judges may be tempted to exercise power with prejudice, either as a result of corrupt practices or simply because of personal predilections. To the extent this is the case, the judicial system may undermine the predictability of contract and, more generally, law enforcement, raising the cost of transactions and slowing market growth.

A free press is critical to an effective democracy by the establishment of independent media institutions that deploy reporters who closely examine and then report on the workings of other institutions, particularly the activities of government and large-scale corporations, providing citizens with information necessary to make good political judgments. A free press is critical to providing transparency in both corporate and governmental conduct. It is a critical component in the working of financial markets by providing transparency about the components necessary for valuation, particularly in the case of corporate valuation. Liquid markets in corporate equity require reliable information on the behavior of corporate officers, as well as on the reported financial information provided by such officers. More transparency typically means more trustworthiness in corporate information flows which, in turn, should dramatically improve the depth and liquidity of capital markets. Stronger capital markets increase productive investment, which provides for more rapid economic growth.

On the other hand, the absence of a free press (or the capture of a previously free press by institutions with a vested interest in suppressing information or producing disinformation) reduces the effectiveness of democratic institutions, even where they are allowed to function, increasing the risk that serious problems will go unaddressed or made worse by policies promoted by captured media outlets. If portfolio investors come to lose trust in the media's information on corporate officers and data, capital markets may shrink and become less liquid, lowering productive investment and slowing growth.

Independent labor unions provide wage laborers with a means to negotiate labor contracts on a less unequal basis with large corporations and to influence the laws that shape the rules of the economic game, including rules related to contract enforcement, worker health and safety, job security, and social security after retirement. However, even in those societies with a long tradition of trade unionism, the globalization of capitalism has undermined the power of unions in negotiation with large corporate structures.

The "race to the bottom" has entailed, in part, a drive to reduce the bargaining options in negotiations between organized labor and large-scale, transnational corporations. The consequences of this are only gradually becoming more apparent, such as growing income inequality and more frequent financial crises, the undermining of social security for retired workers, and falling real wages. The weakening of labor unions has removed an incentive for some workers' to vote in favor of unionization or to oppose efforts to develop non-union factories or other work places. Thus, the absence of independent labor unions in China may be less of a distinguishing characteristic for Chinese capitalism over time.

Democracy is also highly circumscribed in China and a free press is largely non-existent. The judiciary is a component element in the Party-state bureaucracy, with judges' salaries and continued employment determined within that structure and influenced directly and unambiguously by the degree to which judicial decisions satisfy the objectives of Party-state officials. Judges who anger Party-state officials are not likely to last long on the bench. Thus, China is missing key components of the liberal democratic variant of capitalism.

On the other hand, corporate structures have become just as pervasive in China as in other capitalist societies, including the liberal democratic variant, providing an institutional structure for the mobilization of vast armies of voluntary wage laborers creating value on a mass scale. These workers face very powerful employers but have little or no representation, since the only legal form of union is the All-China Federation of Trade Unions (ACFTU), an institution that is closely allied to the CPC and that has a reputation of serving corporate management more than the workers. If the absence of democracy, free press, and/ or independent labor unions increases political risks, then investments in China would need to be properly discounted to take this into consideration. The absence of mechanisms for venting social discontent and providing incentives for implementing public policies to mitigate such discontent increases social tensions in a society, raising the possibility of discontent exploding into anti-governmental and sometimes revolutionary actions, disrupting the production and realization of value.

One solution would be for the CPC to expand sufficiently so as to encompass a membership roughly reflective of the general population. However, despite the CPC being the largest political party in the world, with over 80 million members, the composition of the party is not meant to be representative of the general population. Indeed, any attempt to do so would be at odds with the very ideology upon which the party functions. In Leninist logic, the ruling communist party is meant to be a "vanguard" party comprised of the most politically astute and pure, i.e. committed to "socialism," elements in the population, as judged by the party membership itself, and holding a monopoly on political power. The party is then vested with the power to bring about a transition to socialism and then from socialism to communism (although the latter two stages are very poorly defined and there is never any time limit for the transitions). Former President Hu Jintao muddied the ideological waters a bit when he added the objective of "creating an harmonious society" to the mix, but the old typology remains a core belief for most party members and particularly party intellectuals. If you join the party, you are supposed to pledge allegiance to this teleological purpose of the party. In other words, the party is a closed community, even if a very large one, with a mission statement that is simultaneously rigid and ambiguous, and operates without any significant incentive to implement policies that reflect the will of the people when that will runs counter to the party's own objectives, particularly the maintenance of the party's control over the state.

Another possible strategy for addressing potential or actual dissent is to suppress such actions by the deployment of governmental or governmentally sanctioned violence. Suppression requires the diversion of government resources to unproductive policing, intelligence gathering, infiltration, and imprisonment. It often includes forms of torture and humiliation. Violent suppression of dissent is costly, as the apartheid regime in South Africa was to discover. Indeed, these costs may have played a critical role in the collapse of the Soviet Union and its network of CMEA nations, where various communist parties held a monopoly on state power and used suppression as a tool. A repressed society is typically less innovative in a wide variety of ways, costing the society in the global competition for technological advance. Workers living in such a society are typically less productive and more prone to sabotage, resulting in upward pressure on unit labor costs which may be only partly mitigated by lower wages.

Democracy, a free press, a relatively autonomous judiciary constrained by the rule of law, and independent labor unions are far more cost effective, efficient, and effective means of addressing social ills, encouraging worker cooperation and loyalty within and outside of the workplace, providing an advantage to societies with such institutional structures.

Will it be possible for China's authorities to achieve their goal of continued modernization and eventual advance to a technological-economic level comparable to the United States (if not beyond) with a social system that is devoid of these elements? And, perhaps more to the question that we find of particular interest in this text; does the absence of such institutional structures raise the long-term risk and/or severity of economic crises, despite Keynesian macroeconomic management and the generally higher level of governmental involvement in the economy? At present, a fragile consensus appears to have formed in favor of the authoritarian political model coupled with an underlying state capitalist economy as the best route to rapid economic growth and development. The idealized Western political-economic model, as best represented by Milton Friedman's vision, has lost some of its luster for poor countries.

The risk of political dissent in the absence of these mitigating institutional structures has appeared to be of minimal significance in the Chinese case and it does appear that, in spite of the large number of demonstrations in the Chinese countryside, the vast majority of the population remain relatively docile either in disagreement with the CPC political monopoly or indifferent about it and a significant minority supports it. Thus, the linkage between economic reforms and political democratization appears weak. This lack of correlation is in sharp contrast to the prior consensus that democratization must necessarily follow upon the transition to a capitalist economy. In other words, there was an expectation that capitalism must necessarily generate democracy (if it was not already present). Of course, this consensus was never based on a broad analysis of capitalist societies, the vast majority of which are not democratic, but was more an anecdotally driven argument based on advanced industrial societies where democracy had already evolved, often in advance of the transition to capitalism (although democratization may have provided a positive condition for this transition in a number of instances).

In some ways it can be argued that since China has come to serve numerous supporting roles in the global capitalist networks, including as "sweatshop of the world" and key driver of global demand for manufactured goods, commodities, intermediate goods, etc., the pressure to shift power from democratically elected governments to a loosely configured structure dominated by corporations and multilateral institutions that serve the interests of a narrow subset of the corporate community, has increased. This has the effect of diminishing the role of democracy, a free press, rule of law exercised by a relatively autonomous judiciary, and independent labor unions; more generally, reducing the power and influence of individual citizens in favor of large-scale transnational corporations.

What does the rise of China, then, tell us about the ontological relationship between democracy and capitalism? And how does the interaction of these phenomena shape economic crises? Are such crises more or less likely with democratic processes, a free press, or independent labor unions? Are such crises likely to be more or less severe, longer or shorter? Does the absence of democracy and democratizing institutions make it easier for the Chinese Party-state to intervene effectively to mitigate economic crises or make it more likely that the Party-state will be unresponsive to conditions that could worsen certain types of crises? Given that the long-term sustainability of economic growth in China is of great importance to the global economy, not just to the Chinese, then the correct answers to these questions is no minor matter.

It is a basic assumption of this book (and all of my intellectual work) that we live in an overdetermined universe. This concept of overdetermination *does not* imply simply multiple determinations. It implies that *all* extant social and natural phenomena contribute, in some distinct way, to *every* instance of causality. And everything that happened in the past contributes to everything existing in the present and everything that will come to exist in the future. In other words, overdetermination implies that *every factor is significant in all social and natural processes.* If this ontological assumption is correct, then there must be an alternative thesis to any reductionist argument about a necessary relationship between the aforementioned set of social phenomena (democracy/free press/ rule of law/independent labor unions) and capitalism. Similarly, there is no singular deterministic relationship between capitalism (in any variant form) and rapid economic growth. The relationship between any A and any B must necessarily be contingent on the other social and environmental processes overdetermining the relevant outcomes.

Thus, in the Chinese case, the possible solutions to reducing dissent to an "acceptable" level (or, at least, reducing risk to such a level) such that growth and development are not impeded (and, perhaps, even supported) are multiple, not singular. The rise of capitalism in China, the political monopoly held by the CPC, the predominance of nationalist and modernist thinking are all important contexts within which such solutions must occur. In a similar vein, there must be innumerable combinations of institutional variations, cultural norms, and other social processes supportive of capitalism, and yet other sets (some intersecting the pro-capitalist set) that are supportive of economic growth and development. Sometimes the same sets of social and natural processes support both capitalism and rapid sustainable growth.

On the other hand, there must be innumerable alternative sets that are not supportive of one or more of these outcomes. In other words, as the old saying goes, there is more than one way to skin a cat (apologies to the cat) or to generate a transition to capitalism or to foster economic growth and development. This is precisely why Deng Xiaoping pushed the idea of "feeling for stones while crossing the river," the experimental approach to modernization and economic growth. The experimental/ real options approach made effective use of the Party-state's pervasive influence within the economy and ability to locate experiments virtually anywhere in the economy, test the waters, and then decide whether to generalize the experiment to the rest of the economy.

The CPC has experimented with democracy in villages and urban communities, but has yet to decide if it was worthwhile to generalize these practices. However, even in those societies that have embraced democracy, a free press, rule of law, and independent labor unions as key institutional structures, the degree to which these institutions are allowed to function varies greatly, as does the institutional relationships between such structures and corporate or other structures. Study of actual historical societies, as well as cross sectional analysis of extant societies, can provide us with some of these variations.

For example, in the United States, the degree of democratic people power, press freedoms, rule of law, and labor union rights have varied greatly over time and space, with some states at certain times severely restricting one, two, or all three of these institutions. Similarly the national government has granted varying degrees of latitude for democratic decision making (including who can participate), freedom of the press, judicial independence and rule of law, and the rights and conditions under which labor unions are or are not allowed to function. Indeed, at times it is precisely the absence of one or more of these factors that has driven investment and economic growth in the U.S.

Indeed, there is similar evidence from China that the absence of these factors has contributed to the high and rising level of FDI, as well as domestic investment, driving rapid economic growth. For example, firms may see their operating costs significantly reduced in an environment where labor unions are restricted, judges are more likely to find in favor of the firm in disputes, the press is restricted from disseminating derogatory information about the firm and/or its patrons in the government, and citizens do not have the right to elect leaders and representatives who might fight for tighter regulation of the activities of the business or fewer tax breaks and other concessions. It is not a given, then, that China will fail to sustain economic growth if the CPC monopoly on political power is broken, nor is it guaranteed that a continued CPC monopoly will foster further economic growth and development.

Institutional innovations solve particular problems within a society. But solutions are never singular. For example, one of the positive roles of democracy in stabilizing a capitalist society is by providing a means for citizens to vent frustration and participate in the shaping of public policy (or at least believe they have been granted such power). In a society where ordinary citizens have little or no power to shape the decision making of the corporate institutions that dominate economic and social life (and where many of these same citizens spend the best hours of their days and lives), it may be important for social stability that this day-to-day powerlessness be balanced with the perception, at least, of having the power to shape public policy (the basis of the rules by which corporations function). Recent political revolts in Tunisia, Egypt, Libya, and other countries point up the problems that may be faced in societies where citizens feel disempowered.

Chinese authorities recognize the problem posed by the absence of a means for citizens to express their concerns and desires, influence public policy, and directly impact the composition of key government positions. Thus, these authorities have been seeking alternative means for the transmission of the popular will, as well as means of exposing corruption or other social ills (one of the functions of a free press), such as using talk radio, the aforementioned village and other community based elections, and surveys.

The development and increasing importance of, and broad participation in China's stock markets may also be viewed, in part, as a mechanism for diffusing social tensions, to an extent, by bringing the financial benefits (or potential benefits) to a larger number of people, making them stakeholders in the rise of Chinese capitalism.

It remains to be seen if these mechanisms can mitigate the lack of genuine democratic people power or the absence of a free press or independent labor unions. Every year the nation experiences a large number of protest demonstrations, estimated at over 200,000 in the last year, including many involving rural people protesting arbitrary seizure of land or other exercises in unchecked governmental power or instances where the Party-state has failed to live up to expectations. The central government has responded to these demonstrations in a variety of ways – intervening to reduce rural taxes, moderate land seizures, and, in rare instances, remove officials or judges who have drawn the ire of a significant number of citizens. These actions show that the absence of democratic institutions does not translate into total impotence for citizen political power.

However, anecdotal evidence indicates a lingering dissatisfaction with CPC monopoly political power, especially among the young, who made up the vast majority of pro-democracy forces during the period leading up to the 1989 Tiananmen demonstrations and subsequent bloody crackdown.

Casual conversation with Chinese students over the past two summers teaching in Shanghai (a small and not very random or even representative sample, for sure) indicates a high degree of disrespect for the CPC and a pervasive belief that party officials are deeply corrupt.

The large number of demonstrations and disrespect articulated by some of China's best and brightest young people come in the context of rapid economic growth. It is not difficult to imagine that discontent could grow considerably and, perhaps, even catastrophically if China were to slip into a serious economic downturn, a possibility that, despite thirty years of rapid growth, is not exceptional when one looks at the record for other capitalist economies that have experienced lengthy periods of economic growth. This is where it might be helpful to take stock of past histories of transitions from feudal to capitalist economies. Most of those other transitions were from private forms of feudalism to private forms of capitalism, so it is likely the dynamics of China's growth pattern will remain radically different going forward. Nevertheless, it is always risky to ignore potentially relevant information that is staring one in the face, so to speak.

In any event, thirty years of rapid economic growth has produced a great deal of complacency about Chinese growth. If it is common for economies transitioning from feudalism to capitalism to experience extended periods of economic growth followed by a significant economic downturn, this may be a warning bell for the Chinese economy.

Another reason for caution in assessing the future growth path of the Chinese economy is that the very process of growth and the intertwining of the Chinese economy with global markets alter the conditions for future growth, creating risks that are poorly understood, if recognized at all. It seems not only possible but likely that investment in the Chinese economy will exceed the limits of potential demand growth, particularly given the tendency to over optimism after a long period of abnormal economic growth, such that a large enough share of investments may be more likely to turn net present value negative as demand growth fails to meet the optimistic expectations about revenue growth, particularly given the likelihood that past rapid economic growth is likely to encourage more intense competition in a wide range of markets. Thus, a growing subset of total investments is likely to generate insufficient cash flow to meet credit obligations.

This turn of events could spell serious trouble for the Chinese economy and, perhaps more importantly, for banks and other financial firms. If China were then to experience an economic crisis, it might quickly transform into a political crisis with even more serious economic consequences. The CPC continues to be a patchwork of factions with the ruling modernist coalition more fragile than is often recognized. The glue that holds the ruling coalition together is rapid economic growth, development/modernization, and a carefully orchestrated set of quid pro quo serving the interests of diverse factions, including local political leaders who have gained significant autonomy (leading, in some cases, to abuses of power that have led to the aforementioned protests) as a result of the reforms. Remove that glue and the direction of public policy becomes more problematic. Circular and cumulative causation could turn negative with global implications.

In the past, even the hint of economic disturbances has had implications for public policy. During periods when inflation rates have risen sufficiently to produce political stresses, party conservatives have pressed successfully for a slowing of the reform process, and sometimes have gained reversal of some reforms.

To an extent, it is precisely recognition of this political fragility that has generated net capital flight from China. China's nouveau riche have been sending millions of dollars abroad every year for some time now, accumulating overseas assets, and sending their children for education in the West. What would it take to turn this steady flow of funds leaving China into a flood? Chinese authorities have relaxed capital controls significantly, partly in response to international agreements, further opening the door to capital flight in the event of a rapidly developing financial/economic crisis. China's rich fear that such a crisis might result in a tightening of capital controls, making their response to any hint of crisis likely to be all the more hasty. Capital flight has been a key component of a number of economic crises, particularly in the less developed world, and including the Asian financial crisis of 1997-1998 (when China's doors to capital flight were tightly locked, helping to shield it from the full impact of the crisis). Thus, in more ways than a few, the political risks compound the economic risks.

This interaction and intertwining of political and economic risks is not simply a macroeconomic phenomenon. Significant microeconomic problems may also arise from this dynamic. For example, the risk of labor unrest within specific corporate structures or industries is also a factor with implications for the valuation of corporate investments and the ability of corporate boards to meet ongoing obligations, including generating cash flow to meet interest and principal obligations to creditors related to past investments. Lower valuation for corporate investments is a factor driving overall productive investments, including FDI, lower, resulting in a slowdown in economic growth and job creation. Thus, political risks are a factor in driving investment and aggregate demand and in shaping financial and, more specifically, default risks. Political risks cannot, therefore, be ignored at either the macroeconomic or microeconomic levels of analysis.

Consider the determinants of bankruptcy of a highly leveraged SOE. The SOE faces relatively high bankruptcy risk in part because of a failure to generate sufficient cash flows to meet its financing requirements and partly because its backers within the Party-state are unable to secure rollover financing. The former and the latter are linked, since the ability to secure politically-related funding may be enough to solve the former problem, even eliminate the bankruptcy risk altogether under extraordinary circumstances. Politics shapes the competitiveness of the firm and, therefore, has relevance for analysis of the viability of specific firms and the stability of the overall system.

To the extent that state banks and other financial institutions directly or indirectly controlled by the state can facilitate (or directly provide, in the case of the banks) financing for the SOE's capital budgeting plans (and to meet any pressures to pay existing obligations), the appropriate discount rate for SOE assets may be lower and the overall valuation of the SOE higher. The firm that has political backers capable of directing loanable funds to them in the case of emergencies is likely to face lower interest rates and overall lower weighted average cost of capital, improving the likelihood that investment projects would be deemed net present value positive, leading to more investments and, perhaps, more rapid technological modernization. Thus, the overall competitiveness of such firms would be improved. However, these positive conditions can be reproduced only so long as the political arrangement that allows such access persists.

Cash flows are, of course, always contingent precisely because of being overdetermined by the ever changing matrix of political, cultural, economic, and environmental processes. Corporate structures, which are dependent upon cash flows for their survival, are critical elements in the development of all contemporary capitalist economies. However, the very economic, cultural, environmental, and political processes that overdetermine cash flows and which are constantly in flux and interacting with one another are also shaped by the actions of corporations.

In China, the rapidly changing corporate environment that constitutes the core of the new capitalist economy is intimately involved in reshaping the overall social and environmental conditions that constitute contemporary China, even as these conditions reshape the corporate world. This reshaped corporate world and the society it interacts with is also changing the nature of Chinese citizens, even what it means to be a Chinese citizen. In other words, a dialectical process is at work in China with far reaching consequences. The CPC has traditionally taken the lead in shaping the social environment but as people, institutions, and socio-environmental conditions change, it may become increasingly problematic for the Party-state to manage this complex constellation of processes and interactions.

The linkages between particular political leaders, national and local, as well as particular factions within the CPC and specific corporations are increasingly important aspects of these interactions shaping Chinese political and economic processes. Corporations are fundamentally political institutions.

In China, as elsewhere, corporations are the product of political processes in which the state grants corporate charters, imposes responsibilities and obligations, and retains the right to regulate corporate behavior, giving corporations with close ties to powerful politicians the means to reshape the economic rules to their favor. The decision to convert the Chinese economy into one dominated by corporate structures is as important as the decision to convert it from one in which feudal exploitation is replaced with capitalist exploitation. By inserting corporate structures between the vast majority of Chinese citizens and the CPC, the reforms altered the power dynamics in the nation. This alteration in power dynamics impacts economic policy and the manner in which the state intervenes in the economy, including during periods of economic crisis. It is possible that growing corporate power could ultimately undermine the state-centered nature of Chinese capitalism and alter the potential for economic crises and crisis mitigation.

One of the interesting side effects of the rise in these linkages between politicians/political factions and powerful corporate structures has been an increasing popularity of neoliberalism among some elements of the CPC and the corporate community. Neoliberalism celebrates the rise in corporate power at the expense of governmental power. The fact that in democratic societies this has also resulted in a reduction in the power of citizens to shape the society (via their democratic control over government policies, which are increasingly shaped by corporate lobbying efforts) is downplayed.

The rise of neoliberalism as an ideology shaping the evolution of capitalism, generally, has worked to undermine the power of the state to shape the boundaries of corporate actions (and the citizenry has no direct democratic access to corporate policy making). As neoliberalism becomes more widespread within the ranks of CPC members and other elements in the Party-state, academia, and elsewhere, it will become a more potent tool for party-corporate power groupings to use in undermining factions or political leaders who advocate maintaining a strong state and retaining general restrictions on corporate power.

A growing number of SOEs have evolved into transnational corporate structures where the management bureaucracy controls cash flows, often for their own interests and those of their political partners within the CPC, and shareholders (other than the state) have little or no influence. Neoliberalism is an attractive ideology for many of these individuals.

The linkage between senior corporate executives in powerful corporate structures and well positioned political leaders within the CPC (and select local leaders with extraordinary clout over local markets and/or resources) has the dual and, perhaps, ironic effect of simultaneously reinforcing corporate power and placing political and social objectives higher on the corporate list of objectives than might otherwise be the case. When looked at in this way, the close intertwining of corporate power and factional power within the Party-state need neither lead to the rise of neoliberalism to a dominant ideology nor to a significant weakening of state intervention in the economy. Thus, it is not a necessity that the growing power of corporate executives and directors need necessarily lead to the replacement of the state-centered version of capitalism with one more akin to the laissez-faire myth that prevails in the English speaking capitalist nations.

While most of the focus in analyzing such relationships is upon the CPC-SOE nexus that dominates the Chinese economy, this relationship increasingly includes other corporate structures, including foreign corporations, within the network of mutual support and influence. It is through these linkages that corporations reinforce the power of their political allies and vice versa. Thus, political allies have an interest in protecting their corporate allies from economic or political problems, creating a self-reproducing dynamic supportive of further economic reforms, particularly those that embed new capitalist processes deep within the fabric of society.

This dynamic is further supported by the growing power of corporations to determine job creation, a key metric for CPC legitimacy. Failure to create sufficient new jobs to satisfy the working population is one of the clearest threats to social stability and the CPC leadership must always be concerned about the possibility that higher unemployment could spark social unrest. At one extreme, it is even possible for corporations to go on *capital strike* if corporate executives are unhappy with policy directions, withholding new investment spending and constraining job growth. This possibility, whether used or not, could serve to reinforce the power of corporate allies within the CPC and various levels of the state.

Close ties between corporate executives and political leaders represent a bridge between the old society of feudal loyalties and reciprocity and the new society grounded in capitalist exploitation and market relationships. Over time, as directors and managers within SOEs have adopted practices from the OECD nations, particularly the United States, Germany, and Britain, and developed commercial and productive relationships beyond the borders of the PRC, this tension between the incentives created by the two societies has increased, without any apparent clear resolution. Corporate executives within the SOEs share the grand ambitions of party leaders and are well into a process of transforming their firms into more globally competitive institutions, leaving behind those vestiges of bureaucratic/feudal origins that obstruct their penetration of new markets and innovation of new products.

In order to be globally competitive, most of these executives have come to recognize the imperative of breaking free from the explicit and implicit constraints that had come from being integral elements of an almost all-encompassing state, even as they continue to tap into political patronage wherever possible. Ironically, this process of building transnational or multinational entities with relatively autonomous powers has provided many of these executives with influence over governments that could hardly have been imagined early in the reform process. It is a delicate balancing act, however, since the PRC retains controlling interest in SOEs and, through the banking system, can influence firms owned by local governments and private firms, as well, and in their external economic activity.

Chinese SOEs may have an advantaged competitive position

at home with their links to powerful factions within the CPC capable of altering the rules of the game in their favor but when they operate outside of their national boundaries they come up against the power of states to restrict their activities and interfere with their long-term strategies, including blocking mergers and acquisitions. Of course, the extent of governmental control over corporations, including Chinese corporations, has been constrained by multilateral trading agreements, such as WTO, whose charter and subsequent provisions have been greatly influenced (in some cases dictated) by powerful transnational corporations based in the OECD countries.

The Chinese leadership recognizes these multilateral agreements as double-edged swords, providing them with a means for supporting the internationalization of SOEs and other Chinese-based transnationals, but also providing foreign transnationals and their host governments with tools for opposing Party-state controls over certain aspects of the PRC economy and some expansionary objectives outside of the PRC. To the extent these agreements and/or the obstruction of foreign governments blocks the ability of SOEs and private Chinese transnationals gaining access to advanced technologies, the goal of modernization is stymied, a result that would be particularly worrisome to the Chinese leadership.

A key institutional transformation in the transition to capitalism in China was the replacement of communes and danwei with corporations as the primary sites of value creation and distribution. The link between the legal structure of corporations and capitalist production relations is not innate. Indeed, one of the largest corporations in Europe, Spain's Mondragon, is organized around communal production and appropriation of value. However, the link between the corporation and the commoditization of ownership may facilitate the transfer of the power of appropriation of value and, by doing so, make it easier to make a transition to the capitalist form of appropriation.

As with all institutions, the internal decision making dynamics within corporations are shaped by a complex matrix of interacting factors, including wide arrays of cultural, political, and economic processes that generate some degree of predictability but always in a context of profound uncertainty, both about events external to the corporate structure and behaviors and outcomes within the corporate sphere. What Keynes described as "animal spirits" may be understood as a metaphor for the overdetermined (and, therefore, uncertainty generating) inputs to decision making, including "herd" behavior where decision makers follow the consensus, which act as catalyst for behavior which may, under certain assumptions, be arguably irrational.

Irrational or not, even behaviors that appear to run counter to economic or even physical self-interest can sometimes be quite predictable, because of repetitive responses to similar circumstances. Similarly, corruption is an important determinant of income distribution, investment decisions, and the supply and demand for a wide range of products and services. It may be viewed as irrational from a societal or institutional standpoint, even if rational for individuals gaining from corrupt practices, but because it may follow certain predictable patterns, it need not add to uncertainty in the economy.

Modeling corporate decision making, such as capital budgeting, without some attempt to incorporate these factors, including unique influences that differentiate corporate structures in one social context from those in alternative contexts, is unlikely to be very useful in predicting economic behavior. Corporate directors and managers in China, as elsewhere, conform to social standards determined dynamically within society.

The incentives created by China's state feudal era, the pervasiveness of party organization within a wide range of local and national institutional structures, including schools and factories, the incorporation within the Chinese communist ideology of the Confucian notion, a fundamental belief supporting the old feudal order, that moral leaders (in this case, read as leaders who have been chosen by the vanguard party) are far more important to social stability than codified laws (which potentially could run counter to the interests of the ruling elites), and, more generally, the monopoly over political power held by the CPC shape the behavior of a wide range of economic agents, including corporate management and directors. Patronage, factional relationships, loyalties grounded in political power, and the ability to get around laws (when concrete laws are present, which is not always the case) continue to shape economic activities and contracts, both explicit and implicit. This influence is not simply political. The CPC is a dominant cultural force in China and has consistently worked to reproduce a nationalist and patriarchal mindset, a cultural phenomenon that is apparent to anyone spending even a small amount of time in the country.

Capital budgeting and other decisions of corporate directors and management in China are not simply exercises in "profit maximization" or even shareholder value maximization and are influenced by these political and cultural processes. Many decisions are determined by non-economic objectives, as well as economic objectives outside of the limited realm of profit or shareholder wealth maximization. This implies that the trajectory toward economic crises and the response to such crises need not be purely economic in nature. It is critical that we recognize the overdetermined nature of corporate strategies and governmental policies (and the interaction between these two decision sets) in order to develop a theoretical understanding of "business cycles" in the Chinese context, as well as China's impact upon global macroeconomic stability going forward.

The influences of Party-state bureaucratic rationality, traditional Confucian codes of conduct, extant feudal fealty relationships that have persisted after the dismantlement of economic feudalism, and other non-economic factors compete with economic rationality in the form of a focus upon value maximization and related financial variables, such as cash flow and discounted net present value, as taught in business schools and other cultural arenas, to shape capital budgeting (investment) and other corporate decisions.

The decision matrixes of corporate structures in China are *overdetermined* in unique ways vis-à-vis other capitalist social formations. In other words, decision making models based on simple concepts of economic rationality are unlikely to uncover all of the relevant drivers of the Chinese economy (or any economy, for that matter) and, therefore, have limited or no predictive value (often providing predictions no better than a randomized selection process) in determining variability in investment or other economic variables that define business cycles.

This fact is not an argument against modeling, since modeling simply means to abstract from a complex, overdetermined reality in the form of a set of well-defined concepts, logic, and an algorithm linking these concepts through the logic to derive conclusions about potential causality and/or correlation. Statistical analyses provide evidence of past causality and/or correlation and, therefore, may lend credence to the structure of a particular model or indicate the need for modifications. Human limitations leave us with little alternative but to develop models if we want to improve our understanding and future decision-making, since it is never possible, in an overdetermined universe to incorporate all relevant factors and relationships. As we've already seen, the Chinese economy is complexly determined by political, economic, cultural, environmental, and demographic processes. Furthermore, the Chinese economy is a key determinant of the global economy. Thus, if modeling can help us to understand the impact of alternative public policies (for example, alternative exchange rate, fiscal, monetary, infrastructure, and regulatory policies) then it provides a tool in identifying strategies for both generating sustained economic growth and for mitigating or even avoiding economic crises that could have global implications.

However, our recognition that the world is overdetermined and, therefore, necessarily containing relevant aspects of reality not included in individual models tells us to maintain a healthy skepticism about the universality of any given model, no matter how sophisticated and well-constructed. Uncertainty cannot be eliminated by modeling, only diminished. Macroeconomic reasoning through the development of models, in a context that recognizes the *overdetermined* nature of causality, provides a very useful tool for exploring the interaction of alternative public policies and other social variables with business cycles but is not a panacea.

Nor should we easily dismiss alternative economic models in favor of some orthodox approach, as is too often the case in academia (particularly in economics departments dominated by neoclassically trained economists) as well as other institutional environments. Many economic departments in Chinese universities have substituted the monopoly of one paradigm, orthodox Marxism, with a duopoly, neoclassical economists have joined the orthodox Marxists, but this duopoly represses other paradigms, including alternative versions of Marxian theory, limiting the innovativeness of faculty and students and making it more problematic that academic economists might offer innovative solutions to social and, more narrowly, economic problems, including the prevention or alleviation of economic crises.

Given the overdetermined nature of economies and economic crises, successful macroeconomic stabilization is more likely if alternative theoretical frameworks and models are allowed to be taught and deployed, with the true test of utility of models and paradigms by their success at generating policies that are effective or in predicting outcomes the knowledge of which improves the human capacity to diminish negative social outcomes, such as increases in malnutrition, disease, or other harmful impacts on human beings and improving the capacity to generate positive outcomes, such as higher incomes and improved quality of life.

By disrupting the normal flow of value within the society, a financial/economic crisis problematizes the capacity of an economy to meet the needs of citizenry, to sharply reduce the growth in financial value available to provide incomes that make normal life possible, and any tools that allows us to mitigate the negative impacts of such crises have some degree of social utility. If modeling helps us to identify risk factors that might trigger such crises, then models are very important and may be just the thing to provide prescriptive answers to the question of how crises may be avoided or, if not avoided, ameliorated.

It is important to isolate at least a subset of factors in any economic model, necessarily omitting key variables, in order to make progress in understanding the dynamics of change in a society and generating policy recommendations. Thus, while rejecting the simplistic humanist and primitive behavioral assumptions of neoclassical models, this text will not eschew the modeling approach altogether, but after reviewing key institutional structures in the Chinese economy, will proceed to build a theoretical framework based on these stylized features of the Chinese economy, culture, and polity, particularly the role of the Party-state in shaping capital budgeting and financing decisions within corporate structures and the notion that individual decision-making is always shaped within and constrained by institutional and larger cultural norms.

The text retains an underlying ontological viewpoint that all decisions, even the most basic "individual" human choices, are necessarily *overdetermined* by all extant factors, both those included and those excluded from models.

The complex relationships between the state, industrial firms, and financial institutions initiates and reproduces conditions for economic value creation, price formation, and the determination of levels of income and employment. Financial institutions construct, manage, and distribute financial instruments, such as deposits, loans, insurance, stocks, options (real and financial), and futures that foster broader access to capital among corporate and other entities and provide contractual mechanisms for managing risk. The People's Bank of China has authority to set reserve requirements of and interest rates charged by banks, as well as depository interest rates. Thus, any financial crisis or industrial/commercial crisis with financial origins must arise out of the complex relationships and financial instruments serving as nexus linking financial transactions to capital budgeting decisions and aggregate demand formation within the capitalist economy.

At least one of the critical links is not difficult to identify. The provision and distribution of capital is a key determinant of overall income and employment growth and is the result of decisions within and interactions among a wide range of institutional structures. Regulatory practices and the rule of law as administered by the courts represent critical links between public policy decisions in government and capital budgeting and financing decisions in corporate structures (financial, industrial, commercial, and extractive). Deregulation and corruption (which problematizes the rule of law) both weaken this link and alter capital budgeting decisions.

In general, deregulation of financial institutions has tended to promote stronger risk preference in loan portfolio formation while deregulation of non-financial corporations has tended to create more flexibility in management choices of production techniques, which tends to lower unit costs of production, but may also generate more negative externalities. The former has implications for business cycles as greater financial risks can lead to more frequent and deeper financial crises, which has negative knock-on effects in the non-financial sectors. While the latter condition can mean higher short-term profitability for non-financial firms, weakening or removing regulation over negative externalities, such as water or air pollution. It alters the net present value calculations for alternative production practices and technologies, leading to different choices than would prevail under a stronger regulatory regime, and potentially generates high social costs. Corruption can have a similar effect in allowing for a different choice of production practices and technologies generating higher net present value than would be possible without corruption, even if selected practices and technologies violate existing laws. Whether the long-run gain in profitability is greater than the social costs is debatable.

However, it is clear the CPC has chosen to grant manufacturing and extractive industries a great degree of flexibility under the assumption that the growth gains outweigh the long-run social costs to Chinese society. What is not clear is whether deregulation (with or without a high degree of corruption) in the non-financial sector can have the same sort of negative implications for exacerbating risks for economic crises as is seen with financial institution deregulation, although the impact on the growing environmental crisis in China appears to be unambiguously negative. Both forms of deregulation are likely to have unintended negative consequences at the firm level to the extent financial and/ or non-financial firms fail to adopt appropriate risk management technologies as a tool for better management decision-making.

The greater the level of deregulation (and/or the greater the degree of corruption) in the financial sector, the less control the state has over the distribution, deployment, and underlying risk matrix of capital. A number of recent financial crises in the advanced capitalist nations of Europe, the U.K., and the U.S.A. have been associated with excessive deregulation (and close relationships between legislators and lobbyists bordering on corruption) and related decisions of financial firms to significantly raise the risk profile of their portfolios of assets and liabilities, extending firm specific risks to systemic risks due to the magnitude of interlinked cash flow dependencies between corporate structures.

Reducing government regulation of and influence over financial firm decision sets is a consequence, in part, of the growing dominance of neoclassical economic theory and the neoliberal policies it has spawned, as well as the growing role of cash flows (in the form of political donations) from corporations to politicians and direct corporate interventions (via direct and indirect interventions in advertising and other cultural processes) shaping the popular consciousness and influencing the careers of politicians. The neoclassical framework assumes that market outcomes are necessarily optimal for achieving the best allocation of scarce resources and wealth maximization, although there is no evidence that such is the case, given that every major country that has achieved high income status, including the United States, has done so with significant government involvement in and regulation of the economy.

The much discussed assumptions of neoclassical theory about rationality, frictionless trading, information symmetries (which precludes effective dishonesty, asymmetric access to relevant information, and the potential to benefit from access to technologies that allow for asymmetric access to trading platforms in trading or other relationships), and the insignificance of a vast array of cultural, political, environmental, and economic factors in shaping decision sets and the functioning of the decision making apparatus are the basis for optimism regarding the social and economic consequences of neoliberal policy. These assumptions bear little resemblance to the real world where neoliberal policies are applied. The neoliberal policy framework forms the basis for the *Washington Consensus*, a prescription for shifting power (and, in some instances, ownership) from state institutions to private (typically corporate) institutions in an attempt to approximate the ideal conditions specified in the neoclassical microeconomic model (albeit without critical features, such as perfect competition).

As we have seen in recent periods, the influence of the Washington Consensus over public policy breaks down during periods of crisis when neoliberalism gives way to strong state interventionism (often some version of Keynesianism) and regulatory vigor. The question is whether or not the Chinese model, sometimes referred to as the *Beijing Consensus*, which makes no attempt to approximate the neoclassical/neoliberal ideal but is based upon a relatively strong state that retains a high degree of control and/or influence over the portfolio decisions of financial, industrial, and other firms, even during periods of relative macroeconomic stability, is a better approach to generating economic development, avoiding financial and other types of economic crises, and ameliorating the effects of crises (including global capitalist crises) when they occur.

Furthermore, is the Beijing Consensus a superior policy prescription for generating economic growth and development *with lower overall risk* than prevails under the Washington Consensus approach? And, finally, are there long-term economic or non-economic consequences of the greater degree of state involvement that mitigate short-term growth and risk reduction effects and which could leave China (or other adopters of the Beijing Consensus model) at least as vulnerable to economic/ financial crises as those nations pursuing a neoliberal path? In particular, does the Beijing Consensus model provide for long-term innovation in cutting edge technologies required to sustain economic growth beyond the period of "catch up" where a poor country reaches the level of "middle income" by simply better employing available underemployed or unemployed resources, as well as adopting available technologies (which can be deployed by the more gainfully employed laborers) borrowed from wealthier, more technologically advanced nations?

It would be a mistake to assume that the Beijing Consensus and Washington Consensus are completely at odds. Although these are clearly two distinct ways of thinking about economic policies, there are some aspects in common. It is clear that the strong state in China has been an instrument for pursuing the broad decentralization of economic decision-making authority, as well as political decentralization in the form of growing relative autonomy of local governments and corporate bodies. This movement of decision-making authority from central government to other institutional nodes within the social formation is arguably consistent with the general ideological predilections of neoliberalism (although, in the case of moving more powers to localities, the neoliberal bent towards less government control and regulation need not hold, since local governments are capable of a quite visible and heavy hand in their involvement in local economies).

The Beijing Consensus also shares with neoliberalism reliance upon market exchanges (another form of decentralization of economic decision-making) to determine the price and allocation of most products and services. The two political-economic paradigms part company on the degree to which the state should allow stresses to build up in the economy, however.

Creative destruction is an implicit aspect of neoliberalism but has largely been avoided within the Beijing Consensus in favor of stability and a reduction in the risk of major systemic shocks to employment and income. Chinese authorities have also been quite capable of reasserting authority to combat inflation, including the aforementioned housing bubble, as well as to influence other macroeconomic phenomena.

Nevertheless, the authorities in China may come to increasingly embrace neoliberalism as their country gains in global economic clout. The ideology of neoliberalism provides a ready response to those who would block Chinese exports or direct investment by Chinese firms in foreign markets, both of which are increasingly important elements in the strategic plans of Chinese firms. Thus, whether or not Chinese authorities practice neoliberal policies at home, they may come to promote such policies abroad.

Capital budgeting and financing and consequent economic growth is overdetermined by the interaction of cultural, political, economic, and environmental processes in China. For example, the cultural notion that "Western" fashion and lifestyles are modern coupled with the Party-state's promotion of modernity as ideal has stimulated investment in a wide range of products, from apparel, cosmetics, and toiletries to the construction of "Western-style" housing developments. These developments have been reinforced by the legalization and diffusion over state media outlets of advertising of such products, as well as the widespread diffusion of Western movies and television, often via torrent downloads, influencing tastes and stimulating the rapid growth of new markets. These new markets coupled with the increased autonomy of enterprises and banks seeking new sources of positive net present value cash flows result in altered capital budgeting and financing decisions throughout the Chinese economy.

Innovation and the Capital Budgeting Process

Firms seek to produce the products and provide the services consumers and other firms are willing to buy. The ability to produce these products and provide these services often generates demand for new production technologies, since it may not be possible to meet the expectations of these consumers and firms with existing technologies. However, new technologies often require new forms of knowledge on the part of workers and managers, requiring skill enhancement in the form of education technologies. Thus, an entire array of hard and soft technologies become necessary in order to satisfy the demands of new and changing markets. This generates a positive dynamic within the society where firms invest in new technologies and training for laborers and managers, leading to the expansion of markets for firms producing or distributing such technologies and providing educational services. Firms providing the new technologies and education services will also need to upgrade, further stimulating market development and pushing other firms to change to meet these additional market demands, and so on.

Capital budgeting and financing decisions and the resulting portfolios of assets have direct and indirect impacts upon levels of income and employment. Economic reforms and restructurings have challenged the management in SOEs to make more effective capital budgeting decisions, in terms of generating positive net cash flows, to take better account of changing market conditions, and to select the best combination of hard and soft technologies to achieve cost minimization within the constraints of satisfying the product quality requirements imposed by market demand conditions. Choices of hard and soft technologies deployed shape the productivity coefficients that go into determining unit costs of production and, directly and indirectly, levels of income and employment.

Financing decisions are collaborative between state banks and SOEs, often under the influence of the State Council, which has been known to "jaw bone" the banks into making loans to favored SOEs and for favored investment projects. In other words, the State Council-finance-industry nexus is a determinant, albeit not the sole determinant, of economic growth. This nexus is not unidirectional in its effects: financial firms influence industrial firms but the dynamics also work the other way around. The indirect effects of decisions by financial firms are, in large part, a result of the linkages between these firms and industrial enterprises, linkages which are shaped, in part, by regulatory policies of the state (which are also influenced by political and social ties between state officials and managers/directors within financial and industrial corporate structures) and cash flows from industrial to financial firms in the form of interest payments and various fees.

Additionally, industrial and financial corporate structures (state and private, domestic and foreign) are shaped by the technologies deployed in the enterprise and the larger set of socio-economic structures of the society, including the existing and changing stock of national infrastructure. This infrastructure has been dramatically transformed over the past three decades, with this transformation accelerating over the past couple of decades. This has been particularly the case for information and communications technology (ICT) and transport technologies. The infrastructure in China was already better developed, thanks to heavy investments in that sector during the Maoist era, than most low income economies at the start of the reform era, but the dramatic development of infrastructure has been a critical determinant of the rapid integration of Chinese labor into the international division of labor that epitomizes contemporary capitalism. This international division of labor has become the basis for large transnational corporations subcontracting manufacturing and lowering their unit cost of production, placing downward pressure on worldwide prices of a wide range of intermediate and final products.

Cultural processes are another set of determinants of the pace and success of the transition to capitalism. "Human capital" is a particular concern of the Chinese leadership and both public and private resources have gone towards development of improved educational institutions, supplemented by a huge outflow of Chinese students into Western educational institutions. This focus on education is in recognition of the importance of knowledge to sustaining the economic growth path. If Chinese firms are to move up the technological ladder, with increasingly complex product mixes, then deepening the knowledge base of the work force is critical. This can be brought about, in part, through foreign educated citizens, imported skilled personnel, and innovating new protocols for internal training but, ultimately, it depends upon the availability of domestically trained Chinese personnel with the appropriate skill-sets. But increasing the number of technically trained individuals is not enough.

In order to generate sustainable long term economic growth, certainly to generate higher than global average growth rates, requires invention and innovation. Invention and innovation is not simply a function of having learned a given body of knowledge, but requires creative thinking, the ability to "think outside the box" as the cliché goes. It has been argued that the Confucian tradition that still governs the learning modality in China, as in much of East Asia, fosters high level rote learning but produces substandard creativity. This may be an incorrect assessment, given China's sterling history of invention, innovation, and entrepreneurship for the past 3,000 years. The catalyst for accelerating invention and innovation may transcend the question of learning modalities, but it remains a concern, partly addressed by shipping students to the West for education (see Fig. 12.1 below) and partly by hiring Westerners and Western educated Chinese to teach within Chinese institutions.

Fig. 12.1

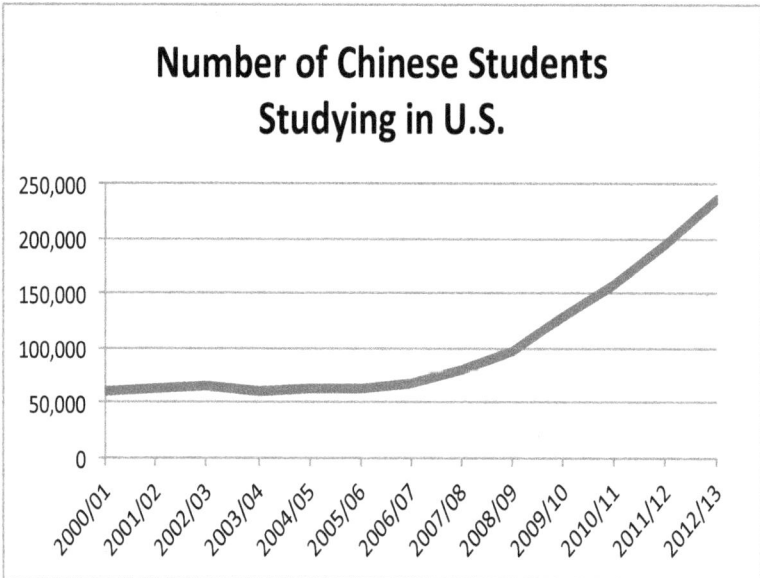

Source: IIE Project Atlas-iie.org/projectatlas

However, if entrepreneurship, invention, and innovation is to thrive in China, serving as a force in maintaining the current abnormal economic growth path, then the domestic cultural institutions will have to play a critical role and a culture of innovation must become more pervasive in the society.

According to the World International Property Organization (WIPO) in 2012, there was continued growth in patents for industrial designs with residents of China leading with 650,000 followed by Germany (76,369), the Republic of Korea(68,737), and the U.S. (45,245). See Fig. 12.2. While China contributes much intellectual talent to the surrounding geographical region, it is also attracting a large number of immigrant inventors from Asia and other parts of the world. See Table 12.1.

Fig. 12.2

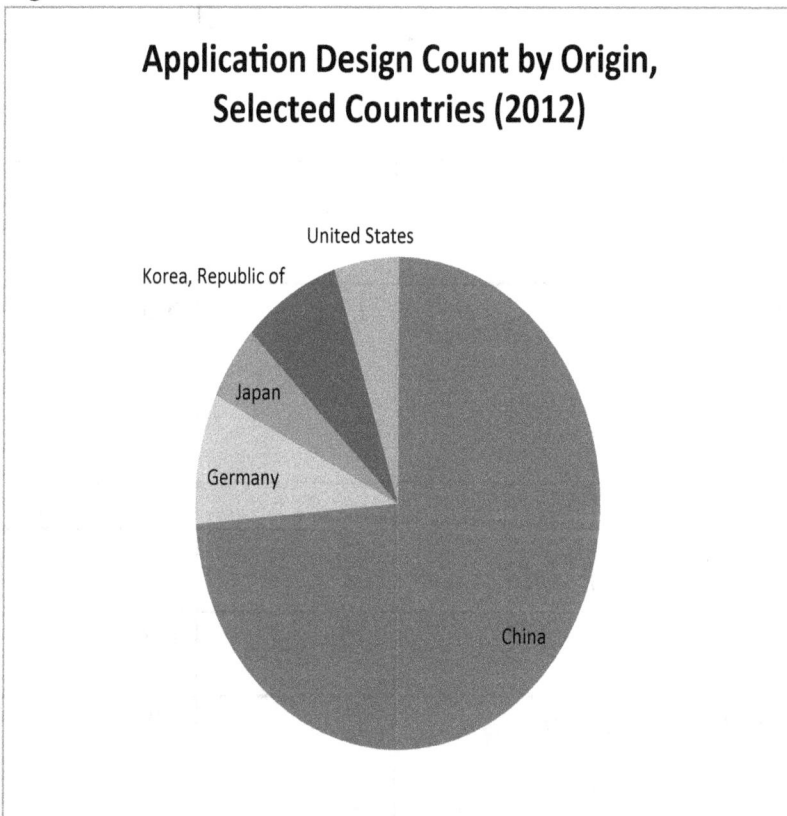

Application Design Count by Origin, Selected Countries (2012)

Source: WIPO

Table 12.1: Inventor immigration rates for top 10 applicants in China, 2006-10

APPLICANT NAME	IMMIGRATION RATE (%)	APPLICANT	INVENTOR
ZTE CORP.	0.2	7551	17803
HUAWEI TECHNOLOGIES	0.8	7277	18858
HUAWEI DEVICE CO.	0.2	570	1372
TENCENT TECHNOLOGY CO.	0	419	1014
ALCATEL SHANGHAI BELL CO.	0.4	380	1095
CHINA ACADEMY OF TELECOMMUNICATIONS TECHNOLOGY	2	317	1002
BYD CO.	0	263	1015
TSINGHUA UNIVERSITY	0.2	242	1571
PEKING UNIVERSITY	0.2	215	818
DA TANG MOBILE COMMNUNICATIONS EQUIPMENT CO.	0.6	205	688

Source: WIPO

Aggregate Demand and The Capital Budgeting Process

Macroeconomic stability and economic growth is overdetermined by various processes of value creation, cash flow distribution, and capital accumulation. GDP or its income equivalent, gross domestic income (GDI), is an aggregate of prices received for final products and services generated in and successfully sold by enterprises (or income received in various social sites) throughout the economy. The flip side of sales is buys. Aggregate demand is a complex function of a wide range of economic, political, cultural, and environmental processes and constraints, including household disposable income; cultural processes shaping consumer tastes, price and income elasticities of demand; marketing and other cultural processes shaping transitory preferences and longer term habits; savings rates, taxation and spending policies of various levels of the state; income distributions within corporate structures, other firms and in the larger social structure; currency exchange rates; and lending practices of the banking sector.

In China, household disposable income has been rising at a rapid rate over the past twenty years, multiplying by a factor *greater than ten* in urban areas and by a factor of *greater than five* in rural areas from 1990 to 2010, leading to a comparable increase in household consumption spending. The rapid increase in household consumption spending has led to steady and dramatic upward shifts in demand curves for a wide range of consumer products, including consumer durables (refrigerators, televisions, automobiles, etc.) whose manufacture and sale generate sizable cash flows to a subset of SOEs, as well as foreign firms manufacturing and selling in China.

Consumption and macroeconomic stability

Expansion in domestic markets for consumer products has been an important factor in allowing SOEs to scale up and reduce unit costs, while increasing access to advanced technologies has allowed for product innovation that has increasingly served the export strategies of these firms. Chinese consumers have been increasingly exposed to marketing and foreign tastes filtering in from Hong Kong. The effect has been a steady shift in preferences towards products and services deemed "modern" or "Western," particularly among consumers in East Coast cities. The interaction of marketing, exposure to Western media, including the ready availability of Western movies, television shows, and digitized magazines and books within Cyberspace, often downloaded in violation of copyright laws, and the large numbers of Chinese students who have studied or are studying abroad (and passing on ideas to friends, relatives, and acquaintances still in China) has led to clear changes in preferences among Chinese consumers. It has even begun to erode some cultural characteristics that have persisted across many different regimes, predating the rise of new China in 1949.

Price elasticities of demand are also reshaped by cultural changes. Products that in the past might have rapidly lost popularity as the price rose may even find increased demand at higher prices due to changes in tastes. As income inequality has grown in China, along with average incomes, tastes for "luxury" products has led to rapidly rising demand for high priced clothing, electronics, and automobiles, for instance, even as the prices charged for these items has risen. The characteristics of consumer demand has been radically transformed and now serves as foundation for the development of a wide range of new consumer markets and related industries and commercial enterprises. The rise of the shopping mall is a quite visible aspect of this transformation.

From the standpoint of macroeconomic stability, the growth of consumer demand is actually a stabilizing force. As Keynes pointed out and statistical analysis has supported, consumption spending is a relatively stable component of aggregate demand that, over short time periods when habits are likely to be slow to change, is highly correlated to income. Thus, it is changes in income that drive changes in consumption spending over these short time horizons, rather than the other way around. Consumers do not, then, generate the business cycle directly but are more reactive to changes that occur elsewhere in the economy. Thus, if the State Council has the goal of expanding domestic markets then it must implement a successful strategy for raising the average incomes of the majority working population.

Investment and macroeconomic stability

The key factor that leads to sharp reversals in the rate of acceleration or deceleration in aggregate demand (and, therefore, in output and income) is investment spending (or capital budgeting decisions). In capitalist economies, capital budgeting decisions are driven by the expectations of corporate directors and management about future cash flows and the risks to those cash flows (that is, the anticipated probabilities of a range of cash flow outcomes, some of which may be negative). The number of factors that impacts these expectations is too large for any economic model or economic analysis to incorporate. Necessarily, we focus on a subset of influences in any attempt to predict changes in capital budgeting.

One of the contradictions of the rapid economic growth taking place in China is the growth in the household savings rate. Economic theory predicts that a high growth rate in income should provide households with insurance against future income needs, reducing the precautionary demand for savings. However, China's savings rate has grown as the economy has become richer. This acts as a drag on household consumption and we have seen a rather steep drop in the share of aggregate demand generated by households over the course of the past three decades, placing greater reliance on investment spending and exports to drive income and output growth.

Consumer credit and macroeconomic stability

One of the factors mitigating the rise in savings and consequent fall in the marginal propensity to consume is the recent rapid growth in consumer credit. The State Council has encouraged the dominant (majority) state-owned commercial banks to ratchet up provision of consumer credit, primarily in the form of home mortgages, automobile loans and credit cards. The increase in consumer credit has helped to diversify the loan portfolios of these commercial banks, although there remains the large percentage of non-performing loans (NPLs) on bank balance sheets. Presently, the state banking sector holds in excess of an average 20% NPLs on balance sheets. To the extent the new consumer loans have a relatively low default rate and generate higher interest earnings for the banks, the move to more consumer credit may actually be a stabilizing force in the banking sector, at least under current conditions.

As indicated above, reforms in the banking sector have played an important role in the finance-industry-export nexus driving high rates of economic growth in GDP in China. The expansion of consumer credit will be an important element in achieving one of the key objectives of the State Council, shifting more of the burden of sustained economic growth to consumer spending and away from investments and exports. However, it is clear that investment remains as important in moderating economic instability and sustaining this growth path as it is in other capitalist economies. Exports remain important as a source of foreign exchange reserve accumulation, which is critical to modernization and expanding the reach of Chinese corporate structures to other parts of the globe, including the search for new and expanded sources of raw materials and other key imports to fuel industrial growth and modernization.

Feudal legacies and macroeconomic instability

Given China's rapid growth rates over the past three decades, it is difficult to imagine that the feudal legacies have been a significant negative influence upon decisions internally within financial enterprises or upon non-financial enterprises dependent upon loans, derivatives, or other financial instruments provided by the financial sector. In order to examine these legacies, and to identify those aspects of the financial structures which are associated with the transition to state capitalism, and which may be implicated in the aforementioned rapid economic growth, it is necessary to briefly review the contours of the communist-era version of a feudal social formation in China.

In the feudal social formation, state dominance via direct

bureaucratic control mechanisms was virtually absolute and, like so many other aspects of feudal social relationships, relatively inflexible. The state monopolized the formal financial sector and banks were integral parts of the state bureaucracy. Bank budgets were component elements of the larger state budget. "The banking system transferred feudal capital to managers in state enterprises to satisfy administratively mandated costs of production." (Gabriel, 2006: 133-134) Loans and other transfers of funds were largely internal movements of value within the bureaucratic structure, since the recipients of loans and various parties to monetary transfers were, for the most part, state controlled enterprises that were also elements within this same monolithic bureaucratic structure. The lack of flexibility that came from operating within such a bureaucratic structure under the constraints of a centralized state budget shaped a wide range of economic decisions, including those involving investments, which were, in turn, influenced by political factions and ties of fealty between officials within the bureaucratic hierarchy. Pricing of inputs, outputs, and labor were determined, to a great extent, endogenously within the bureaucratic structure generating extraordinary stability, but at the cost of innovation, flexibility, and efficiency.

As China underwent the transformation to a predominantly capitalist economy, the state first retained this monopoly over major financial institutions, using banks as policy instruments in the transition, and only later reformed the structure to create competition among financial enterprises and greater autonomy for state-owned banks. These changes were a response to the budgetary problems created by the state feudalist bureaucracy. Under the feudal system, banks served as political tools to serve the interests of specific factions within the Party-state and often made negative net present value loans that destroyed more value than the receiving firms created. Under this system, economic growth was a lower priority than meeting political objectives, such as full employment or national security. In other words, the system was set up to pay for political objectives, including meeting the reproductive needs of specific political factions within the

Party, out of resources that might otherwise have been invested in modernization and greater value generation in the short and long term.

While it is possible to argue that these policies might have generated positive (value enhancing) externalities in the society, perhaps even generating social value comparable to the economic value lost from inefficient deployment of resources, it is more likely that these decisions lowered overall national wealth and damaged the ability of the Chinese economy to produce future resources necessary to modernization and higher household incomes. Indeed, economic growth and higher incomes also produce positive externalities, so the real gain to the society from successful growth producing policies is likely to be greater than that measured purely in terms of GDP growth. And what are we to make of the argument, still made by many on the Left, that the old system was less exploitative than the contemporary capitalist economy?

The identification of the underlying class structure under the pre-reform regime as feudal negates this justification, leaving no ideological platform upon which to support the sacrifice of growth and income under the previous structural regime. Thus, while it is impossible to know the results of paths not chosen, the extraordinary economic success experienced since the reform process began in 1978, wherein the rigidities of the feudal structure were gradually removed, indicates that some value may have been lost by not beginning the reform process sooner.

Given the long standing CPC objective of modernization, an objective that predates the reforms and is embodied in Zhou Enlai's *Four Modernizations*, it is clear that the rigidity of financial relationships and centralization of financial decision making under the state feudalist bureaucratic arrangements, among other institutional rigidities of pre-reform periods, did not serve key objectives of the party. The reformers wanted a more flexible and decentralized system in which managers of enterprises could be incentivized to increase surplus value available for targeted investments, particularly investments in new technologies (the raw material of modernization), and laborers could more easily be shifted to higher productivity/higher value creating positions. The interaction between structural reforms, decentralization over financial decision-making, and the creation and expansion of labor power markets (with the concomitant increase in rural to urban migration) served as catalyst for rapid economic growth.

Thus, while feudal bankers served as agents for policy implementation, primarily pursuing the narrow objective of reproducing the bureaucracy, as a whole, or particular factions within the Party-state bureaucracy, in particular, the cost for placing these objectives at the core of the financial structure was a diminution of value available for distribution to meeting the objectives embodied in Zhou Enlai's Four Modernizations. As long as value was flowing to projects based on political criteria, the returns on such "investments" was likely to be low or even negative. In addition, political objectives overrode cost concerns, such that existing projects or activities were likely to be implemented in a cost inefficient manner, resulting in waste of available resources.

These two political/fealty effects of the feudalist bureaucracy reduced resources available for technological improvements or expansion of productive facilities. Industrial, agricultural, military, and research and development modernization were starved for funds under this system. If financial institutions were to shift objectives towards modernization and economic growth, then the internal incentive structure of banks had to be changed and systemic flexibility introduced. Reforms had to be extended to the banking and the larger financial sector if these goals and objectives of the modernist leadership were to be successfully achieved.

The waste of value within the bureaucratic network where banks were incentivized to make policy loans and industrial firms were incentivized to favor output and employment maximization over value maximization would become all the more problematic if the guaranteed employment under feudalism was abandoned in favor of capitalist wage labor power markets with limited job security. In the feudal system full employment was guaranteed. Employment was coupled with a wide range of family services, including education, medical care, and subsidized food and clothing, which were all seen as elements in an implicit feudal social contract. Value had to be distributed to meet the systemic requirements of this feudal social contract. Industrial and other enterprises operated under soft budget constraints under this system. The soft budget of individual enterprises was, however, a hard budget for the overall feudal bureaucratic structure. Thus, the old bureaucratic system generated a sizeable amount of surplus value to meet the demands of the feudal social contract but, by doing so, reduced the available value to meet other objectives, such as modernization.

Modernization in the pursuit of macroeconomic stability

The modernist leadership recognized that one of the necessary changes was the imposition of harder budget constraints for both financial and industrial corporate structures. Harder budget constraints would serve as catalyst for changing the focus from political policy-oriented (or fealty driven) investment decisions, many of which were clearly not value maximizing and would negatively impact firm balance sheets, to value-oriented investment decisions that would generate necessary cash flows to both financial and industrial corporate structures, positively impacting firm balance sheets and providing value needed for the aforementioned modernization project. The modernist leadership recognized that this change of focus could not take place if these corporate structures remained within the state bureaucracy where internal cash flows and bureaucratic solidarity could cover over failures to meet cash flow requirements within constituent enterprises.

The modernist leadership had already recognized the power of altering incentives from earlier reforms that allowed rural workers to become self-employed farmers and retain a portion of their output. Shifting incentives away from the fealty based system to a system based on retained cash flows would connect capital budgeting decisions and work effort (both of which impact productivity and overall value creation) to the level of cash generated, rather than just satisfying political objectives, such as pursuing the pet projects of higher level officials or protecting the jobs of specific sets of workers. In previous attempts at reform without granting enterprise management greater autonomy from the bureaucracy, efforts to raise the priority of value creation within the bureaucracy, which might often conflict with political objectives, had been repeatedly short-circuited by the internal political machinery by which managers were promoted based on ties to higher level officials. Bank officials demonstrated this fealty by making policy-oriented loans to industrial enterprises or projects favored by their patrons. Thus, it was recognized that in order to sever these ties of fealty, the state had to grant greater autonomy to both industrial enterprises and state banks. It was recognized that only by separating these corporate structures from the protective cocoon (and chains of fealty) of the state bureaucracy could the chains of patronage be broken.

Breaking these chains of patronage does not, however, imply severing the links between these corporate structures and the state in total. In particular, the State Council retained indirect authority over all corporate structures for which the state held controlling ownership interest, even in those cases where the corporate shares were sold to the general public on stock exchanges, which will be discussed in a later chapter. The People's Bank of China (PBOC) retained a considerable amount of control over the leadership makeup of the state banks, as well as their portfolio decisions. As long as the State Council had the dominant power to determine directors and, therefore, influence the executive leadership of the corporate structures then it retained indirect control over policy direction, and the PBOC retained direct control over many bank decisions.

For example, in recent years, the State Council, acting as executive authority of the state, has instructed all or a subset of state-owned industrial corporations (or corporations where the state had sufficient shares to elect the directors) to forego layoffs or other labor force reductions; to increase investments in specific areas; and to pursue partnerships with foreign parties. Similarly, the PBOC has instructed the large state-owned banks to increase or decrease, depending upon policy objectives, loans in specific areas or to specific firms. In other words, the state remains the dominant actor in the economy, but directives have become less tied to fealty relationships than under the prior system.

The banks and their role in aggregate demand

In any case, the role of predominantly state-owned banks remains closely linked to the policy objectives of the state. These state-owned banks are, to a significant extent, instrumentalities of the Party-state leadership. This has advantages and disadvantages. The advantages for the Party-state are that it is easier to implement certain policies and, given the indirect nature of using financial instruments, can sometimes bring about desired behavioral changes in corporate structures without the heavy-handedness of feudal-era direct controls over productive firms. It is clearly advantageous for the big banks to remain linked to a state with extraordinary financial resources that can be made available to them without the need for legislative action (as is the case in many more advanced capitalist economies). Access to large amounts of capital provides returns to scale. And even a relatively small return on invested capital can become a very large aggregate profit when the capital available for investment is relatively large. But there are also clear disadvantages to remaining an agent of the state, even if relatively more autonomous than under the feudal bureaucratic structure.

For instance, during the early reforms, strict controls over bank interest rates restricted the ability of bank management to take advantage of oligopolistic market power inherited from the old system where competition had been suppressed and the persistence of policy loans (dictated by political authorities, even after the reforms) forced banks to transfer funds (in a manner not unlike feudal-era practices) to state enterprises, even in circumstances where bank managers recognized that the loans were doomed to become non-performing loans (NPLs). The period after 2003 saw the gradual opening up of the financial sector to private (non-state) corporate structures as competitors with reformed state owned (if not completely controlled) corporate structures.

Furthermore, the necessity to prepare domestic financial institutions for foreign competitors under WTO resulted in acceleration of reforms that would foster greater competition and more flexibility in bank practices, including the setting of interest rates, lending practices, and types of savings and demand deposit accounts. This increased competition and flexibility changes the finance-investment-growth nexus. Thus, the impact of reform upon output and employment growth and price stability would be expected to be different as the banking sector undergoes these types of reforms.

Decentralization: More local control, less demand on central cash flows

In order to understand the capital budgeting implications of these reforms, it is important to note that decentralization of direct controls over and/or regulation of businesses was a necessary step in the process of building a governing pro-reform coalition within the Communist Party of China (CPC). The modernist Marxists within the CPC had to form a coalition that could counteract the power of the various factions within the party who benefitted from and wanted to retain the feudalist bureaucracy. To build this coalition required offering something attractive to powerful but relatively neutral elements within the party, such as the People's Liberation Army (PLA). The PLA was enticed by the promise of fulfilling Zhou Enlai's Four Modernizations, in particular the modernization of the military.

In addition, local-level CPC leaders are a significant and influential segment of the party. These local leaders wanted decentralization of state power, such that they could gain greater control over local resources and greater independence of policy-making and implementation. To gain the support of local leaders the modernist leadership promised to initiate a process by which state-controlled rural and urban industrial enterprises could be transferred into the control of the local governments with the authority to restructure the enterprises. Thus, local government authorities gained greater control over the cash flows generated by these local enterprises and were motivated to pursue policies that would assist such enterprises in increasing net cash flows. This local level control and regulation would eventually be extended to new banks and other financial firms created under the reform process fostering more competitive conditions in the financial sector and greater financing options for local firms.

This decentralization would also have the effect of reducing cash flow demands upon the central budget and providing the means for faster adjustment of locally controlled resources to meet local needs and locally determined objectives. Whether or not this is better than the old system remains to be determined, but certainly the rapid modernization of infrastructure throughout the country and overall rapid economic growth indicates some degree of success for these policies.

Although enterprise and bank reforms began as an endogenous reform process, driven by competition for leadership of the CPC and appropriate interpretation of Marxian theory and related governmental policies, more recent reforms (after 2003) have taken place, in part, in the context of participation in the World Trade Organization (WTO). Under the WTO agreement, Chinese authorities committed to a gradual opening up of the financial sector to foreign financial institutions.

As of 2011, foreign corporate structures have become significant participants in China's financial sector, particularly in the market for insurance and other non-bank financial services. Foreign banks have the right to compete with domestic banks for the business of domestic firms, although the continued strong role of the state in both banking and the industrial corporate sector makes it difficult for foreign firms to secure the largest domestic corporations as clients. Nevertheless, the modernist leadership in China has explicitly recognized that the competitive conditions created under WTO serve as an incentive for domestic firms to focus on those objectives most likely to result in improved value-creation potential (often interpreted as increased competitiveness) and, therefore, view WTO as an important instrument in meeting their domestic reform objectives.

The transition from feudalism to capitalism is noted for increasing economic competition and flexibility. Feudal economic relationships are relatively rigid social arrangements wherein direct producers are bound to the service of a specific boss and do not have the freedom to choose alternative employment in that sector. In the Chinese case it was the state that served this lordly role (in historical terms, it was not unusual for the state to serve as feudal lord). From 1959 to 1978, agencies of the state bureaucracy served as receivers and first distributors of value generated within industrial and agricultural enterprises, as well as revenues generated by financial, transport, merchant, and other large scale enterprises. In cases where enterprises were not controlled by the central government, they were controlled by provincial or local authorities. Rural and urban workers were assigned to work places by the state, these work places provided for a wide range of household needs, and worker mobility was tightly controlled by a state imposed household registration system. The rigidity of this system resulted in relatively low productivity and, thus, suppression of the value creation potential of the Chinese population.

Thus, the state directly monopolized all aspects of the value nexus. Given the prerogatives of feudal hierarchical organization, this produced an economic system where personal ties of fealty between various levels of managers within the bureaucratic structure were more important than value maximizing capital budgeting decisions or increasing aggregate demand.

Therefore, it is unusual for a regime dependent upon such arrangements to initiate the transition process to capitalist social relationships, with all the related risks of altering existing social relationships. The Japanese Meiji Restoration is one of the most prominent historical cases where such was the case. The Meiji Restoration did not shift power from the ruling elite in Japan, but rather shifted the value nexus from feudal institutional structures to new capitalist corporate structures, related banks, and a powerful state bureaucracy. It was with this new structure that the modernization of Japanese industry and infrastructure was implemented and rapid economic growth for over a century was generated.

The contemporary Chinese transition to capitalism has produced far more aggregate value, as well as average annual growth, than the Japanese transition. This value growth has been underpinned by a dramatic movement of the site of value receipt and distribution from state agencies (from within the state bureaucratic structure that had previously engulfed the whole of the economy) to autonomous firms; an equally dramatic devolution of control over many local enterprises from the central government bureaucracy to local governmental structures; and a massive Arthur Lewis-like migration of "surplus laborers" from the rural areas to the cities. Thus, control over capital budgeting (productive investment) processes was also shifted at the same time that downward pressures were exerted on urban labor (due to the aforementioned migration). The discipline of market relationships coupled with relatively low unit labor costs and the shift in the locus of control over key aspects of economic growth provided a context for economic success.

However, it might not have succeeded if not for the concurrent opening of the Chinese economy to the global capitalist marketplace, which became all the more vibrant with trading activity in the wake of the collapse of the Soviet Union and CMEA. This opening combined with these other processes to make possible the modernization of Chinese institutions and markets, provide important political cover for the CPC reforms, and generate the hard currency reserves that would insulate the Chinese economy from currency-based financial crises.

This shift and decentralization in economic power has been accompanied by changes in broader economic relationships and institutions, as well as non-economic aspects of the Chinese social formation (cultural, political, environmental processes and relationships). As already indicated, the reform and restructuring process has transformed the link between financial institutions and industrial firms, the key sites for the generation of value within the society. This nexus between financial institutions and industrial firms and, in particular, the way investment decisions at such firms have changed under the new environment is a key focus of exploration in this text. Exploring financial restructuring as a catalyst for changes in the investment landscape is part of the process of identifying the economic reforms as a specific Chinese version of the transition to capitalism with determinate consequences for modernization and economic growth. Ultimately, it is a goal of this text to understand the dynamics of transition/transformation in China and to analyze the potential that rapid growth can continue without a major economic crisis, as has often accompanied such transitions in the past. Indeed, the focus on financial institutions and processes is critical to this analysis, given that crises in capitalist economies have, typically, been endogenously generated within the financial sector.

On the cover of David Harvey's *A Brief History of Neoliberalism* is a photograph of Deng Xiaoping along with Ronald Reagan, Augusto Pinochet, and Margaret Thatcher. Obviously these are supposed to be icons of neoliberalism. It would not be difficult to construct a narrative in which the latter three serve as such icons of neoliberalism, but it is not so clear that such would be the case with Deng Xiaoping, leading figure of the post-Mao reformers within the CPC who took control in 1978 and began pushing for economic restructuring *in the context of continued dominance by the Party-state over economic affairs and a perpetuation of strong direct state involvement in every sector of the economy.*

This strong state approach contradicts the fundamental tenet of neoliberalism, calling into question any narrative of China's economic growth path that attributes it to neoliberal policies. Nevertheless, there has been a tendency in both popular and academic writings and speeches to confuse the modernist Marxian strategy behind the post-1978 reforms in China with neoliberalism, which argues for giving wide latitude to *private* corporate structures over economic affairs and a minimal role for the state. The CPC has clearly not embraced neoliberalism, although there may be elements within the larger CPC membership who embrace neoliberal theories, just as there remains a Maoist faction within the CPC who are none too happy with the economic reforms, but neither of these subsets of party members has representatives in the top leadership.

The current leadership has taken an unambiguously *anti*-liberal stance on the role of the state. The current leadership in China clearly believes in a strong state that intervenes at numerous points in the economy and explicitly monitors and aggressively regulates both individuals and corporate structures. In particular, the modernists have consistently retained within the state bureaucracy a large degree of control over those financial institutions that play a critical role in shaping the decision sets of industrial, merchant, extractive, construction, and service enterprises throughout the economy. Greater reliance on indirect financial and fiscal policy mechanisms (which are sometimes difficult to separate) allows the Party-state to manage aggregate demand and supply in a manner that is less heavy handed than under the previous command central planning mechanisms but considerably more aggressive than would be allowed for under any version of a neoliberal model.

To reinforce the point, this Chinese version of corporate capitalism should not be confused with the so-called Anglo-American/neoliberal version wherein corporate structures dominate economic, political, and cultural life and the regulatory reach of the state is relatively restricted. This Anglo-American/ neoliberal model is operative in the United States, Canada, the United Kingdom, Ireland, Australia, and a few other places, although even here we find a wide degree of variation over time and space: the United States has, at times, seen a relatively great degree of state involvement in the economy and at other times much lesser involvement, and at present there are clear differences in the degree of state involvement in the U.S. economy vis-à-vis the U.K. economy.

Perhaps one could make the argument that *Chinese capitalism* is closer to the Japanese version of corporate capitalism where economic life is dominated by the keiretsu (conglomerations of industrial, commercial, and financial institutions) working in close coordination with the state (particularly through various powerful state agencies, such as the Ministry of Finance or the former Ministry of International Trade and Industry, now part of the less powerful Ministry of Economy, Trade, and Industry), although even that comparison oversimplifies.

To understand the complexity of the Chinese economy requires being well-versed in its history, past structural innovations linking the Chinese state to industry and commerce, such as the creation of a professional bureaucracy overseeing state owned and controlled monopolies in backbone industries during the Han Dynasty, and some of the problems encountered in numerous past efforts to reform the system.

When the People's Republic of China (PRC) was founded in 1949, the only model for communist party rule was the Soviet-style centralized command and control system, one aspect of which was the absence of any clear boundary between Party and state (a reflection of the Leninist principle of a *vanguard party*), as well as between the Party-state and various economic enterprises. In the Soviet model, the state directly controlled all aspects of business enterprises, including the receipt and distribution of value. The integrated nature of government agencies and enterprises reduced uncertainties in the determination of a wide range of economic variables and guaranteed that value flows could be directed to various nodes (whether state agencies or enterprises) as needed, reducing systemic risk from spontaneous value imbalances or unemployment of resources or laboring potential but increasing the risk that planned variables, including quality variables, could be in disequilibrium conditions vis-à-vis the underlying needs of households, enterprises, and other economic units. The Soviet model was also notorious for its inability to encourage innovation, even when invention occurred at a high level of frequency, producing a lag in technological advance when compared to more decentralized economic systems.

Between 1949 and 1958, the CPC-controlled state copied the Soviet style of governance, placing large-scale enterprises that had been run by the defeated Nationalist government or powerful families with direct ties to that Nationalist Party under direct state control. In the period from the Great Leap Forward in late 1958 up until the beginning of the reform process in late 1978, the CPC-led state took on extraordinary powers over workers in both the city and countryside, exceeding the bounds of the Soviet model, which Resnick and Wolff identified as a form of *state capitalism*, and created an economic system that I have identified as a form of state feudalism (Gabriel 2006).

If anything, the state feudal system in China created the potential for even greater control over the economic and social lives of citizens. This did not, however, translate into greater social stability because internecine struggles within the CPC, particularly Mao's assault upon the Party-state bureaucracy and other social institutions, including schools and even households, with the Great Proletarian Cultural Revolution generated an extraordinary degree of social and economic instability.

However, even the Cultural Revolution did not result in any permanent dismantlement of the bureaucratic network of institutions underlying China's Soviet-style system. Mao was never powerful enough to do this. Nevertheless, the Cultural Revolution did weaken the bureaucratic structure (and traumatize the bureaucrats) sufficiently that it was possible for the reformers to set in motion an internal transformation of that system; to begin reorienting the bureaucratic network from feudal relationships to capitalist relationships; make a relatively painless transition from administered prices and wages to market exchange determined prices and wages; and to effect a decentralization of control over value flows that would strengthen the capacity of local governments, state enterprises, and eventually state banks so that they could act with greater autonomy under the discipline of harder budget constraints. Inducements to innovation and upgrading of technologies deployed throughout the economic system followed from these reforms and the increased competition that came out of the reforms.

Banks and other financial institutions have played a critical role in financing this transformation. These institutions were formerly integral parts of the state bureaucracy in both the Soviet state capitalist system and the Chinese state feudal system, serving as institutional instruments for reproducing the existing system. In this role, banks and other state-run financial institutions implemented state budgets and long-range plans, determining allocations of investment and decisions about innovation. Banks were also instrumental in reproducing the political hierarchies in both societies, including serving to reproduce particular factions within the respective communist parties. Thus, banks and other financial institutions can be seen as relatively system neutral.

The intermediation function that they perform is necessary to a wide range of systems. However, the modernization objective of the current CPC leadership requires that these financial institutions play a role in innovation that may not be universal to their functioning in other economic systems and is certainly different from the role of finance in Soviet-style systems, whether capitalist or feudal.

In order to encourage modernization via innovation and technological upgrades, the reformers had to find ways to directly challenge the old power structures, including breaking the economic bonds that served to reproduce many of the more powerful factions within the Party, without generating the sort of chaos that had come out of Mao's Cultural Revolution. The banking and larger financial system provided one of the vehicles through which this reorientation of the system towards greater innovation and technological upgrade could be effected.

Thus, the wide scale restructuring of China's economy has taken the form of releasing banks from their traditional role as instruments for meeting the project investment objectives of powerful political leaders, which diminished the importance of innovation and technological upgrades or, in some cases, actually stymied such modernization. Bank management was given greater autonomy to finance state enterprise modernization and financial institutions played a critical role in the restructuring of the state enterprise conglomerates through overseeing asset divestitures and spin-offs.

CHAPTER 14
HARD CURRENCY AND MODERNIZATION

Expansion and liberalization of a wide range of markets and the related opening up of the Chinese economy to foreign participation have been important elements in the reform process. Foreign participation in the Chinese economy has included contractual relationships linking Chinese firms to transnational firms headquartered within member nations of the Organization for Economic Cooperation and Development (OECD), the world's "advanced capitalist nations" club, where hard currency and advanced technology are pervasive. The contractual relationships linking Chinese firms to OECD firms have included subcontracting and joint venture agreements that provided channels for hard currency cash flows (as well as providing the basis for enhanced cash flows to transnationals and other firms in the OECD nations). Chinese firms with access to hard currency could modernize internal technology, gain access to critical natural resources, and access information critical to expanding marketing of Chinese products in the OECD universe. Over time, Chinese firms have become players in the international market for corporate control, acquiring firms in other nations, including the OECD universe. The overall effect of these relationships has clearly been supportive of Chinese firms becoming significant participants in the global economy.

As I argued in my 2006 book, these relationships have also linked the Chinese government to OECD-based transnationals. Whether or not the Chinese national, regional, or local governments have, in part or in whole, been "captured" within the sphere of influence of these transnationals remains to be seen, but it is unambiguously the case that these firms have increased influence on various levels and agencies of the Chinese government since the opening up process began. It is also true that the Chinese government and Chinese firms have increased influence upon the transnationals and, to some extent, the home governments of these transnationals, so the influence goes both ways.

The globalization of the Chinese economy has served the modernist agenda by stimulating rapid and unusually large accumulations of hard currency reserves that have flowed into the coffers of the People's Bank of China (PBOC). This hard currency accumulation has served the modernization objectives of the Party because the central bank has been able to exchange hard currency for yuan from member banks who could then lend hard currency (dollars, euro, yen) to favored industrial borrowers. These domestic firms could use the hard currency to purchase advanced technology from OECD-based sources or to acquire imported natural resources, for which Chinese firms have a growing appetite, or even to engage in mergers and acquisitions activities in foreign markets.

Indeed, in recent years hard currency has provided SOEs with the wherewithal to acquire OECD-based corporations as part of a growing foreign acquisitions strategy. The acquisitions are, perhaps, an even more effective means for modernization because Chinese firms can absorb not only material technology but also human talent, in the form of highly trained employees of the acquired firms, that is so critical to further invention and innovation. Mergers and acquisitions activities in Africa, South America, and Australia-Asia have also intensified, primarily involving firms in natural resources sectors.

Thus, hard currency accumulation combined with high levels of household and institutional savings have supported four key objectives of modernist Marxian theory: rising organic composition of capital, rising per worker productivity, the ability to self-finance modernization with domestic savings, and direct control over technological knowledge upon which future inventions and innovations are based. Chinese firms with the means to access soft (intangible) technology in the form of knowledge, both in patents and in the form of skilled workers employed by acquired OECD-based firms, are in a stronger position to compete in a world where technological transformation is taking place at an exponential rate. The result of this process has been rapid modernization of productive technologies and infrastructure generating greater production efficiencies and opening up new sources of value creation.

The success of this strategy can be measured, in part, by the rising income levels in China, particularly along the eastern coast. The growth of a relatively prosperous middle class and a much smaller but increasingly powerful wealthy class, typically with close ties to the Party-state, has reinforced the modernist faction's hold on power within the CPC and their continued implementation of economic reforms.

The availability of hard currency (even when combined with high savings rates) does not, in and of itself, bring about modernization and/or the creation of sustainable economic growth, much less the growth of a thriving middle income class. If this was the case, the major oil producing nations, with ready access to large amounts of hard currency earnings, would all be models of rapid sustainable economic growth. The institutional and infrastructural conditions to achieve sustainable economic growth are more complex than simply acquiring access to hard currency. A necessary but not sufficient condition for such sustainable economic growth is the existence of a financial system providing ongoing financial means for productive investment and firms driven to be both innovative and competitive leading to increased sales and higher net present value over time. If firms are creating more value, this is reflected in higher gross domestic product. After all, it is greater value, in the form of realized sales by firms and self-employed individuals, which is being measured in the gross domestic product statistics used to gauge relative economic success.

CHAPTER 15
PRODUCTIVE INVESTMENT

Productive investment can be subdivided into investment in property, plant, and equipment; investment in training and the general education of the work force; investment in research and development (which, for accounting purposes, is often counted as an expense rather than as a productive investment, as it should be for economic purposes since research and development is no different from other forms of productive investment in serving as catalyst for economic growth and development); and investment in inventory and other forms of working capital. When successfully implemented, these forms of investment enhance the value creation potential of enterprises and, due to the diffusion of technological knowledge, of the larger society (and eventually of the global community). The financial system provides the means for financing all of these forms of investment and mitigating risks that could undermine future value realization arising out of these investments.

In order to improve the likelihood that these investments will actually result in value growth, there must be mechanisms for the proper evaluation of value creating potential and the organizational effectiveness of firms in implementing investments. This requires skill at assessing risk because all investments are dependent upon future events for which there can be no absolute certainty. The tools used for such evaluation represent forms of technology. Thus, for financial institutions to be good stewards of the accumulated savings (and hard currency) of the society, there must be access to this evaluation technology, training in the use of such technology by agents of the financial institutions, and incentives to use the technology and make decisions based upon the proper use of such technology.

Financial sector reforms in China have incorporated all of these component elements in some form or fashion. However, the reforms have not eliminated all the vestiges of the old feudal bureaucratic structure and some retained elements from the old system may act at counter purposes to these new financial technologies, creating risks that are poorly recognized but potentially devastating to the Chinese and, by extension, the global economy.

While it may seem obvious that such technologies would be part of any reform process, it is important to remember that prioritizing value creation required the displacement of alternative system objectives, in particular the displacement of the feudal-era primacy of fealty to higher level officials and the related division of the bureaucracy and related corporate bodies into factions of officials with interrelated loyalties and obligations. The shift from the feudal structure to a capitalist structure is ongoing and has encountered difficulties inside bureaucratic structures, particularly within central and provincial government agencies.

The Soviet model of command-central planning was implemented, albeit in variant forms, in China, the nations of Eastern Europe and the former Soviet Union. The Soviet model can be viewed as a risk minimizing system, in the sense that it was designed to control as many social variables as possible and, in some cases, to use extraordinary coercion to force citizens into compliance with the edicts of the Party-state. Capital allocation decisions were determined within the planning bureaucracy, as were a wide range of other economic variables. To some extent all of the social formations to adopt this model suffered from poor capital allocation decisions (from a private net present value standpoint, externalities excluded).

Poor capital allocation decisions resulted in relatively anemic productivity growth and a history of non-performing loans and/or excessive subsidies from the central budget to financial institutions and industrial enterprises. These problems were manifest in China, just as in the other Soviet-style economies, but in China were also exacerbated by the feudal social arrangements discussed earlier. The old feudal economic and political structure was wasteful – costing the society resources that could have been utilized to raise standards of living (and, more broadly, the quality of life) for Chinese citizens. However, as Chris Bramall has eloquently pointed out in his discussion of Maoist China, the command and control model was actually very effective at investing in certain forms of infrastructure, providing the basis for initial growth that set the stage for long-term value creation once the reform process was developed. In other words, the rapid economic growth and strong investment path of China is, in significant part, a consequence of investments made during the pre-reform, Maoist era.

Most of the economies that had operated according to this Soviet model have made transitions to some version of market economies, albeit most typically from a version of state capitalism to private market capitalism, rather than from state feudalism, as was the case with China (Resnick and Wolff 2002; Gabriel, Resnick, and Wolff 2008, 2011). The restructuring of financial sectors has played an important role in altering investment processes in transitional economies, including China. In general, these transitions have sacrificed some of the risk minimizing characteristics of the old system in favor of the flexibility and capital allocation efficiencies of a decentralized, net present value oriented structure of financial institutions and the financial relationships linking such institutions to other firms and to households in the economy.

In the Chinese case, this has included facilitating the transfer of decision making authority from state bureaucracies to more decentralized and cash flow focused agencies, such as corporate directors and senior executives, who contract for loanable funds and other financial services with banks, and make a wide range of decisions related to the allocation of capital and the deployment of laborers. Invariably this shift in investment decision making has improved the effectiveness of investment decisions in generating value (measured in either microeconomic terms, as net cash flows to corporate structures, or macroeconomic terms, as gross domestic product), often compelled to do so by loan contracts or other newly created obligations.

Restructuring has also altered the sectoral pattern of investments, significantly increasing investments in consumer goods and the incidence of foreign direct investment (FDI). The latter has served to place some of the investment decision making in the discretion of foreign agents, creating further macroeconomic management complications for government officials. At the same time, investment has become more sensitive to global economic conditions and markets, as well as global political and cultural conditions. This is one of the outcomes of the larger process of globalization (where capitalist firms have become more decentered, in geographic terms). This globalization of investment is, perhaps, never more apparent than during economic crises.

Given that global political, economic, cultural, and environmental conditions are complex, volatile, and inter-related, the effect of greater globalization has been to increase the level of uncertainty in the economic system and, in particular, investment patterns and magnitudes. It has become all the more difficult for decision makers within corporate structures to feel confident about future product demand, pricing flexibility, cost structures, interest rates, political and even environmental conditions. These decision makers have increasingly turned to hedging schemes as a way to mitigate these uncertainties, but hedging is an inexact art and the associated probabilities, in any event, unknown. Investment is, to a significant extent, a function of expectations about uncertain future events. Greater uncertainty about the variable values that go into investment calculations results in greater sensitivity to any shift in such variables, given the perceived wider range of potential future values, both in positive and negative directions.

In other words, if we think of the relationship of investment to any variable as a partial derivative (of a constantly changing function) then the globalization process has resulted in an across the board increase in the magnitude of these derivatives and of the second derivatives (or rates of acceleration of changes in variable values) such that tipping points from states of relative stability to states of instability, including crisis situations where breaks in the value nexus occurs, becomes all the more likely. This has generated both more frequent investment booms and more violent busts, with the inflection points coming more suddenly and frequently than before.

However, investment decisions in China continue to be guided, to a significant extent, by political policies of the Party-state, which continues to value relative stability and holds enough control, at least at present, to mitigate some of the volatility of the (unknown and constantly changing) aggregate investment function. Perhaps there is reason for less concern about the predictability of future investment spending in China because government bureaucrats can ignore a wide range of factors that are not so easy to ignore by private agents (or even agents within state owned enterprises who are subject to hard budget constraints and, therefore, the prospect of bankruptcy).

However, government bureaucrats are not completely insulated from the effects of economic crises or the capture of public policies by increasingly powerful domestic and foreign firms. The real question is whether the state-centered model in China is less likely to generate such crises and/or reduce the magnitude of the domestic effects of such crises.

It is clear that investment decisions within public corporations (those with publicly traded shares) are sensitive to changes in a wide range of variables, from measures of consumer sentiment to measures of demand for intermediate goods to indicators of future political shifts in a wide range of countries and any number of other factors deemed relevant, results in more volatility in investment spending, as projects are postponed or terminated when indicators are perceived as negative and approved or expanded when these indicators are perceived as positive.

SOEs are more likely to push forward with investment projects when such projects are backed by their largest shareholder, the government. The Chinese government has shown a strong tendency to encourage more investment spending during times of external economic crises, such as the 1997-1998 Asian economic crisis or the more recent U.S.-centered global economic crisis, as well as to adopt economic stimulus spending to further boost aggregate demand. This state-centered counter-cyclical spending has dampened the effects of crises on the Chinese economy. If decentralization of investment spending decisions reduces the predictability of such investment and the related levels of hiring and aggregate demand in the economy, then continued liberalization of the Chinese economy could make it more vulnerable to economic crises.

Nevertheless, the cash flow nexus connecting corporate structures in China to corporate structures outside of China, as well as connecting government agencies (and bureaucrats) to both domestic and foreign corporate interests, has reshaped the priorities of countless economic agents, in the government and outside of it. It is also not difficult to understand how managers and directors in newly autonomous corporate structures (even though they might remain, to a significant extent, state owned) would be incentivized to work for successful reform when the end result might mean they would gain both greater income, status, and power to shape their work environment than was the case under the old feudal structure.

As previously noted, local officials were supportive of the reforms because decentralization of the economic structures enhanced their political position and gave them more control over locally generated cash flows, either directly or indirectly. The growing linkages between local governments and local firms and powerful transnational corporate structures has enlarged these cash flows and exerted further influence on the political agendas set at local levels and beyond.

Military officials within the People's Liberation Army (PLA) continue to play a critical role within the Party-state and have been largely coopted by the reformers because higher value creation and related cash flows to the defense budget has allowed significant progress to be made in meeting another of Zhou Enlai's Four Modernizations: modernization of national defense structures. Although China's military spending budget pales in comparison to the United States, it has been growing faster than defense budgets in OECD nations and China is no longer viewed as militarily weak. The country is even building its first aircraft carrier (whereas the United States has eleven).

Thus, a wide range of agents in the society have been incentivized to support the process of transition from the feudal to the capitalist structure and, perhaps more to the point, have become dependent upon the current growth strategy of the Party-state. These incentives and dependencies are strong enough that it appears likely the transition will continue and the capitalist structure will be strengthened in coming years, making a reversal to the old structure unlikely, even in the event of a major economic crisis, and despite a significant opposition both outside and inside the Party.[41]

In fact, economic transition in China has benefited a significant subset of the same political, managerial, and military elites that held high level status under the previous system. It is doubtful that reforms would have been implemented if this had not been the case. However, the transition has also benefited an expanded segment of the society and provided the means to build a modern infrastructure that serves the society at large, creating a much wider level of public support for the reforms than would have been the case if they only served to enhance the well-being and status of elements of the old elite. Thus, historically high long-run economic growth rates attributed to the transition have also played and continue to play a critical role in legitimizing communist party rule and reproducing social stability.

On the other hand, it is clear that such decentralization has positive effects on innovation and competitiveness, both of which are associated with the concept of modernization and with the long term sustainability of economic growth. In other words, the transition from state-centered to market-centered investment may result in some level of trade-off between stability and volatility (or risk).

There were many inherent shortcomings of the centrally planned economy, like the defective functioning of a planning mechanism dependent on processing huge amounts of data and making correct allocation decisions about future demand, incentives that often fostered value destruction, rather than value creation, and the absence of hard budget constraints that might have reduced agency costs and systemic waste, but one of the strengths of the central planning system was its greater predictability than the market system. For the leadership of most communist party ruled regimes, including the leadership

---

41 Bo Xilai was considered a leading proponent of factions with closer links to the Maoist past, although this may be an oversimplication. In any event, his downfall will likely weaken factions opposed to the modernist reformers.

in Beijing, this predictability was a definite positive of the old system. In the past this predictability was cherished to the point of strangling the innovative capabilities of the system. The CPC leadership is certainly not less interested in maintaining stability than their "comrades" from past decades or those former party bosses of the old CMEA nations, many of whom have gone on to entrepreneurial riches in the less economically stable "post-communist" societies.

In fact, given China's history, social stability is an important objective of virtually all the political factions on both mainland China *and* Taiwan. However, fear of social instability is balanced by a strong desire for modernization precisely because of the humiliations of the Opium Wars and other periods when more technologically advanced foreign military forces were able to impress their will upon the Chinese nation. The tension between trying to find a path to continued social stability and simultaneously modernizing the economy (and military) has been an important part of the social and political fabric of China for much of the past two hundred years. The decision by the leadership to initiate a transition in the type of economy they were governing was a definite nod in the direction of pushing the limits of modernization without losing social stability.

The leadership recognizes that in the long run, failure to modernize would be, in itself, destabilizing. In a world of rapid technological advance, failure to adopt modern ways could ultimately undermine the Party-state and related institutions and leave China vulnerable, once again, to foreign domination. Nevertheless, the leadership will only go so far (or so fast, which isn't exactly the same thing) in adopting new institutional relationships and structures that foster decentralization of political, as well as economic, power. The Beijing leadership has no intention of relaxing controls to such an extent that social tension is allowed to surface in more dangerous forms than has already been witnessed in various mostly rural locales. This is one of the reasons that the Chinese state has retained a strong role in the economy during this process of transition, with only the slightest drift away from the Leninist model of

Party-state governance.

The reforms of the period after 1978 have seen the gradual decentralization in economic authority and the transition from *state run* to *state owned* enterprises, as well as the dramatic growth in private enterprises and enterprises controlled or closely associated with local governments, but has done little to alter the underlying feudal culture that shapes all social relationships, including business and governmental relationships. The ascendance of capitalist ethics and related relationships is taking place slowly under the influence of globalization. Decentralization of the financial system is proceeding in a similar slow fashion. Growth of stock markets and associated financial institutions, as well as the growing role of foreign invested financial firms within the domestic economy and the financial culture they bring with them, are likely to have a strong influence upon the way business relationships evolve. Financial reform is likely to foster rather dramatic changes in decision making processes and outcomes within a wide range of corporate structures in China but the changes will not come overnight.

After the 1949 revolution, China's financial system was consolidated under a single bank, the People's Bank of China (PBOC), in what is sometimes described as a mono-bank system. A number of branches catering to the needs of specific regions were later established, decentralizing key functions of the PBOC. The decentralization would be further enhanced in the late 1950s with the establishment of four additional state banks to provide a broader range of banking services to specific sectors of the economy/bureaucracy. The "Big Four" state-owned banks consisted of China Construction Bank (CCB), Bank of China (BOC), Industrial and Commercial Bank of China (ICBC) and Agricultural Bank of China (ABC). These big four took over some of the PBOC's commercial banking business as it began its transformation into a more narrowly focused central bank, albeit one that remained far from the traditional model. The State Council served as overlord over the banking system and the banking system served as primary regulator of the industrial, commercial, construction, and extractive sectors, playing a critical role in both implementing national political policies and minimizing systemic risk.

The PBOC functioned as both the central bank and a lending institution to non-financial enterprises from 1950 to 1978. During this period, the PBOC served as the primary financial organ of the state bureaucracy, regulating other financial institutions and simultaneously financing long-term investment projects of state-run firms with budgetary grants and loans out of the central budget. The other four banks served a lesser, though closely-related, role of channeling state funds to favored projects in the industrial, commercial, extractive, and other sectors. In other words, the PBOC and the big four were integral parts of the same bureaucratic structure as state-run firms in non-financial sectors, serving as component nodes in a financial network designed for redistributing value within the bureaucracy and channeling value (in the form of loans and grants) to state-run firms at the command of the central authorities, most notably the State Council, which served as the primary executive authority.

By the end of 1979, in the early stages of the transition from state feudalism to state capitalism, PBOC and the big four banks were separated from the Ministry of Finance. The big four began transitioning to commercial bank status, and the PBOC was granted the full authority of a central bank (Naughton 2007). This financial restructuring was an important step in the decentralization of the state bureaucracy, serving as another condition for transitioning state-run firms into more autonomous SOEs and for increasing privatization of value appropriation and distribution and investment decision making, reducing the role of the bureaucracy in these processes.

However, the party bureaucracy has retained a significant degree of influence over hiring and promotion of key bank executives. This has made it possible for key factions within the Party to populate the top executive positions within the big banks with supporters, guaranteeing that financial decisions retain a strong political flavor, even as reforms have increased the role of valuation analysis and other professional criteria for lending decisions (Ping 2013). For instance, Liu Mingkang, who served until 2011 as the first chair of the China Banking Regulatory Commission, was a former director of the Bank of China and also a former deputy head of Fujian Province in 1993. These same political factions vie for positions in the State Council. Under the old system top-level bank executives were appointed by the State Council and many of the current top executives in the banking system owe allegiance to specific factions, directly or indirectly. Prior to the 1990s, the industrial system was dominated and, to a significant extent, controlled by these four banks through the nexus of financing, further extending the reach of political factions, as well as the terrain over which they competed.

The historical role of the Big Four

Until relatively recently, when the big four banks were spun off from the Ministry of Finance (MOF) to become commercial entities, each had its distinct role within the bureaucratic structure that largely differentiated it from the other three. CCB executed the cash payment and receipt orders of the Capital Construction Finance Department of the Ministry of Finance, which in turn received these orders (primarily for infrastructure projects) from the State Council. The BOC (which had served as a central bank during the Nationalist government before 1949 and was subsequently subsumed within the PBOC) issued foreign exchange certificates (the only legal currency allowed to foreigners, under a dual currency regime, before 1990) and otherwise served as the agency regulating foreign exchange for the bureaucracy. ICBC was established to take over most of the commercial transactions previously conducted by the PBOC, while ABC was responsible for financing State Council approved rural business investment. Prior to the commercialization of the big four banks, banking capital consisted primarily of bank notes, essentially functioning as scrip of the bureaucracy. Only the PBOC and the BOC had any significant capital beyond scrip, mostly in the form of meager amounts of foreign exchange reserves and gold.

From the late 1950s to 1986, the commercial loan and credit authority that had been concentrated within the PBOC was gradually disseminated among the four state banks. Households had little alternative to placing their savings on deposit in these banks, earning a low rate of interest set by the same bureaucracy that controlled the banks. Thus, wide scale participation in financing official investment was a fundamental structural attribute of the system, placing no burden on the bankers to either properly evaluate loans or to serve the interests of their depositors (who had no alternative savings venues, other than the family mattress, so to speak).

The creation of joint-stock commercial banks

The reformers in Beijing recognized the need to change this situation and between 1986 and 2001, 11 joint-stock commercial banks (JSCBs) were established. These JSCBs were commercial banks set up as partnerships of other corporate structures, each of which had a unique relationship with specific subsets of government officials and local interest groups. Most JSCBs were owned by diverse groups of SOEs, government agencies, and non-SOEs (Peng 2007). The JSCBs added flexibility to the financing system by providing an alternative source of funds for SOEs and enterprises owned by lower levels of government, such as provinces, municipalities, and county administrations. Although this reform did not separate politics from banking, it did allow for more agents to participate in setting the objectives of bank lending, therefore making a broader range of investment spending and entrepreneurial endeavors more likely.

The benefits of bank expansion

Expansion of the number of banks and increasing the flexibility of financing are critical elements in fostering more value creating investments (and, perhaps, in a more significant sense, adding to the possibilities for innovative activities) by providing options for firms that might lack necessary social and political ties to officials of the big four banks. On the other hand, because the new banks are joint-stock companies owned by other corporate structures and local or provincial governments then these new banks are subject to similar non-financial pressures to make loans to associated firms or to satisfy policy or personal preferences of a subset of government officials. This is the balance that drives much of the financing in the Chinese banking system, with the shift towards value creation and away from policy loans continuous but hardly complete.

Nevertheless, more banks are probably better than fewer in bringing this result about and certainly making financing possible for a wider range of firms has implications for future growth and employment creation, key objectives of the Party leadership. Therefore, it is likely that banking sector reforms will continue in a similar vein, with more banks allowed to compete for depositors and borrowers. This could bode well for entrepreneurs. On the other hand, as the number of banks and other financial institutions expand, broadening participation in capital financing, the predictability of future capital costs and capital availability may be more difficult to predict, adding another element of uncertainty to the economy.

In the late 1980s, the modernist leadership, particularly then Premier Zhu Rongji, led the successful struggle within the CPC to establish a domestic stock market. The primary objectives for the stock market were to provide a vehicle for transformation of the planned economy into a market economy, to facilitate the conversion of solely state-owned enterprises into joint-stock and limited liability corporations with only partial state ownership, and to raise capital for the modernization of these enterprises. This institutional reform would serve as part of a larger plan to restructure and downsize the SOEs during the 1990s, reorganize the internal decision making structure with greater decision making autonomy to firm directors, and reduce the internal costs of maintaining these firms as component elements in the state bureaucracy.

At the same time, initial public offerings would provide an injection of new capital for SOEs and serve as a direct nexus connecting corporate management to a burgeoning market for corporate control. To eliminate the temptation for the bureaucracy to siphon the funds from the listing firms, control over funds raised in the IPO were placed under the exclusive control of the firm's directors or, in the case of firms within holding companies, under the jurisdiction of holding company directors. Government bureaucrats were not allowed to access these funds, even when the state held sufficient shares to control the firm.

The Party-state and the establishment of stock exchanges in the transition to capitalism

Two domestic stock exchanges were established in 1990: the Shanghai Stock Exchange (SHSE) and the Shenzhen Stock Exchange (SZSE). Both exchanges have experienced rapid growth in the number of stocks traded and total volume of trading since opening for business. See Figs. 17.1 and 17.2.

The total value of equity trading in these markets now exceeds that in Tokyo, previously the largest equity trading center in Asia.

Figure 17.1

Source: Shanghai Stock Exchange

Figure 17.2.

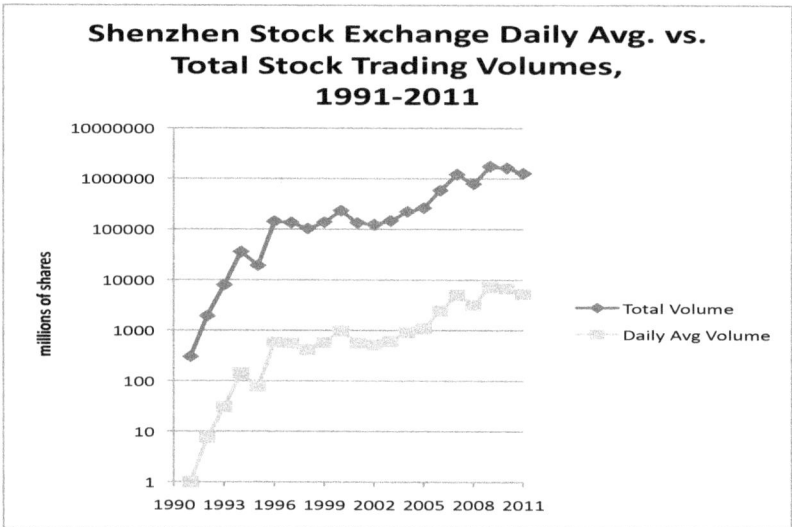

Source: Shenzhen Stock Exchange

Whereas many financial markets in more advanced capitalist economies were the result of institutional innovation designed to meet capital needs originating within a growing corporate sector that operated largely outside of direct governmental control (or even significant indirect control), China's stock market was developed from the top for the primary purpose of facilitating the financing of large SOEs and granting further autonomy to enterprise directors and managers charged with building more modern, more competitive enterprises capable, ultimately, of competing in global marketplaces.

The stock market was carefully planned and implemented by the Party-state to serve its goals and objectives, including but certainly not limited to expanding the supply and demand for financial capital to fuel the transition to and expansion of capitalist class processes within China and the modernization of existing plant and equipment deployed within SOEs. It is not, in any sense, the result of spontaneous market forces, equilibrating supply and demand conditions generated by autonomous economic agents acting with little or no governmental influence, or historical inevitability. As with so many of the institutional changes that have constituted a transition from state feudalism to state capitalism, the development of stock markets was the result of compromises among the ruling factions within the CPC.

The conjuncture of financial market reform with the transition to capitalism is predicated upon the partial privatization of capital allocation decisions which represented a shift in economic power within the society. The money capital flowing into SOEs linked those firms to economic agents that had not previously been empowered to shape capital allocations; in particular it empowered the buyers of corporate capital securities. These buyers have gained influence over the determination of the cost of capital for both SOEs and private firms in the Chinese economy. This influence over the cost of capital introduces a channel by which these private economic agents can directly influence capital budgeting decisions and, therefore, aggregate investment demand in the economy.

Again, given the importance of investment demand to growth rates of the economy and the creation of employment, these new connections between SOEs (and private firms) and private economic agents involved in the financial markets, including the new equity markets, has fundamentally changed the dynamics of the Chinese economy.

Nevertheless, as has already been indicated, the financial markets in China were developed largely as instrumentalities of the state rather than as the outgrowth of an independent corporate sector. Any attempt to model the behavior of financial markets in China must take into account the role of the Party-state in determining which firms can raise funds via stock markets, as well as state directed access to bank financing.

To the extent the Party-state continues to exert this authority over financial markets, decisions about capital budgeting will continue to be strongly influenced by public policy decisions, as well as valuation criteria exerted by private economic agents who make up the market for corporate securities. The mix of influences, public policy versus private valuation criteria, upon capital budgeting/investment decisions is significantly different in China than might be anticipated in most capitalist economies of the current period. The investment function in China is, therefore, not simply a function of market generated variables but must include *at least* one policy variable (and probably multiple policy variables to capture the relative influence of different levels of government and different agencies within each level). This has direct implications for business cycles in China, although one must also recognize that this relationship is fluid. It is possible that, over time, investment in China will drift away from state direction and become simultaneously more flexible and more volatile, producing both more innovation and more frequent economic crises.

Expansion of the equity markets to serve both SOEs and private firms has deepened the link between aggregate investment demand and private portfolio investors. Because employment, sales and cash flow growth rates of private firms exceeds that of SOEs, the private firm share of GDP has been growing, indicating that a drift towards a lower percentage of state directed investment in overall investment demand is proceeding and the importance of private investment is increasing.

The shift to private investment and reduction of moral hazard

In the early period of the transition to capitalism in China, this shift to private firms was slow, particularly given the exclusion of private firms from big four financing and then from the new equity markets. The restructuring and expansion of the banking sector and opening up of equity markets to private firms has created opportunities for private firms that had previously not existed. This has provided a new source of investment and economic growth that is likely to continue to expand over time but also represents a decrease in state control over investment and employment creation resulting in less predictability of aggregate demand. Increased instability may be one of the costs of deepening the capitalist economy such that rapid growth is more likely to be sustainable over the longer term, albeit with heightened potential for recessions or worse.

Expanding the sources of capital is also an attempt by the Party-state to reduce the importance of the Party-state-commercial bank-SOE relationship. This latter relationship led to loans that were often driven by politics and personal connections, resulting in an accumulation of non-performing loans (NPLs) that created a financial burden on state finances and a form of moral hazard. The problems of the banking system are well known and many analysts believe the problems grave enough to eventually precipitate a financial crisis that could then trigger a broader economic crisis. It is not surprising then that one of the objectives of the Beijing leadership in the transition process was to reduce the magnitude of these NPLs without exacerbating the potential systemic risk from removing the role of the state as guarantor of these loans.

However, it is unclear that the equity markets will not introduce an additional source of systemic instability, since it is possible that equity valuations may impact not only the ability of firms to raise equity capital but could influence lending and other financial relationships.

The Party-state leadership is not only addressing the financing problems of SOEs with the development of equity markets, but is also expanding the network of relationships linked to the new capitalist economy, building a larger coalition in favor of the reform process (and, by extension, of the factions that are currently dominant within the CPC). The leadership recognized the moral hazard problem that originated in the old feudal bureaucratic structure, where all firms, financial and non-financial, operated within a singular budgetary regime, as well as the fact that a large number of economic agents depended upon that system and, at least some of which, were less than supportive of the reforms. In the old system, no firm faced financial consequences from negative net present value decisions, so long as the firms' leadership fulfilled the politically determined objectives passed along from the national leadership and often embodied in the five year plan. This arrangement reduced risks to individual economic agents, as well as systemic risk.

However, systemic costs were very high, due to soft budget constraints and the absence of incentives for management of state-run enterprises to make positive net present value decisions. The leadership sought to improve the efficiency of the system by hardening budget constraints, pushing firm directors and executives, including those in the banks, to take value creation seriously, without simultaneously generating a sharp contraction in investment with a concomitant rise in unemployment. This change was initially traumatic for many people and generated some degree of resistance. The creation of new financial relationships, including the creation of equity markets, has expanded the opportunities for participation in the new economy, enlarged the number of people who potentially benefit directly from value creation within SOEs (and other firms), and helped to neutralize those economic agents who continue to oppose the reforms.

Large SOEs were required to restructure their financing and governance system in a gradual and orderly process guided by state agencies and under the ultimate control of the State Council. Development of the stock market and the subsequent sale of a portion of state shares to the private sector was one of the steps in this process of restructuring. However, the Party-state retained a modicum of control over all aspects of the financial process (the supply and demand side of the markets for securities), as well as the functioning of the partially privatized SOEs. Strict rules governing which firms could "go public" and who could purchase shares were elements in this process of retaining control and, essentially, rationing finance capital. Capital budgeting decisions, the determination of product mix and pricing, human resource decisions, and a wide range of other management decisions were constrained by the imposition of targets and restrictions originating within the Party-state bureaucracy. In other words, the transition from bureaucratic control over capital budgeting and other management decisions was not something that happened over night, but has been gradual.

However, over time, equity markets have grown more important in the economy and the relative autonomy of SOEs has increased, partly because as SOEs have become more important centers of value creation and private firms have expanded, public policy has ceased to be the sole province of the Party-state bureaucracy, more elements within the Party have been "captured" by corporate interests, including the SOEs, and the channels for SOEs and private firms to influence public policy have expanded. The decentralization of governmental authority that has also been a hallmark of the reforms (see Gabriel 2006 for an extensive discussion of this) has worked to intensify the shift in power over public policy.

The continued shift away from state authority can also be seen in the continued reform of the equity markets. Early on, the state's micromanagement of the stock market went so far as restricting the range of IPO prices, presumably to reduce the risk that the IPO could be unfairly manipulated to cheat SOEs that were going public, shifting value into the hands of private economic agents, including firms engaged in merchant banking and the buyers of the new securities. These administrative rules and interventions can be viewed as either creating more stability in the system by enforcing boundaries around decision choice sets, which was clearly one of the intentions, or of generating more unpredictability because government policy is formulated under conditions of relatively low transparency and policy makers do not directly or predictably respond to signals originating from market-based sources. In this latter point of view, the Chinese approach to stock markets is understood as generating significant *political risks* to market participants, a factor that could actually lower the value of the partially privatized SOEs by increasing the discount rate applied by buyers. By introducing a new set of political risks associated with buying and selling securities, the Party-state alters the decisions and reaction functions of market participants and, therefore, changes the vectors of prices and quantities generated by stock market transactions and the volatility of these prices and quantities exchanged. These political conditions and lack of transparency would also result in alternative investing strategies for market participants, calling into question any attempt to apply models formulated on the basis of less political and more transparent stock markets.

The confidence factor in the creation of financial markets

The Chinese government recognizes the correlation between confidence in the fairness and efficiency of securities markets and the relative willingness of portfolio investors to participate in such markets. This recognition has translated into a continuous push for improvements in the regulatory regime and the institutions vested with the authority to enforce that regime. By all indications, the government has had some success in raising the confidence level of both domestic and international portfolio investors, at a minimum creating the impression that the system is not rigged, despite the Party's continued enforced dominance over the economic institutions of the state and of publicly traded SOEs. The public relations success in developing financial markets that attract wide scale participation is even more impressive given the general perception of a culture of corruption in most aspects of economic life in China. Confidence translates into larger sums of capital flowing into securities markets and this undoubtedly raises confidence in other financial markets where loanable funds and insurance are provided to SOEs and private firms.

Thus, the development of regulatory agencies and related rules of the game, combined with a successful public relations campaign to raise confidence in these agencies' abilities to enforce those rules of the game, augurs well for the fund raising efforts of firms in China, including fund raising beyond China's borders and fund raising for firms that are engaged in transnational economic activities. To the extent these efforts are successful, firms may face more stable financing prospects and reduced overall risk.

In pursuit of this stabilizing function of securities markets, the Party-state has formulated the following principles for the development of domestic securities markets: i) the development of a legal and prudential regulatory system that creates confidence in the fairness of securities transactions; ii) standardization of trading technologies based on the best practices; iii) world class supervision; and iv) the fostering of self-discipline (in following rules and practicing corporate "good behavior" or "virtue" – a concept with direct corollaries in Confucianism, a key driver of social stability in past versions of feudal culture) on the part of managers and directors at publicly traded corporations and bureaucrats operating the equity markets.

The financial market and the creation of differentiated share ownership

The expansion of securities trading to new instruments, particularly the development of a bond market (with the corporate bond market only becoming a source of capital in 2004, but having expanded rapidly since that time), and the development of a more flexible market for foreign exchange transactions were implemented to deepen the role of markets in providing for the financing and hard currency access necessary to firms engaged in technological innovation and global expansion.

The sale of equity of China's largest state banks to foreign investors was put into place in 2005, reinforcing the general impression that the trend in financial institutions, as in other sectors, was towards greater levels of privatization and transparency than had previously been the case and providing substantial new financial capital for the role of these banks in the capital accumulation plans of SOEs and, to a lesser extent, private firms (Peng 2007).

The Party-state has clearly focused on solving long-term capital financing and budgeting problems of the SOEs, in particular, and the larger social structure that has arisen under reform, more generally. However, it remains unclear how far the Party-state will go in the privatization process. The Party-state initially attempted to strictly control who could buy into the *partially* privatized (non-state agents were minority shareholders) SOEs. Domestic investors could buy "A" shares, foreign investors were restricted to buying "B" shares (with hard currency), and shares trading in Hong Kong were classified as "H" shares. These three classes of shares, at least on paper, had the same rights and obligations, but segregating private owners was another step in guaranteeing the state would maintain controlling interest in publicly traded SOEs.

The creation of "B" shares is actually a more liberal move than one might assume. Many poor, industrializing (and sometimes transitional) economies are closed to foreign portfolio investors, including India, which is often seen as the favored rival to China in the competition for most powerful "Third World" nation. Thus, the internationalization of China's equity markets can be seen as an important signal that the Party-state would go further with reforms than might at first have seen likely. More recently, equity trading has been liberalized but the state retains controlling interest in a large number of very powerful and increasingly transnational SOEs.

As China's SOEs grow into more active and prominent transnational firms, further internationalization of equity markets is all but inevitable, given the linkages between accessing foreign markets and technologies and such liberalization, both from an economic and political standpoint. As early as 2001, the Party-state transformed "B" shares from an instrument for restricting foreign ownership to an instrument for attracting hard currency by allowing Chinese citizens to legally purchase "B" shares with hard currency. Expanding the rights of Chinese citizens to participate in the equity markets beyond the right to purchase "A" shares was an explicit recognition of the growing importance of a well-to-do stratum of the Chinese population, households with extraordinarily high incomes engaged in the accumulation of substantial wealth, with access to hard currency, and not very different from well-to-do foreign portfolio investors. The growth of this relatively well-to-do stratum, the highest level of which is quite wealthy, has changed the economic, political, and cultural dynamics of the People's Republic in ways that are not altogether predictable.

The instrumental role of a stock market in the transition to capitalism

A stock market can play an instrumental role in the transition to a capitalist economy in a variety of ways. First, prices can provide signals of the confidence in corporate management, as long as there is sufficient liquidity and prices fairly accurately reflect supply and demand for particular equity shares, encouraging management to take actions that increase shareholder value, providing a means for shareholders to signal displeasure at egregious cases of management abuse of power (agency problems), assuming there is sufficient transparency for such cases to be exposed. For initial public offerings, at least in the absence of state imposed pricing limitations, the initial pricing of shares and subsequent trading prices after those shares go public can provide signals helpful in gauging the viability (or, at least, the popularity) of business strategies and, by influencing the extent to which future firms can tap securities markets, may improve the overall efficiency of capital allocation. Second, the public issuance of shares can provide investment resources for enterprises that have insufficient retained earnings to finance positive net present value investments and/or are unable or unwilling to go to the banks for financing. Third, the stock market plays a crucial role in asset diversification for savers, reducing risks associated with less diversified portfolio investments and, therefore, lowering required returns and the cost of capital calculated on the basis of these required returns.

The first of these benefits provides an incentive for corporate management to implement strategies for raising overall firm value, producing more income and, potentially, more employment as a result. The second provides direct investment funds that drive growth in value and job creation. The ability to raise investment funds in the securities markets (either in the form of equity shares or public bond issues) can provide a means for reducing the risk that the firm could face a liquidity shortfall or even a full-blown liquidity crisis, particularly when such problems occur as a result of the timing of cash flow receipts and expenditures, rather than due to some underlying fatal flaw in business planning or execution. Ironically, such liquidity problems are one of the likely results of rapid economic growth, as firms find their costs accelerating faster than revenues can be realized. Under such circumstances, a well-functioning financial market (or banking system) can be critical.

Party-state interference and illiquid market risks

However, a stock market does not automatically provide any of these benefits. The Chinese government has, generally, exercised a great deal of control over the development of the stock market and, in particular, in the selection of who can issue shares. This Party-state's control over the role of the stock markets in channeling capital to firms can short circuit the first of the conditions above. Rather than institutional relationships between sell and buy side firms and the general conditions of securities markets determining initial public offerings, the Party-state has the power to select that subset of firms allowed to go public, as well as to place bounds on the pricing of subsequent IPOs. It exercises these powers.

Further complicating the impact of securities trading upon capital allocation decisions, including initial public offerings, is the relatively thin market in buyers and sellers of securities and the relative absence of complementary institutions, such as a free press, an efficient and independent legal system, and a group of mature institutional investors, all of which play critical roles in improving market efficiency at sending appropriate signals that firms are operating on the basis of value enhancing strategies and without bearing greater than anticipated risks.

Of course there are no guarantees that deep markets with appropriate institutional structures will send the right signals all the time, but the absence of these conditions only makes it all the less likely that market signals will the appropriate signals to guide improved capital allocation decisions. Economic agents (individuals, firms, or government agencies) adapt to the larger institutional context within which they operate. In a relatively illiquid market context, where market prices are more likely to be subject to manipulation, economic agents will attempt to gain access to insider information relevant to the manipulation, follow some simple heuristic that is believed to provide information compatible with the manipulated market results, act on rumors of the direction in which the manipulation is likely to move prices, or avoid the markets altogether due to the absence of inside information or any reliable heuristic. To the extent the latter is the case, the market will remain relatively illiquid. Securities markets in China are widely believed to be subject to such manipulation. It should not, therefore, be surprising that the securities markets in China remain relatively underdeveloped with relatively poor liquidity and that equity prices are likely to diverge significantly and often unpredictably from fundamentals of the underlying firms, as those who do participate in trading are guided by the methods described above.

The irrational exuberance of Chinese equity prices

In the early period of the stock markets, the limited supply of shares, relative to demand for equity, added a supply constraint factor to the determination of prices and tended to drive up prices, which caused many market participants to operate on the basis of the same expectation that an upward trend in prices would persist even without a firm fundamental basis for such valuation. During the boom market of 2000, Chinese shares traded at an average price to earnings (P/E) ratio well above 40 (Green 2003).

The high P/E ratios may be understood as rational, from one point of view, given the unusually rapid rate of growth of the Chinese economy and underlying firms, as well as the limited options for portfolio diversification by Chinese portfolio investors. It is, after all, rational to pay more for faster growth in cash flows, which overall rapid growth of the Chinese economy make possible. One may also look at the early boom in stock prices as simply an element in the learning and adjustment process of economic agents unaccustomed to stock markets, in general, or to an emerging stock market in a context of unusually rapid economic growth, in particular.

The struggle by Chinese portfolio investors to adapt to the new economy and stock market may also be a product of cognitive changes in individual decision-making during a transitional period where capitalism is being established on a wide-scale manner for the first time.

Finally, the early boom in equity prices may simply be ascribed to a supply-demand bottleneck as a fraction of China's unusually large accumulation of household savings (relative to income) was shifted into the equity markets in a short time frame. In any event, it is difficult, if not impossible, to decipher the underlying motivations for buy and sale decisions in equity markets and there is no firm basis for ascribing rational information analysis to portfolio investors in either developed or emerging equity markets, much less a society undergoing a transition of economic systems.

The value of publicly traded corporations can appear quite straightforward. Stock valuation is the net present value, properly discounted, of future cash flows generated by the portfolio of investments that comprise the productive assets of the corporation in the context of management expertise at coordinating this portfolio and exploiting synergies. However, the variables that generate this valuation, operational cash flows and the underlying growth rates that determine the changes in cash flows from one period to another, the risks that these cash flows might deviate from some mean value, and all the inputs necessary to determining current and future cash flows, including institutional components shaping the effectiveness of marketing, training and management, and research and development, are uncertain (and not subject to any knowable probability distribution). These variables are embedded within an overdetermined and, therefore, constantly changing matrix of other economic, political, cultural, and environmental processes.

Political factors in the valuation of assets

Calculating the value of corporate assets in China requires *estimates* of not only current but future input costs, sales revenues, taxes, managerial compensation, and other distributive payments to agents whose activities are necessary to securing the cash flows, as well as the underlying growth rates of all these variables. All of these factors are influenced by Party-state policies, at both the national and local levels. These factors and the valuation derived from them are also shaped by *guanxi* relationships, which are also constantly changing, and which are integral to the relationships between firms, banks, and the various agencies of the Party-state, including those at the local level.

Stock prices in China, as elsewhere, are partly a reflection of expectations about corporate valuation, but in a context where politics plays such a critical role in not only the components of valuation but in the changing constellation of rules of the economic game within which the relationships that determine those components are embedded. Stock valuation becomes as much a political, as an economic, phenomenon. This is all the more the case because banks continue to dominate capital financing in China and banking relationships with firms remains, to a significant extent, political.

In the Chinese case, if individual investors restrict their valuation activities to calculating expected future growth rates without taking into account potential political changes, then it is likely their results will be inferior to agents who do take a more broad-based analytical approach. Observed stock prices represent the interaction of a wide range of agents deploying alternative strategies for determining intrinsic stock values or simply anticipating, based on some heuristic, future stock price changes, including heuristics that are based purely on political activities that impact stock price movements. As with all stock markets, the collective wisdom, or lack thereof, is embodied in observed stock prices.

The transitional nature of the Chinese economy and the emerging nature of the Chinese stock markets provide some justification for the difficulty in valuation and, at least in the initial stages of marketization, higher levels of variability of stock prices. In the case of China, these conditions are added to by the state centered nature of the economy and the fact that most publicly traded firms were and continue to be state owned, with minority shareholders having ambiguous rights.

The liberalization of the market for corporate control

The primary purpose of the stock markets was to raise funds for state owned firms, to allow these firms additional non-state resources to use for modernization, and to provide an institutional means for broadening support for reforms by directly giving Chinese households a monetary stake in the success of publicly traded firms owing to the reforms. The more household wealth was tied to the stock valuation of state owned firms, the more citizens became cheerleaders for any policy that might add to that valuation. The most effective means by which the state encouraged citizens to put their money into domestic stock markets was by limiting the rewards to bank savings accounts via interest rate repression and by using capital controls to keep domestic portfolio investors from investing overseas.[42] In addition the central government restricted which firms could go public, thus limiting the fruits of this reform to select state owned firms.

The equity markets also provided an institutional mechanism for wedding Chinese firms to each other, mimicking the form of Galbraithian bureaucratic capitalism pioneered in East Asia by Japan. Before 2005, a significant percentage (from 50-75%) of state owned firm shares were non-tradeable and a majority of the tradeable shares were held by large state-owned conglomerates in an informal system of interlocking shareholdings similar to the keiretsu system in Japan (sans a shareholding big bank participant). As a result, the vast majority of equity was not formally traded, making it difficult for an effective market for corporate control of state owned firms to arise.

However, these conditions have changed and Chinese capitalism continues to evolve towards a more liberalized market for corporate control, with fewer shares held by political entities and a higher percentage of SOE shares held by private parties. The incoming leadership, led by Xi Jinping, may further liberalize the market for corporate control within China. Over time a larger percentage of shares in state owned firms have been floated in the public markets and this trend may continue to the point that the state ceases to hold controlling shares in all but a small number of firms designated as of strategic value. SOE conglomerates have already shifted from being passive shareholders in other firms, buying securities purely for the purpose of jacking up prices and valuations in the equity markets, to active participants in both domestic and foreign securities markets, partly for the purpose

---

42 China is not unusual in this regard. Controls over foreign inflows and outflows of capital are common among countries outside of the OECD set of most developed/high income nations.

of accelerating acquisitions. SOE directors and senior executives are leading the way to a more developed and active market for corporate control and they are doing so with the blessings of the Party-state. As investment banks, both domestic and foreign, adapt to this changing market for corporate control in China, new avenues for channeling capital into the Chinese economy will be coupled with lucrative opportunities for banks to generate fees and long-term investment banking relationships with SOEs and other Chinese firms.[43]

Negotiating the global market for corporate control

In the early days of the securities markets, SOE equity accumulation was facilitated by the continuation of soft budgets, with the state serving as a financial backstop allowing SOE management to shift some portion of their revenues into equity markets without bearing much risk, given that any miscalculation of the risk associated with such portfolio investments ultimately being born by the state which stood ready to cover bad loans or other cash obligations that could not be met due to bad investment decisions by firm management. In other words, in those early days of Chinese capitalism, the SOEs participated in the equity markets under a veil of protection from the state. As long as the state protected the SOEs from bankruptcy, SOE participation in the equity markets represented a form of moral hazard. To some extent, these protections continue for the largest and/or most critical SOEs, allowing them to become more active in global markets for corporate control than might otherwise be the case. This serves the interests of the Party-state, allowing for increased Chinese control over strategic resources and technologies via

---

43 This trend towards a larger and more active market for corporate control in China may actually be part of a global trend within emerging markets. If this is the case, the revenue opportunities in emerging markets from fees generated both from IPOs and mergers and acquisitions could more than mitigate any lost revenues in the more developed markets of the OECD where tightened regulations in the wake of the 2007-2009 economic crisis are anticipated to negatively impact sales and trading revenues, as well as reduce overall financial leverage with a further negative impact on earnings.

the acquisition of companies with such resources, patents, and personnel. In the absence of political barriers or a debilitating financial crisis, Chinese firms are likely to become even more active in global markets for corporate control in the future.

At the same time, SOEs have taken steps to insulate themselves from this same global market for corporate control. Chinese conglomerates have quite consciously copied the keiretsu model of shareholding and interlocking directorates. SOEs are active buyers of their own stock and that of their brethren SOEs, without much regard for fundamental valuation, primarily to protect themselves from outside control. The degree of interlocking directorates is also quite high, with a relatively small number of individuals often holding the seats in numerous SOE boards of directors.

Thus, securities markets have been successful at meeting the initial requirement of officials, generating capital for SOEs in the process of modernization, without threatening Party-state dominance over the economy. However, Chinese officials recognize the need to meet the expectations of public officials in those external markets where they generate exports and acquire technology, as well as the requirements of globalization, epitomized by WTO. State dominance over firms trading in the Shanghai and Shenzhen markets, the aforementioned tendency towards keiretsu-style stock ownership and interlocking directorates, problematizes Chinese officials' commitment to a more open economy; so does the relatively weak regulatory regime and lack of transparency, with little incentive for SOE disclosures of relevant information to the public. The regulatory system has been designed primarily to protect the rights of the government as dominant owner of companies with minimal interest in providing protections to minority shareholders.

As has often been the case in the orchestrated transition to capitalism, Chinese authorities are keen to simultaneously satisfy their desire to retain control and to make foreign "partners" happy that China is "opening up," thus maintaining Chinese access to foreign markets and technologies. Taking steps to expand the market for corporate control in China is a tool for maintaining this access, if for no other reason than quieting critics in those markets where Chinese firms are becoming more active buyers. After all, both global markets for corporate control and trading relationships are always political to some extent.

The commoditization of ownership shares, as well as claims to shares of government bonds via the development of the bond market, strengthens the relationship between Chinese state firms, banks, and the Party-state with private parties, including those overseas. The processes by which the rules of the global economic game are altered involve an interaction between the internal politics of countries, negotiations between countries, including the formulation and amendment of international agreements, and the various channels by which corporate structures influence governments. The more the Chinese economy opens to foreign participation, the more executives from those foreign firms will gain access to Party-state officials and the more influence these executives will be able exert over future reforms in China. The more Chinese firms become involved in foreign markets and economies, including by establishing subsidiaries and hiring locals, the more Chinese corporate leaders will gain access to foreign political leaders and the more influence these corporate leaders will be able to exert over policies in those foreign nations. It's a dynamic and reciprocal process.

Non-state owned enterprises and access to equity markets

A similar interactive process is taking place inside of China, where SOEs are interacting with a rapidly growing private sector of domestic firms, as well as foreign firms, as competitors, customers, and/or collaborators. Domestic non-state-owned enterprises (NSOEs) were unhappy about being blocked from raising capital in the new equity markets, which were dominated by SOEs, and the dynamic nature of the rapid growth process, as well as the way private firms' growth allowed them increased access to Party-state officials, provided a path to addressing this issue.

NSOE access to capital and the domestic market for corporate control has been addressed by the development of an over-the-counter (OTC) market for equity in non-state-owned Chinese enterprises (NSOEs), which has become a major financial market reform. NSOEs and a subset of SOEs whose shares were not floated in the official securities markets have been informally traded since the mid-1980s. The development of an OTC market will broaden the number of firms with access to capital and deepen the trading in shares of NSOEs. At the same time, this new market will add an additional layer of risk for both portfolio investors and firms.

Perturbations in the financial markets, due to any number of catalysts for changed investor sentiment, could, potentially, reverberate through the real economy and cause difficulties in raising anticipated capital. And this problem is not restricted to a slowdown in IPOs during an extended period of declines in equity markets. Falling equity valuations may impact the willingness of banks or other investors to provide capital and can trigger negative outflows of capital from financial institutions, particularly when foreign portfolio investors are heavily involved in capital markets or domestic portfolio investors have the ability to withdraw domestic capital and send it abroad. This is one of the risks that come with the rewards of equity markets.

Nevertheless, it is clear that Chinese portfolio investors would prefer to have greater access to a broader range of domestic and foreign firm equities. In terms of domestic equity markets, this is indicated, among other things, by consistent excess demand for IPO shares. The excess demand stimulated an innovative response in China's financial markets. A derivative instrument, called subscription rights certificates (SRC), was created to absorb some of this excess demand. In order to get access to IPO shares, portfolio investors were required to first purchase an SRC. In a way the SRC can be understood as a ticket positioning the portfolio investor in the queue for IPO shares in the same way a ticket is used at the local deli to mediate between customers queuing up for orders. The difference is that in this case the customer has to pay to get in the queue. Thus, the very process of queuing up becomes a fund raising event. Thus, financial firms and the SOEs were both in a position to raise higher sums of money from IPO issues than might have been the case with a better balance between the demand for and supply of new equity issues.

The above described situation also indicates that portfolio investors in China were less interested in questions of fundamental valuation than in simply being in on what was perceived to be a good thing, in the same way investors in technology stocks in the late 1990s would have been willing to pay for SRCs to get access to the latest Internet stock IPO, if investment banks in the U.S. had recognized this potential source of pre-IPO funding and come up with this innovation before Chinese firms. The generally positive attitude of Chinese investors towards new domestic equity issues is reflective of a broader positive attitude towards the transformation in the Chinese economy, a vote of confidence in the reform process (if not necessarily in the reformers). The pro-reform factions leading the Party-state had, therefore, hit upon a successful method of raising funds for upgrading domestic firms, as well as a good way to not only broaden support for the entire reform/transition process, but to make the process more exciting and financially lucrative. Economic, political, and cultural goals were simultaneously addressed by the particular manner of the development and expansion in equity markets.

The OTC equity market: risks and rewards

The need for expanded job creation was also addressed by these reforms, as NSOEs and SMEs, of all types, are key job creation centers, generating more jobs per yuan than their larger SOE brethren. SMEs alone are estimated to account for 80% of new jobs created (Davis 2012). Thus, if the capitalist economy is to generate sufficient jobs to keep unemployment to acceptable levels, then capital must flow to these firms and the reforms have provided another channel through which that happens. The OTC equity market has opened a lucrative door to capital for NSOEs and small to medium sized firms (SMEs) of all types, whether some version of state-owned (including county and municipally owned firms) or private firms. This new channel for raising capital was the basis for further boosts to investment spending and employment growth. Of course, the more these markets play a role in providing capital, the more the demand side of the capital market comes to depend on these markets to behave themselves, which equity markets occasionally do not.

In any event, the OTC market must necessarily be more open than the primary markets if they are to serve as channels for capital to the relatively smaller, more dynamic firms that the Chinese economy depends increasingly upon to generate jobs and growth. In keeping with this role, the OTC market has relatively lower requirements for listed companies and does not require the approval of central government authorities. Theoretically, the OTC market targets portfolio investors with higher risk-bearing capacity, particularly institutional investors with the wherewithal to provide substantial capital to unlisted SMEs that might otherwise fail to address financing problems, despite having positive net present value investment opportunities. Governmental control over listings on the major markets leaves a large number of seed-stage companies unable to meet public listing requirements on the Shanghai and Shenzhen exchanges, restricting the ability of venture capital and private equity (VC/PE) investors to monetize their investment in these relatively small but potentially quite lucrative firms. The ability for VC/PE investors to develop an exit strategy from an investment in a start-up, to eventually be in a position to take a firm public on some market via an IPO is critical. The OTC market provides just such an exit strategy for VC/PE investors.

This is no minor matter for that special breed of investment firms that focuses upon highly risky, but often very innovative start-up firms, just the sort of firms the Chinese government recognizes are critical to technological innovation, even if a bit of a political risk. After all, the same innovative spirit that drives these new entrepreneurs to found companies and experiment with new business models could also be manifest as a political rebelliousness, under the right circumstances. It is clear that the reformers leading the Party-state recognize both of these aspects of entrepreneurship and have decided to rely upon financial institutions to both encourage the economic innovativeness and keep the potential political rebelliousness in check by strictly controlling financial capital and using this lever to keep the new entrepreneurs within the confines of their business plans.

Thus, the OTC market is likely to continue to grow in importance, become an integral part of the larger financial system (within which the state continues to play a guiding role), and foster a growing amount of capital infusions into the burgeoning capitalist economy from VC/PE firms, both domestic and foreign. To the extent this is the case, the OTC markets are a condition for expanding financing for SMEs and, in particular, for more innovative but high risk firms, such as high technology ventures. Given that SMEs generate more employment per yuan of capital investment than larger firms; the development of the OTC market could also have the potential impact of increasing job growth. And by maintaining a high degree of state involvement in the financial markets, including the OTC market, the Party-state hopes to satisfy the objective of fostering more innovative firms without losing too much control over the financial flows that may determine both the ultimate direction of long-term economic developments and the shorter term potential for economic instability (or Schumpeterian creative destruction, which some would argue is necessary if a genuinely innovation-driven economy is to come into being).

Whether or not the Party-state retains enough control to limit creative destruction, the growth of the OTC market may have positive impacts on innovation, given that new technologies, including social technologies, are often adopted in relatively smaller, seed-stage firms earlier than in larger firms. The disruptive influence of SMEs upon markets is likely to force many of the larger SOEs to be more innovative than might otherwise be the case. Thus, increased funding opportunities for the types of firms tapping the OTC market can have a positive impact on an economy's long term economic growth and employment creation prospects. Innovation may serve a critical role in stabilizing economies by providing new sources of cash flow and employment as older sources decline as a result of increased competition, demand shifts, or other factors. The willingness of the Party-state to allow the growth of the OTC market, despite the possibility it may be seen as a competitor with the major equity markets over which the government exercises direct control and with which it has increased capital flows to key SOEs, may indicate recognition of these potential benefits.

At the same time, the OTC equity market is not without externalities. Since China's OTC equity market is distributed over 200 agencies nationwide, with a great deal of duplication of services and highly variable trading information, it becomes difficult to regulate and fairness of trading and information flows are difficult to assess. Problems with prudential regulation are exacerbated by ambiguity about which level of government and which regulatory agencies within each level is responsible for this new and rapidly changing set of institutional relationships and trading systems.

In order to strengthen the regulation of non-publicly listed limited companies, China Securities Regulatory Commission (CSRC) set up Securities Regulation Department II, responsible for regulating the non-publicly listed limited companies and their stocks. It remains to be seen if this new system will significantly improve regulation of the OTC market, generate uniform evaluation criteria across these disparate trading platforms, fill the regulatory vacuum, and result in more predictable procedures for both trading and information flows. However, if the OTC market is to effect the efficient movement of capital from PE/VC firms into seed-stage firms, these issues must be positively resolved.

CHAPTER 19
ALTERNATIVE FINANCIAL INTERMEDIARIES

The continued deepening of financial intermediation is epitomized by rapid growth in financial firms and a gradual weakening of dominance by the big four state-owned banks. This has included continual expansion in the presence of foreign invested firms. The role of both formal and informal financial markets in providing a condition for value creation has always been a critical element in the functioning of the Chinese economy. It has not been uncommon, in China's long history, for periods of financial market liberalization to be followed by periods of repression. In this sense, recent experience has parallels in China's past.[44]

The creation of credit cooperatives

For much of China's history, it was a primarily agrarian society, so the flow of money capital was largely a rural phenomenon, with both borrowers and lenders based in the countryside. For much of this history, informal moneylending (a form of microfinance) served as a primary means for these capital flows. Under such circumstances, authorities had limited control over capital movement and economic problems, including crises, were also more difficult to control. The Party-state's subsumption of banks within the larger governmental bureaucracy and its attempt to monopolize capital flows during the state feudal period was, in part, an effort to control such problems and to avoid the destabilizing effects of crises generated by "spontaneous" market forces, although this was not completely effective for political reasons.

China's rural development was severely damaged by the Great

---

44 In recognition of this historical oscillation in policies, as well as for other reasons, China's wealthy may be particularly keen on diversifying their portfolios with foreign-held assets.

Leap Forward and the Great Proletarian Cultural Revolution, both of which not only disrupted capital movements but also caused large-scale disruptions in production, triggering a massive economic crisis and ultimately resulting in the loss of millions of lives. Thus, while the state feudal system may have short circuited a financially triggered economic crisis, like the West's Great Depression, it substituted an even more damaging politically triggered economic crisis. However, just as the West's Great Depression led to a long period of reforms that ultimately resulted in economic growth and greater prosperity, a similar dynamic appears to be working in Chinese society, as the experience of the Mao-era economic crisis has served as the anti-thesis driving post-Mao reforms.

As part of a strategy to reverse this damage (to serve as thesis to the anti-thesis) and advance development of rural China, the Party-state has successfully encouraged the emergence of rural credit cooperatives (RCCs), functioning in a similar manner to credit unions in U.S. in raising capital and similarly to small banks in farming communities in the U.S. in making loans to rural enterprises that might not otherwise be in a position to access capital. Urban credit cooperatives (UCCs) have also proliferated. RCCs and UCCs provide the financial system with increased flexibility and outreach to more marginalized clients and sectors in the economy. In general, a deeper financial system should provide more efficient channeling of funds to positive net present value projects, resulting in more rapid value growth and job creation than in a financial system dominated by a few large players who favor lending to a similarly small set of firms. Nevertheless, this sort of deepening also complicates regulation and may not mitigate the potential for financial crises. Indeed, the more rural enterprises, including farmers, depend on the capital markets for financing, the greater the potential for capital market disruptions to reverberate throughout the rural economy and turn into full-scale crises.

Insurance companies as non-bank financial intermediaries

The reforms have not simply increased risk by decentralization and expansion of the number of financial players. Some financial sector reforms have actually addressed the problem of uncertainties and related risks in a very direct manner. The reform process has created institutional means for risk mitigation. In particular, the reform process (and meeting requirements for WTO) has resulted in expansion in the role of insurance companies as non-bank financial intermediaries. Insurance companies provide the means for enterprises, as well as households, to mitigate some of the risks from uncertain economic consequences in future, making it that much easier to plan economic activities. This function of insurance is not new to post-revolutionary China. It should be noted that the People's Insurance Company of China (PICC) provided a precedent for such institutions long before the reform process was initiated. But the reforms have greatly expanded the number of insurance providers and the scope of insurance products/contracts, offering economic agents in China more options for risk mitigation and, therefore, a more complex set of economic choices.

Financial innovation: Trust investment corporations (TIC)

In addition to the expansion of insurance providers and products, financial reforms have resulted in a broader expansion in non-bank finance. Perhaps no financial sector innovation epitomizes the transition to capitalism more than the creation of trust investment corporations (TICs). TICs were established by the central and regional governments as a way to broaden and deepen the role of the state as a financial capitalist.

The first TICs were established by the state owned banks, after being granted permission to do so by the central government. The TICs operate as subsidiaries of the state owned banks. The objective of rationalizing the financial capitalist role of the state via these new institutions required granting TICs a degree of autonomy from both the government bureaucracy and from their parent banks. This relative autonomy was deemed necessary to allow properly trained staff within the TICs to avoid political influences that might counter efforts to build positive net present value portfolios. The degree of autonomy required for these subsidiaries to serve as independent finance capitalists in a wide range of portfolio building transactions, including taking ownership stakes in foreign corporations for purely economic, rather than political, reasons is probably not entirely possible under the current system where the parent banks remain subject to Party-state directives and influences and political factions continue to play a critical role both inside the Party-state and within corporate structures. The role of guanxi in shaping relationships between Party-state officials, commercial bank officials, and trust investment corporation executives is such that every decision made is potentially tainted by political objectives, including support or opposition to loans or portfolio transactions that might impact certain factions within the CPC, and/or familial or other non-economic social ties. Nevertheless, China International Trust Investment Corporation, CITIC, the largest trust investment corporation in China, has become a relatively powerful financial institution in both the domestic economy and abroad.

The risks and rewards of expanded access to capital

On the one hand, reformers have not broken the role of guanxi in shaping financial decisions. The distribution of finance capital in China remains, to a significant extent, a product of social and kinship ties, particularly connections to the powerful factions within the CPC guiding policy formation and implementation. On the other hand, the objective of expanding access to capital to finance further economic growth, including providing channels by which SMEs can gain such access, has enjoyed some degree of success, in spite of the powerful role of non-economic factors in capital allocation. Rapid expansion of non-financial intermediaries has opened much more varied channels of capital for a wider range of firms and made the web of connections between firms more complex. While this expansion may not have reduced the role of non-economic factors, it has made it possible to gain access to capital on the basis of a wider array of non-economic, as well as economic, relationships.

In other words, a firm that does not enjoy ties to members of one of the ruling factions within the CPC may, nevertheless, have other social or kinship ties that open doors to one of the newer domestic financial institutions or even to foreign financial institutions. Thus, the expanded financial system has generated greater flexibility by allowing a wider range of firms to access financial services, particularly loanable funds, and expanded overall lending beyond the lending quotas imposed by the PBOC. The expansion of access to financing has benefitted both firms and consumers, providing for an expansion in aggregate demand through higher levels of investment spending and, by expanding household credit, more rapid growth in consumer durables spending. Expansion of aggregate demand serves the objective of placing more emphasis on domestic demand growth and thus lowering the reliance on exports to drive growth and employment creation.

The obligations created by an expanded system of loans and other financial contracts are not unambiguously positive. On the one hand, firms and households are in a stronger position to participate on the buy and sell sides of capital, product, and labor-time markets. A stronger and expanded financial system makes more total transactions possible and grows the size of the domestic economy. On the other hand, these obligations add another element of risk, creating the possibility that if obligations are not met by certain parties a chain reaction of default could occur and trigger a systemic crisis. Such a chain reaction could lead to a sudden slowdown in demand growth and disappoint expectations of corporate sales and cash flow. Investments made in an environment of optimistic expectations about future growth rates could be deemed ex post failures and a condition known as overinvestment come to prevail in the economy.

Overinvestment is always a ex post problem, since it is rare that a firm's management would invest if they did not think the appropriate level of revenues was forthcoming. Nevertheless, overinvestment is not just a possibility, but, in an environment where growth expectations have been formed over such a long period of time, as is the case in contemporary China, it is a virtual inevitability. Disappointment must happen at some point. Growth expectations are simply too high and too well established in the imagination of investors.

China has been growing so rapidly over the past three plus

decades that the target growth rate established by officials in the Chinese government of 7.5% appears relatively low. The worst growth experiences over this period of time (during the dual crises of 1996-1998 and 2007-2009) have been near the current target growth rate. Nevertheless, 7.5% is a very rapid and unprecedented growth rate over such a long period of time, much less in a country the size of China. This rate of growth is simply not sustainable, in part, because the rapid growth is itself creating conditions that make it more difficult to maintain, such as rising commodity prices, stresses on the natural environment, localized labor shortages, trade tensions with the United States, social unrest related to growing income inequality, land seizures related to property development, and so on. It should not be surprising when the problems being generated by this growth process forces a sharp slowdown in growth and rates fall well below the current target, but the fact is it will be a surprise to a lot of people in decision making positions about investment. And executives responsible for capital budgeting do not normally react well to surprises, particularly when those surprises hit the top and bottom lines of income statements.

Even a positive rate of growth that is well below 7.5% could trigger a reversal in the extraordinary rate of growth of investment, which has been *the* driving force in the Chinese economy. A sharp downward move in investment spending, not an uncommon characteristic of capitalist economies, especially after a long period of above normal growth, would generate immediate cash flow imbalances in the economy, perhaps most problematically within the banking system. Key SOEs might find it difficult to meet obligations; non-performing loans (NPLs) in the state banks could balloon again and the cash flow problems could quickly spread and become a generalized financial/economic crisis. FDI would also be negatively impacted, as would cross-country short term capital flows, which because of WTO are gradually becoming more important to overall capital flows within China.

This expectations adjustment driven downturn is not a worst case scenario, but a likely scenario. The only question is whether or not, in such a circumstance, the government will be in a position to arrest the decline in aggregate demand and employment destruction before the crisis became serious enough to threaten social stability and perhaps then spiral out of control.

The rapid expansion in financial institutions outside of the control of the central government has been, in many ways, a product of expanding capitalist relationships within the economy. As capitalist corporations have become more important sources of revenues for local governments, as well as sources of less reputable unofficial support for local, provincial, and national government officials and their family members, these firms have become more influential in policy formation and execution (which sometimes means they can effect the way laws or regulations are or are not enforced).

It is in the interest of many of these firms, particularly SMEs who were ignored by the big banks, to see financial reforms implemented when the result is expansion of their sources of capital. Local officials, in particular, are often closely linked to particular SMEs and since one of the consequences of the early reforms was to strengthen the role of local officials in governance then these officials are now in a strong position to support those SMEs with which they are linked. China's entry into WTO only reinforced this dynamic as the financial system was opened to greater competition and foreign firms provided yet another potential source of support for officials, at all levels of government.

However, this expansion of the financial system also raises new risks, opening new channels for the transmission of problems within the financial infrastructure, including new ways for financial difficulties originating abroad to impact capital markets in China. As the 2007-2009 crisis originating in the United States so clearly demonstrated, particularly when one explores the way the US crisis reverberated throughout the European financial system, this is not a minor issue by any stretch of the imagination. There is clearly the potential for significant impacts on the Chinese economy as both negative and positive financial results (whether originating within domestic or foreign financial institutions or markets) are magnified within this expanded and expanding financial system.

Thus, while rural and urban credit cooperatives have become important sources of financing to SMEs, particularly former township-village enterprises, the expansion of lending relationships has also created some increase in systemic fragility. Because the rural credit cooperatives keep their reserves with the Agricultural Bank of China, one of the big four, any problems within the cooperatives is likely to impact that bank and its contractual obligations to other financial and non-financial enterprises. The predicted economic slowdown may pose particular difficulties for the SME sector and credit cooperatives because margins for many of these firms are rather thin and liquidity ratios relatively small.

The expansion in the number and type of financial intermediaries, like many other of the financial innovations that serve as positive supports for further economic development and the continued deepening of Chinese capitalism, is also a source for more systemic instability and potentially more violent fluctuations in economic activity.

At the same time, the moral hazard problems that are so common for financial institutions, given that such institutions are typically stewards of other people's money and are often provided with governmental protection in the event of particularly poor investment decisions, may be an even larger problem in China than is typical of capitalist economies, although this is arguable. Most capitalist countries go through an early stage where political corruption and cronyism are key factors in business development. The privatization of public policy and public resources may be no more problematic in China than in the early stages of U.S. capitalism. Nevertheless, from a macroeconomic perspective, moral hazard problems that may lead financial firms to make riskier (but potentially more profitable) capital investment decisions only adds to the potential destabilizing effects once the Chinese economy begins to markedly slow.

The globalization of the Chinese economy is best epitomized by the rapid growth in foreign direct investment (FDI). The modernist coalition in the CPC has recognized the importance of FDI, particularly as a vehicle for the diffusion of advanced technologies inside China, and has attempted to create conditions conducive to FDI growth. They have been brilliantly successful. China has now surpassed the United States as the world's number one destination for FDI. Transnational corporations operate in a highly competitive environment and corporate management must continually seek means of gaining advantages that would allow the firm to secure cash flow growth via higher operating margins and expanded revenue sources. Globalization has provided a means for attaining these goals.

The advantages of direct investment in China: Value and expanded markets

The opening up of China during the transition process offered an opportunity for transnational firms to take advantage of relatively skilled, disciplined, and low wage labor sources combined with an unusually strong infrastructure (for a poor nation). Rapid FDI growth in China was also pushed forward by intangible factors, such as the perception that China was the world's most important untapped market and a failure to set up operations in China would create a competitive disadvantage. As more and more firms relocated operations to China, either directly or via subcontracting relationships, agglomeration effects added to the advantages of locating future investments in China. The accumulation of resources and talent in and around industrial parks provided a relatively unique environment for transnational firms to offshore production. In other words, success at attracting FDI breeds success at continued growth in FDI. This has certainly been the case with China.

Foreign direct investment can occur in a number of ways. Corporations make these investments in order to create value. This value can be the result of immediate advantages available in the foreign country, such as proximity to raw materials or markets for finished goods, cheap labor, favorable regulation, or direct transfers from the home government as an enticement to engage in FDI. The value may also be generated in a longer time frame. For example, the corporation engaged in FDI may see longer term advantages from investing in the target country. This is often the case with foreign investment projects in China. Executives at transnational corporations often decide to invest in China in anticipation of benefits in the long term, such as a close working relationship with Chinese officials or executives in SOEs. It is now commonplace among corporate leaders in the West that success in China depends on cultivating relatively long-term business and social relationships with individuals in positions of power in the country. Never has it been so obvious that success depends on "who you know." It is also a widely held perception among corporate executives and directors that China is a critical market for generating long term growth in cash flows for their corporations and failure to gain a strong foothold in the Chinese economy may be a fatal mistake.

FDI: The establishment of joint-ventures (JVs)

The state centered nature of the Chinese economy may necessitate a close relationship with officials of the Party-state and this may not be possible without FDI. Distributions of cash flows related to FDI become the glue that holds together the relationships between the transnational corporate structures and domestic political and economic structures inside China. However, senior executives in transnationals were in the past often reluctant to invest in a directly controlled subsidiary operation in China because of difficulty in finding management personnel to carry out the necessary tasks or because Chinese officials might discriminate in their treatment of the subsidiary, disadvantaging the transnationals operations in the country, or for other reasons. This has become less likely over time, as foreign firms have gained more experience and closer ties in the country, but it still can be the case that the leadership of some foreign firms remains reluctant to operate facilities directly. In such cases, the executives may negotiate a joint-venture agreement with a Chinese firm, simultaneously satisfying the need to invest directly in China to begin securing their bona fides with Chinese officials and securing a business relationship with a state owned firm, providing yet another channel for gaining guanxi with Chinese officials.

The establishment and expansion in JVs has played an important role in diffusing both hard and soft technologies throughout China, particularly along the relatively prosperous eastern seaboard. This is one of the key reasons the Chinese government has, in the past and sometimes in the present, encouraged joint ventures. For foreign firms, JVs have proven an effective means of entering the Chinese market, often bypassing much of the red tape encountered by transnationals attempting to establish directly controlled subsidiaries in China. Transnationals have also used the JVs as "ports of entry" into the Chinese market, later using the connections created by the JV to establish subsidiaries. Thus, JVs and subsidiary operations are not mutually exclusive.

The various forms of joint-ventures

A very common method of creating an international joint venture is to establish a corporation in the target country with its equity divided between two (or more) corporations, one of which is a foreign corporation. This type of JV is called an *equity joint venture* (EJV). The creation of EJVs has been a favored method for transnationals to enter the Chinese market. Chinese firms have found these types of partnerships useful for a variety of reasons, in particular as a vehicle for knowledge transfer. Again, this satisfies a key Party-state objective and, therefore, Chinese officials have encouraged the growth of such ventures.

An alternative to the EJV is the *contractual joint venture* (CJV). The contractual joint venture is a *partnership* between two or more corporations. As usual, the partnership is based on a carefully negotiated contract that specifies all the liabilities, rights and responsibilities of the corporate partners, including the form of administration within and division of profits from the partnership. The negotiations over the contract can be quite complex and, unlike equity joint ventures, profit sharing is not based on the percentage of equity ownership of the participating corporations but is specified in detail within the contract, often as a simple percentage of shared net cash flows.

Joint ventures have been promoted by Chinese authorities because they perceive this arrangement as an effective means for technology transfer from foreign transnationals to Chinese SOEs and contribute to the larger diffusion of technologies (hard and soft) within the society. Foreign firms have recognized it as a way to more efficiently enter the Chinese market (for instance, by avoiding the red tape of obtaining a business license, since the JV is allowed to operate under the domestic partner's license), gain valuable access to market intelligence, and forge closer links to the Chinese authorities and larger power elite. JVs provide both parties with greater flexibility in arranging the management and financing of the joint venture and in implementing exit strategies from the partnership.

Foreign firms often find it difficult to fill management positions with local employees to their liking, although this is becoming less of a problem with many Chinese students being educated abroad. Nevertheless, forming a JV has been another way to solve this staffing problem, since the Chinese partner can provide a portion of the staff. Perhaps more importantly, this can significantly lower manpower costs since Chinese firms continue to pay less than foreign firms, although the gap has been narrowing over time as domestic Chinese firms have become both more flush with cash and more eager to access high quality talent to execute their ambitious business strategies. Clearly, the development of JVs, subcontracting relationships, and foreign firms operating in China, has all contributed their effects upon employment practices in domestic Chinese firms.

In practice, a foreign investor does not need to set up a new corporation in China under joint venture structures. The foreign investor and Chinese partner participate in the joint venture by doing business using the Chinese business license under a cooperative and contractual arrangement. This would allow each partner to contribute in those areas where they have the strongest competitive advantages and expertise. This has led the way to the emergence of more technologically advanced and efficient means of creating value in the Chinese economy and diffusing these practices to domestic firms.

Risks in joint-venture arrangements

It is not all rosy with JVs, however. Chinese JV partners have been known to drive very hard bargains in negotiations over contract agreements, recognizing their guanxi is valuable to the potential foreign partner. Tough negotiations and/or the effective use of stalling tactics by potential Chinese partners when they do not immediately gain desired concessions can ultimately result in the foreign partner paying higher contributions up front than might have been anticipated. "Misunderstandings" can result in more contributions required of foreign partners over time than were explicitly called for within the contracts signed, but which may be required to avoid early termination of the partnership. The Chinese government is typically on the side of the domestic partner, which is likely an SOE, in any event. Over time the problems with differing interpretations of contracts has been reduced, but can still come up at the most inopportune moments, particularly if the Chinese partner is convinced the foreign partner has more to lose from terminating the contract than was the case earlier in the process. These risks could make JV arrangements more costly than license and contract manufacturing arrangements. And then there is the waste of managerial time trying to iron out disagreements between partners. This is another source of risk for the foreign firm, although experience is making this less and less a surprise factor.

FDI: The wholly foreign-owned enterprise

Another form of FDI is through the wholly foreign-owned enterprise. This refers to corporate structures established in

China by foreign investors, exclusively with their own capital, according to the *Wholly Foreign Owned Enterprise Law of the People Republic of China*. The law does not relate to subsidiaries (operations that are not separately incorporated) of foreign corporations. Therefore, a wholly foreign-owned enterprise can only be formed with capital originating outside China. Thus, this law also does not apply to JVs.

Corporations seeking to perform the full range of corporate activities within China and to do so with a relatively autonomous corporate structure that may independently implement a business strategy, including pricing and output decisions, may choose to do so with a wholly foreign owned enterprise. The cash flows of the wholly foreign owned enterprises are freed from the constraints of either subsidiaries, whose accounting must be subsumed to the interests of the larger corporate structure of which they are a component part, or JVs. These cash flows can serve to secure the interests of the wholly foreign owned enterprise through its own management and relationships formed between that management and local, provincial, or national political leaders or agents of SOEs or other domestic firms. The ability to secure these relationships without any direct connection to the corporate owner may be an advantage, under certain circumstances, particularly if the corporate owner should decide in future to sell the wholly foreign owned enterprise, in whole or in part (such as via an IPO). The value of the wholly foreign owned enterprise is enhanced by the corporations' ability to do business solely in RMB (receiving and distributing cash flow in RMB), whereas the cash flows of subsidiaries depend critically upon exchange rate conditions and, technically, are subject to command and control from the financial officers of the parent corporation.

In other words, the decision of a corporation to take advantage of the Wholly Foreign Owned Enterprise Law is partly related to efficiency and control and partly a function of the market for corporate control. It follows that granting foreign corporations the right to own wholly owned and, technically, independent corporations operating solely within the boundaries of China further complicates the market for corporate control, on both the buy and sell sides, since Chinese corporations can, potentially, buy these foreign owned firms at some point in the future. These firms are also potential buyers of domestic Chinese firms or the assets of Chinese firms. In this latter case, Party-state officials might have recognized that these foreign owned but domestically operating firms might add more buyers to the market for assets of SOEs.

In any event, the Chinese government's decision to extend the right of establishing new corporate structures within China to foreign corporations is yet another instance of liberalization, partly in response to international agreements and partly in pursuit of the modernization objective. The overall effect of expanding the rights of foreign corporations within the domestic Chinese economy is to further deepen competition and to release a bit more control over the domestic economy.

FDI and knowledge transfer

Competition among foreign firms to gain footholds within the Chinese economy, sometimes to take advantage of relatively cheap but well trained and disciplined labor potential and sometimes to gain entry into China's rapidly growing markets, has been intense, as has been efforts by these foreign firms to adapt to the unique socio-economic and cultural environment of China. This adaptation has included a willingness to accept that a major role of foreign firms in China has been to act as conveyors of modern technology. To date, well over 1,000 research and development centers have been established in China by foreign firms. The Chinese employees of these foreign firms represent potential sources for the transfer of technological knowledge, as well as potential entrepreneurs innovating modern technologies (hard or soft) in the Chinese economy. The entrepreneurs within Chinese firms play a role in the growth of Chinese transnational corporations, firms engaged in outward FDI, which is yet another channel for the modernization of the Chinese economy, as well as a pathway for solving macroeconomic disequilibria that we've discussed in earlier chapters.

The modernization of the Chinese economy is advanced by FDI to the extent there are spillover effects, particularly through the diffusion of technologies from the foreign firms to domestic Chinese firms, and the degree to which foreign firms take market share from domestic firms does not create a stronger negative impact than this spillover effect. One of the means of detecting the impact of FDI is through its effects upon total factor productivity. Eunsuk Hong and Laixiang Sun demonstrated that FDI had a significant positive impact on TFP within and across regions in China.[45] The diffusion of technological knowledge takes place by both direct and indirect channels, including the spread of positive productivity impacts beyond the Eastern coastal regions of China where the highest concentrations of FDI are located.[46] Research by Koichiro Kimura has demonstrated that FDI in market areas where the technological knowledge gap is widest between domestic and foreign firms tends to have a negative impact on the growth of domestic firms.[47] Thus, the Chinese government must try to balance incentives for increased FDI with efforts to improve the relative competitiveness of domestic firms. The role of the financial sector in improving the technological foundation for domestic firms is one of the areas that have been targeted for improvement, as indicated by the financial sector reforms we've already discussed.

The benefits and contradictions of FDI

The expansion of foreign capital accumulation within China has had a direct impact on a wide range of macroeconomic variables, including the demand side of domestic money capital markets and intermediate goods markets. Foreign firms have also become more

---

45 Hong, Eunsuk and Sun, Laixiang, "Foreign Direct Investment and Total Factor Productivity in China: A Spatial Dynamic Panel Analysis," in Oxford Bulletin of Economics and Statistics, December 2011, v. 73, issue 6, pp. 771-791.

46 Puman Ouyang and Shihe Fu, "Economic Growth, Local Industrial Development and Inter-regional Spillovers from Foreign Direct Investment: Evidence from China," in China Economic Review, June 2012, v. 23, issue 2, pp. 445-460.

47 Koichiro Kimura, "Does Foreign Direct Investment Affect the Growth of Local Firms? The Case of China's Electrical and Electronics Industry," in China and World Economy, March-April 2012, v. 20, issue 2, pp. 98-120

active participants in the market for corporate control, therefore impacting the demand for equities and other financial assets whose equilibrium market prices and yields have, therefore, been influenced by this foreign participation.

Thus, the disequilibrium problems in the Chinese economy can be managed, in part, by both increased foreign participation in the economy and by modernization of domestic firms (and infrastructure), but the very nature of FDI and the growing foreign decision making clout within the Chinese economy may work at cross purposes with the government's efforts at macroeconomic management, since foreign firms are likely to act with a much higher degree of autonomy than domestic firms, whether SOEs, NSOEs, or SMEs, private or state owned.

If the nature of the disequilibria and the structure of the Chinese economy were such that FDI could contribute to making available the technologies necessary for an economic and technological fix for at least a subset of the problems facing China, such as the energy and water problems mentioned earlier, and if domestic investments could be properly targeted and financed to push forward projects that implemented these technologies, then FDI would be an unambiguous positive for the Chinese economy and, in a larger sense, for the global economy. But the real problem arises because there is no guarantee that FDI won't actually contribute to problems of disequilibria in economic and ecological terms. To the extent FDI results in more energy consumption, more water usage and pollution, diversion of resources to the export sector, including skilled labor, it may just make the macroeconomic management problems faced by Chinese authorities all the more difficult.

CHAPTER 21
DEVELOPMENT OF PRUDENTIAL REGULATION

A key condition for increasing confidence in the securities markets is the establishment of the infrastructure for proper oversight and related transparency of securities markets. This confidence factor is, in turn, a key condition for increasing the role of those securities markets in directing capital flows to the growing capitalist economy.

The role of securities markets in shaping improved financing and investment decision making within Chinese firms, particularly the newly publicly traded SOEs, will be advanced by the enforcement of international standards of accounting and reporting of financial data, strict prohibitions on insider trading, and unbiased enforcement of capital requirements on and regulations of financial firms involved in the securities markets. The Party-state must establish regulatory authorities capable of making relatively quick decisions about refinements in policy regimes to meet changing market conditions and enforcement actions required to keep the regulatory machinery from being derailed by political or other types of interference.

The dynamics of capital allocation in the Chinese economy, at the current stage of development, are such that politics continues to play as important a role as does economic calculations. The securities markets push the system more in the latter direction because portfolio investors have very little patience with obvious misallocation of scarce capital and are likely to punish any publicly traded firm by driving down share prices and, where relevant, bond prices. However, if securities regulators are not effective at creating an atmosphere of transparency and fairness in the financial markets, then securities prices are likely to be so mispriced that this positive role of the securities markets is short-circuited.

Oversight: Creation of the Chinese Securities Regulatory Commission

The Chinese Securities Regulatory Commission (CSRC) is responsible for oversight of capital markets in China, although prior to 1999 the authority of the CSRC came from its position as an agency of the State Council, rather than via any national law, and local government agencies often had overlapping authority. The CSRC was originally subsumed within the bureaucratic machinery controlled by the powerful State Council, and operated as the executive agency representing the State Council in enforcing securities laws and regulations. The actual setting of these regulations was placed within a larger body called the State Council Securities Commission (SCSC), which was also an agency of the State Council. Because the membership of the State Council is shaped, to a significant extent, by major factions within the CPC politicking to get their representatives on that body to secure access to state power and critical intelligence, it is a given that the agencies controlled by the State Council would be subject to influence of such factions. This is a serious problem for an agency whose purpose is to build confidence that securities markets are fair and transparent.

Securities regulation was further complicated by the presence of another powerful state institution involved in securities regulation, the PBOC. The PBOC had oversight responsibility over those institutions involved in investment that were linked to the state banks. The presence of the PBOC as a regulatory body in competition with the CSRC added to confusion over who had the ultimate authority to interpret rules, which were in flux, and to the general impression that the Party-state could exercise the regulatory function in a manner that was hardly fair or transparent.

In recognition that some clarity needed to be brought to securities regulation, the State Council gradually expanded the CSRC's authority to cover most securities transactions. The agency began to regulate the Shanghai and Shenzhen Stock Exchanges in 1993, emulating other securities regulators, including the U.S. Securities and Exchange Commission (SEC). At the end of 1993, the CSRC was given authority over China's futures markets (combining investigative and enforcement powers associated with the SEC and similar powers over certain derivative contracts associated with the U.S. Commodity Futures Trading Commission). In the middle of 1995, the CSRC expanded its oversight to the bond market when the State Council transferred control over 25 bond trading centers to the authority of the CSRC. The CSRC also came to exercise oversight authority over mutual fund companies and investment trusts in an attempt to close any avenues through which participants in public financial markets might evade such oversight. While the State Council's expansion of the CSRC's powers eliminated some of the jurisdictional confusion, it did not solve the problem that came from the CSRC being under the control of a State Council viewed as the product of factional politics and associated special interests.

In 1998, the State Council restructured its securities regulatory machinery, merging the CSRC and the SCSC. Later that year the National Securities Law was passed, addressing the problem of having the new agency under the thumb of the State Council. The National Securities Law provided for the newly constituted CSRC to both take full responsibility for securities regulation and to be an autonomous governmental agency, separate from the State Council and the PBOC. The provisions of the law were implemented in the summer of 1999 with the PBOC and local governments ceding authority to the CSRC in overseeing securities markets and the institutions involved in securities trading. The National Securities Law also set clear guidelines for the issuance of securities, removing the State Council from this process and further reducing the role of politics in decisions about which firms could list on the major markets or issue specific types of securities. The elimination of ambiguity about who had authority in these areas was an important condition for improving transparency and the perception of fairness of securities trading and reporting, which are necessary conditions for expanding access to capital in these securities markets.

Securities regulation: Creating transparency by improving disclosure

By regulating securities markets and imposing reporting requirements on corporate structures that have issued or hope to issue securities in China, the CSRC has become one of the forces shaping the evolution of Chinese capitalism. In particular, CSRC rule enforcement has become one of the most important factors shaping corporate governance and the overall culture at listed companies. In this regard, the CSRC has not only adopted stringent disclosure regulations and international accounting standards, but has provided advice to listed companies on proper ways to interact with shareholders and the media. Given that SOEs dominate among listed corporations, these interventions are having a direct effect on the way SOEs are managed and the public perception of SOEs.

In the past, it has been commonplace for SOE management to provide misleading or incorrect information to the public and/or to violate the conditions set forth in prospectuses, including by using capital in ways that do not comport with conditions set forth in company documentation,[48] causing skepticism among portfolio investors. Portfolio investors' willingness to invest in securities, particularly new share or bond issues, is inversely proportional to the level of skepticism they have about the disclosures of issuing firms. Therefore, if CSRC enforcement leads to higher quality information in various disclosure reports, including better written and followed prospectuses, and a reduction in outright deception, such as hiding debts, as has too often been the case in past initial public offerings, then these and other improvements in disclosure

---

48 One of the reasons for the real estate bubble referred to earlier in the text is the way SOEs have sometimes used capital raised for industrial purposes (where investors evaluated the prospectus associated with fund raising on the basis of industrial endeavors) for real estate transactions, instead. Firms with no particular expertise in real estate have been enticed by the attractive growth rates experienced in certain real estate markets, such as the Shanghai market, without much regard to either their own prospectuses or the underlying risks of investing diverted funds in such a manner. The CSRC has played an instrumental role in reducing this misuse of capital. (Naughton 2007)

should reduce the level of portfolio investor skepticism and result in improvements in the depth and overall liquidity of Chinese securities markets.

The China Insurance Regulatory Commission: Creating prudential regulation for the insurance market

The transition from a feudal economic system in which systemic dependence was so rigidly constructed that neither enterprises nor individuals bore much economic risk to a capitalist economic system in which risk was pervasive required a wide array of institutional changes. One of these changes has been the establishment of an insurance sector capable of providing risk mitigation in exchange for the payment of premiums. However, if insurance companies are to be reliable providers of risk mitigation and reduce the overall need for precautionary holdings by individuals and firms (funds which would not be available in capital markets), then they must be tightly regulated. Even in the United States, home to one of the more laissez faire versions of capitalism, insurance companies are among the most highly regulated businesses. Thus, for the Chinese authorities, prudential regulation of the insurance sector is another key area of financial sector reforms.

The key institution in this area is the China Insurance Regulatory Commission (CIRC), which was established the same year that the National Securities Law was passed, 1998. It was a busy year for regulatory reform. The CIRC, like the CSRC, was first authorized to carry out regulatory functions by the State Council.

Unlike the CSRC, the CIRC remains directly under the authority of the State Council, leaving the agency open to the same sort of influences as was a concern for the CSRC when it was part of the State Council bureaucratic structure. However, while the securities market is a relatively prominent institutional structure that facilitates the buying and selling of relatively generic securities, a role that depends critically upon portfolio investor confidence, both domestic and foreign, and positive media coverage, the insurance market is, generally, less prominent, trades in more idiosyncratic products, and depends more on firm-client relationships unmediated by an attentive media. Nevertheless, if left to their own devices, insurance company executives are no less likely to engage in excessive risk bearing than executives in other financial institutions, particularly when compensation is linked to abnormal profits in the context of moral hazard.

The State Council recognizes the problem and depends upon CIRC to formulate appropriate strategies for regulating insurance firms in such a manner that it does not stymie the development of the sector but protects against excessive risk bearing that might ultimately undermine the ability of these firms to serve their social role. And that social role is primarily risk mitigation. As a secondary role, insurance firms add substantial amounts of money to the capital markets, providing further financial fuel for the continuation of rapid economic growth.

In this regard, the CIRC oversees the establishment of new insurance companies, the expansion of existing insurance companies, and the functioning of insurance company asset management units and subsidiaries. As part of the WTO process, CIRC has the task of overseeing representative offices of foreign insurance companies, which have expanded rapidly in China and view the China market as an important area for future growth. The State Council has gone from protecting domestic insurance monopolies to fostering more competition, only partly due to WTO, in pursuit of a more efficient financial system overall and, in particular, to foster better practices by domestic insurance companies in providing cost effective risk mitigation for a wide range of economic agents.

The transformation of the banking system into one that is more autonomous, decentralized, and directed to making more positive net present value loans was the first stage of the restructuring of the financial system as a condition for the transition to capitalism. The second stage was the development of equity markets to broaden the base of direct support for capitalism (as SOEs become partly privatized and the portfolio investors begin to identify their interests with those of the SOEs with which they have bought shares). The third stage saw an expanded role of the insurance market to provide broader risk mitigation and a more active asset management role for insurance companies. The fourth stage involves the development of a more broadly accessible bond market through which not only the national government and its agencies may raise funds but also local governments and firms, including banks, may also be able to borrow.

Fig. 22.1. The Restructuring of the Financial System

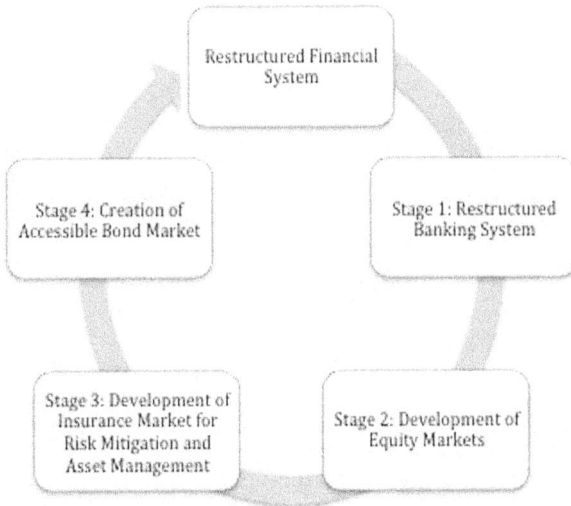

Local governments have been an important part of the modernist coalition from the earliest days of the reform movement under Deng Xiaoping and continue to be critical supporters of reform. The modernist leadership relies heavily upon local party and government officials to pursue a wide range of development projects and help in maintaining high reinvestment rates for the economy overall.

Looking for autonomy: The role of local government and corporate bond markets

The market for local government bonds expanded dramatically in 2009, growing by 80% over the previous year. Similarly, the market for corporate bonds grew markedly during the same year. In 2013, China overtook the U.S. as the world's largest issuer of corporate debt. It now has more corporate debt outstanding than any other country with an estimated $14.2 trillion outstanding at the end of 2013 compared with $13.1 trillion in the U.S. (Hong 2014). See Fig. 22.2.

Fig. 22.2: Total Outstanding Corporate Debt, 2013

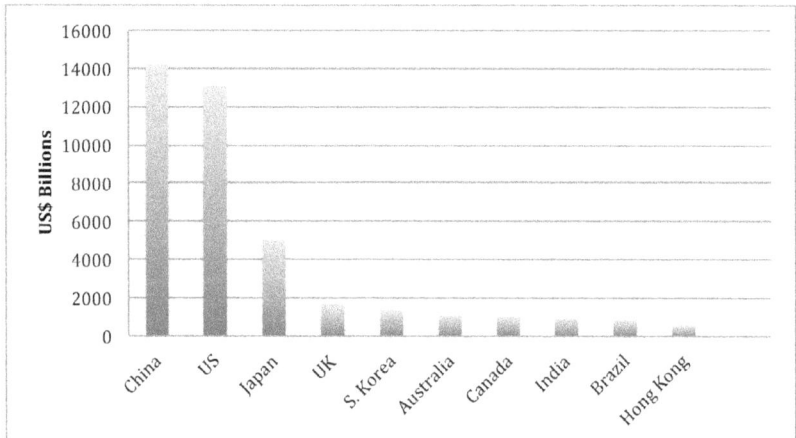

Source: Standard & Poor's

Expansion in the channels through which firms, particularly SOEs, may access loanable funds, domestic and foreign, could relieve some of the pressure on China's state banks, with an estimated RMB 700 billion (US$ 111.4 billion) in bad debts on their balance sheets.[49] The development of corporate bond and commercial paper markets allows firms to secure loanable funds outside of the banking system and therefore removed from the often intrusive oversight of bank managers. This would reinforce the autonomy of SOEs from the state bureaucracy, which the banks are still viewed as representing, and therefore provide greater flexibility for firm management in executing their business strategy, an important factor in an environment of globalization, and rapid technological and market change.

Bonds, in particular, are issued through intermediaries, typically investment banking enterprises, who take on the task of finding the sources of capital, in exchange for a discount over the retail price of the bond and the payment of fees. In general, investment bankers are much less likely to intrude into the borrowing firm's strategic planning than might be the case with banks. It is a commonplace that bank managers can be quite intrusive and this has certainly been the case with the relationship between China's state-owned banks and SOEs. The banks played the role of coordinators and enforcers of the grand economic plans of the state feudal system from 1958 to 1978 and are still perceived as overseers. The securities markets offer the SOEs a way to become even more autonomous from the still massive bureaucracy of the state.

Aside from a fully-developed stock market, a well-functioning bond market is crucial to the success of a capitalist economy, expanding the capacity of the financial system to serve as intermediary and provides portfolio investors, particularly institutional investors, with a more diversified array of investments. As Anita Davis, writing in *Asiamoney*, points out: "China's bond market is already the world's third-largest, with RMB 25 trillion (US$ 3.97 trillion) in debt outstanding." The growth of China's bond market has been impressive and has already gone a long way towards solving one of the key objectives of the reformers, relieving the central government of the obligation to cover

---

49 Anita Davis, "Building China's Bond Market," in *Asiamoney*, October 2012.

budget deficits generated at various levels of government, including municipal governments. Forcing local governments to seek bond financing puts pressure on local officials to develop more coherent strategies for public spending and taxation, improving the efficiency of government administration. The same argument could be made for the increased use of bond financing by the central government.

Bond markets and the capital budgeting process

The role of bond markets in the capital budgeting process of firms, and indirectly in investment driven economic growth and development, can be explained with Figure 4.1. As the bond market develops and deepens and financial institutions become more adept at evaluating the risk associated with bond issues, the effective cost of debt can be reduced, along with the related weighted average cost of capital for Chinese firms. As firms face lower weighted average cost of capital, investment projects gain in net present value such that more projects are acceptable investments (positive net present value) and the magnitude of capital budgets at circle α expands. Expanded capital budgets for SOEs, NSOEs, and particularly SMEs could improve the chances for sustaining the current growth path for a longer period of time, provide the capital for further modernization, and thus improve the competitiveness of Chinese firms in the global economy. This is a critical objective of the Party-state and is necessary if Chinese firms are to continue to develop into world-class transnationals.

The bond market: Shifting risk, reducing moral hazard

On the other hand, as firms take on more debt, whether from bank loans or the bond market, the risk of default grows. However, traditionally bank loans were only available to SOEs and the risk of default on bank loans was mitigated by the likelihood that the central government would cover any critical cash flow shortages, simultaneously reducing the effective risk of default and creating a moral hazard problem. The moral hazard problem always raises the possibility of negative net present value investments. Shifting

SOE financing more towards the bond market can reduce moral hazard if the central government is less likely to intervene to save firms that default due to bond borrowing than due to defaulting on loans to state banks.[50] And NSOEs and SMEs that raise funds in the bond market may not have previously had access to bank loans and therefore gaining such access raises the amount of capital available for productive investment by firms that generate the vast majority of new jobs. Either way, the bond market can have a positive impact on the behavior of firms, particularly capital budgeting decisions. These effects are reinforced by the way servicing debt (making interest and principal payments as they come due) can focus management on generating positive cash flows by improving management practices, such as cost control or more effective product design and marketing.

The bond market as an instrument of monetary policy

The bond market also provides the monetary authorities with an indirect mechanism for monetary management via open market purchases and sales of government bonds. This is a more subtle instrument of monetary policy than direct controls over credit by the PBOC, providing the central bank with more flexibility in the exercise of monetary policy. In the past, the PBOC has instructed state banks to tighten or loosen credit, as well as employed the relatively blunt instruments of changing reserve ratios. It is likely the PBOC will continue to employ these more direct instruments but the utilization of open market operations may become more common over time, particularly if inflationary pressures can be kept in check by doing so (which remains to be seen).

Corruption and the cost of debt

One of the headwinds faced by China's burgeoning debt market is the relatively high level of corruption. Ciocchini, Durbin, and

---

50 Of course, as long as personal/social ties between bankers and SOE executives serves as a key driver of financial and other economic relationships, there is little incentive for SOE management to shift to bond financing as a primary or even a significant secondary source of fundraising.

Ng demonstrated in their 2003 paper that corruption raises the borrowing costs for governments and firms in emerging markets.[51] Thus, among the many challenges that the relatively high level of corruption poses to sustained economic growth in China is the possibility that it raises the cost of debt. Other studies have shown corruption to have negative impacts upon foreign direct investment.[52] However, China has done unusually well at attracting FDI, so it is possible that, at least in the case of China, corruption is mitigated by other factors, such as the overall magnitude of China's rapid economic growth and accumulation of hard currency reserves.[53]

---

51 Ciocchini, Durbin, and Ng, "Does corruption increase emerging market bond spreads?" in *Journal of Economics and Business 55* (2003), pp. 503-528.

52 Mauro, P., "Corruption and Growth" in *Quarterly Journal of Economics, 110(3)*, 1995, pp. 681-712.

53 Ciocchini, Durbin, and Ng do find a positive correlation between foreign exchange reserves as a percentage of GDP and country credit ratings, indicating that the larger the reserves/GDP ratio the lower are borrowing costs for government and firms in an emerging market.

The 2012 presidential candidacy of Mitt Romney, the former CEO of Bain Capital, a private equity firm, brought private equity (PE) into the forefront of media coverage in the United States. However, it is likely that the 2012 presidential campaign had very little impact on Americans' general knowledge of private equity (or finance) and most Americans probably remain unclear about exactly how PE works or the role that it plays in an economy.

The role of PE in financing investment, modernization, and the transformation in patterns of ownership is complementary to the other forms of financing we've discussed so far, but plays a fairly unique role in the transition to state and mixed (state and private) forms of capitalism, particularly in opening additional channels of investment for SOEs, providing additional policy options for the state in managing the macro-economy, and in expanding the diversity in ownership types beyond the state ownership that has predominated in the Chinese economy.

Private equity in the market for corporate control and the importance of informational advantage

Despite the aforementioned publicity related to Mitt Romney's campaign, the PE sector typically operates out of the public limelight. PE involves transactions in the market for corporate control that, generally, involve non-publicly traded corporations: privately held equity is transferred to the PE firm for a negotiated price. In order to realize abnormal returns (positive alpha), PE firms must, necessarily, underpay for corporate assets. This is more likely when the PE firm's management has an informational advantage over the sellers or when social ties between PE management and officials allow for special deals to be negotiated. The continued dominant role of guanxi in Chinese business makes it all the more likely that these conditions will hold and abnormal returns are realizable.

Thus, one should not underestimate the ongoing importance of PE in reshaping Chinese capitalism. Since 2004, PE firms, seeking abnormal returns through close social ties with Party-state officials, have become increasingly active participants in the burgeoning Chinese market for corporate control. In fact, fundraising for Chinese PE deals dominated in the Asian PE market with $312 billion raised between 2003-2013. See Figure 23.1.

Figure 23.1 Funding for Private Equity Deals, 2003-13

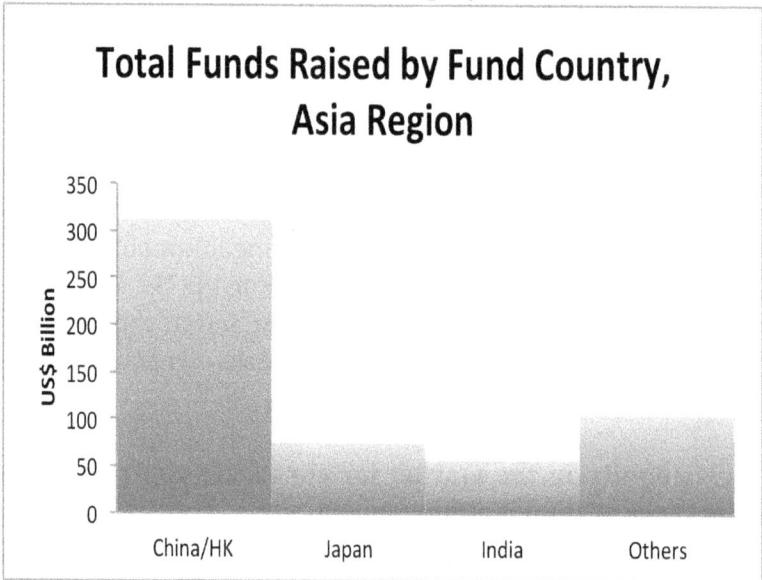

Total Funds Raised by Fund Country, Asia Region

Source: PwC (2013). *excludes allocation from non-China specific funds

The importance of the successful development of Chinese equity and bond markets to private equity firms

The long-run success of PE firms in China depends on a wide range of factors, including many of those we have already discussed. PE is directly connected to the continued development of equity and bond markets, for instance, as sources of IPOs, secondary offerings, and for capital financing purposes. PE exit strategies depend upon a healthy and vibrant equity market, one in which it is likely that stocks will experience periodic "bull" markets where stock issuances, whether for IPOs as a PE exit strategy or for secondary offerings to finance restructurings and capital accumulation, are more likely to raise sufficient funds to make abnormal returns possible. Other exit strategies for PE firms, such as management buy-outs or resale to other financial or non-financial institutions are less reliable in emerging market contexts, including China. This makes continued successful development of a vibrant Chinese equity market all the more important for PE firms.

Since PE is critically dependent on portfolio investors for capital, the success of the Chinese authorities at improving prudential regulation is also important to building the necessary trust for PE firms to access larger quantities of capital from both individual and institutional investors.[54]

"Broadly speaking, China has benefited from the private equity industry, as local firms received expansion capital, management support and best practices," says Erik Bethel, Managing Director of *ChinaVest*, a Chinese American investment bank that is considered one of China's venture capital pioneers. The current leadership's objective of modernizing the practices of Chinese firms, to produce social conditions that push management to adopt best practices, is fostered by a healthy PE sector. The recognition that different types of ownership are fungible, yet produce different results under different circumstances, is an important component in the current leadership's version of modernist Marxian theory: private forms of ownership are not seen as antithetical to the objectives or overall mission of the CPC. This is the reason the door to PE, among other institutional innovations, is open in today's China.

PE investment: The allure of China

PE has been booming in Asia. According to executives at

---

54 Institutional investors include pension funds, sovereign wealth funds, hedge funds, insurance companies, and various other types of private investment companies.

McKinsey and Company, a major consultancy, private equity in Asia increased 63% in 2011.[55] Thus, the growth in PE in China can be seen as part of a larger trend in the global economy of capital flowing towards Asia, particularly East Asia. Ji Lin, vice mayor of the Beijing municipal government, commented at the 3rd Global Private Equity Forum in Beijing, November 14, 2010: "Sustainable economic growth, abundant investment opportunities, and a positive government attitude would make China one of the most appealing countries in the world for global private equity investors."

One of the reasons PE firms would be attracted to China, and perhaps even more importantly one of the reasons that domestic PE firms would expand operations, is that it is not difficult to identify underperforming corporations in the country, particularly in the SOE sector. The state feudal system created an atmosphere of bureaucratic inertia and inefficiency, yet at the same time bequeathed a legacy of potentially lucrative assets and infrastructure. If PE firms can develop close working relationships with local experts and management in some of these firms, allowing privileged access to information about firm operations, strategies, and markets, then it is possible for valuation methodologies to be applied that would allow the PE firms to set reasonable maximum target prices for acquisitions and, given the reforms to the market for corporate control, have a strong likelihood of negotiating a price below this maximum. After acquiring the underperforming firms or assets, the PE firm could reorganize management and business practices, raise workforce productivity, and raise the value of these firms or assets and then resell them for a profit.

Growth of China's PE industry is, therefore, a function of institutional reforms that have opened up the market for corporate control; social ties that have provided PE firms access to critical information for valuation and guanxi for negotiating deals;

---

55 Stephen Aldred, "Asia Shares of Private Equity Deals Jumps," Reuters, Monday, June 4, 2012, 10:24pm EDT, http://www.reuters.com/article/2012/06/05/mckinsey-privateequity-idUSL3E8H306D20120605.

regulatory reforms that have improved PE access to capital; and equity markets within which acquired firms can be taken public (in some cases for a second time after having been previously acquired in the public market and then taken private by the PE firm) through IPOs. The growth of China's PE industry is also a function of foreign portfolio investors' search for abnormal returns (alpha) via international diversification, particularly within emerging markets where such abnormal returns may be more likely than in the more developed capital markets of the OECD universe. Among the emerging markets, China's rapid growth rates, expanding domestic markets, and history of underperforming SOEs may provide among the most lucrative opportunities for such investments.

CHAPTER 24
SOVEREIGN WEALTH FUNDS IN CHINA

Since the 1980s, global financial markets have seen an explosion in innovative investment vehicles, greatly expanding the number of participants in investment funds, including so-called retail investors with relatively low income levels who have been able to participate first in mutual funds and later in a much broader range of funds, including the increasingly popular exchange traded funds. It should not be surprising to find that governments would eventually recognize the value to be gained in direct participation in capital markets.

Sovereign Wealth Funds (SWFs) are state owned and operated (or, alternatively, state affiliated) corporate structures managing special-purpose investment portfolios funded by the state and for the benefit of the national treasury. The SWF provides the government with an expanded source of revenues beyond traditional fiscal (taxes and fees), monetary (printing fiat money), and borrowing (issuing government bonds) sources. Modern portfolio theory is grounded in empirical evidence that a more diversified holding of government assets provides higher returns with lower risk. The emergence of SWFs has provided governments with an institutional means for engaging in the same sort of portfolio management as has been available for private corporations and wealthy individuals, allowing governments to take advantage of modern portfolio theory, invest in a wide array of assets, including stocks, corporate bonds, real estate, precious metals, derivative instruments, other securities, and private equity partnerships. SWFs are not restricted to the purchase of domestic assets and typically will target a significant percentage of investments in cross-border assets, particularly foreign assets that are viewed as serving strategic objectives of the home government.[56]

_____

56 The strategic objectives of SWFs can often conflict with building a portfolio in

The focus on foreign assets, combined with the lack of transparency about SWFs, has created some controversy, as some politicians, particularly in the United States, have questioned the motives of SWFs and perceive them as ultimately a threat to the existing global political and economic order (Truman 2007; Mihai 2013). Nevertheless, the utility of SWFs to national governments is becoming increasingly apparent and it is, therefore, likely that the number of SWFs and the total amount of capital under the control of SWFs will continue to grow. See Table 24.1.

Table 24.1: Top 20 Sovereign Wealth Funds by Assets Under Management

Country	SWF Name	Assets $Billion	Inception	Origin
Norway	Government Pension Fund	$893	1990	Oil
UAE- Abu Dhabi	Abu Dhabi Investment Authority	$773	1976	Oil
Saudi Arabia	SAMA Foreign Holdings	$737.6	n/a	Oil
China	China Investment Corporation	$652.7	2007	Non-Commodity
China	SAFE Investment Company	$567.9*	1997	Non-Commodity
Kuwait	Kuwait Investment Authority	$410	1953	Oil
China- HongKong	HongKong Monetary Authority Investment Portfolio	$326.7	1993	Non-Commodity

accord with modern portfolio theory, resulting in a suboptimal portfolio in terms of risk-return characteristics. However, if the home government considers the strategic objectives in the longer term interest of the home country, generating positive externalities that are not quantified in the SWF's risk and return variables, the fact that risk and return from the SWF may be suboptimal, considered in isolation, may be irrelevant.

Country	SWF Name	Assets $Billion	Inception	Origin
Singapore	Government of Singapore Investment Corporation	$320	1981	Non-Commodity
China	National Social Security Fund	$201.6	2000	Non-Commodity
Singapore	Temasek Holdings	$177	1974	Non-Commodity
Qatar	Qatar Investment Authority	$170	2005	Oil & Gas
Australia	Australian Future Fund	$95	2006	Non-Commodity
UAE-Abu Dhabi	Abu Dhabi Investment Council	$90	2007	Oil
Russia	National Welfare Fund	$88	2008	Oil
Russia	Reserve Fund	$86.4	2008	Oil
Kazakhstan	Samruk-Kazyna JSC	$77.5	2008	Non-Commodity
Algeria	Revenue Regulation Fund	$77.2	2000	Oil & Gas
Kazakhstan	Kazakhstan National Fund	$77	2000	Oil
South Korea	Korea Investment Corporation	$72	2005	Non-Commodity
UAE-Dubai	Investment Corporation of Dubai	$70	2006	Oil

Source: Sovereign Wealth Fund Institute (2014). * Best guess estimation.

SWFs currently have more total capital under management than hedge funds and PE firms combined.[57] This has been the result of

----

57 SWFs had $3.5 trillion under management in 2009 and the amount has grown since then, whereas hedge funds managed $1.9 trillion and PE firms managed $0.8

two interrelated processes: 1) rapidly expanding foreign exchange reserves due to accelerating export growth, particularly among oil exporters during a period of relatively high oil prices; the so-called BRIC nations (Brazil, Russia, India, and China), and East Asian nations that went through a financial-foreign exchange-economic crisis in 1997-1998, successfully restructured their economies to generate export expansion, and whose governments sought a means for managing burgeoning foreign exchange reserves without levels of currency appreciation that could short-circuit the export expansion; and, 2) a paradigm shift among emerging market governments about how best to redeploy surplus foreign exchange earnings to improve the long-run economic prospects of their nations.

This paradigm shift has affected policies in a wide range of nations. Today, even the relatively small nation of Botswana has an SWF. Norway's SWF is probably the most important from the standpoint of augmenting fiscal revenues since it is designed to smooth out oil revenues over a long time horizon such that revenues will be generated beyond the terminal period when oil revenues are exhausted. At present, about 90% of the total value of assets in SWFs comes from oil exporting nations and Asian nations.

Sovereign wealth funds and their connections to the global financial system

At issue here is how the rise of SWFs, and particularly Chinese SWFs, interacts with the rest of the global financial network of institutions and markets. We've already seen that the SWFs have grown extraordinarily fast and now command more capital than hedge funds and PE firms, both of which are understood to be significant financial players shaping global economic structures. There is no reason to believe that SWFs would have any lesser role and, given their connections to state power, there is every reason

---

trillion. See Jason Kotter and Ugur Lel, "Friends or foes? Target selection decisions of sovereign wealth funds and their consequences," in *Journal of Financial Economics*, 101 (2011), pp. 360–381.

to assume that their influence will go beyond the boundaries of traditional financial relationships.

SWF participation directly impacts securities prices and indirectly shapes the demand for various types of securities. Any time a major player steps onto the financial markets, this player must begin to influence the behavior of the other players, including the demand side and the supply side of securities markets. Of course, in this case the governments who deploy the SWFs are also involved in the supply side, both through issuance of debt instruments and, via privatizations, issuance of equity securities.[58]

SWFs also become clients of other financial firms, often outsourcing all or part of their funds to private fund management companies, providing these firms with increased capital and greater capacity for leverage. SWFs contract with research and consultancy companies for a wide range of financial services, including trading, clearing and settlement services, independent valuation of assets, market analysis, hedging and risk mitigation management or assistance, and the management of physical assets, such as real estate and commodity reserves. SWFs represent lucrative sources of new funds for firms providing international accounting and/or legal assistance. Similarly, SWFs may provide firms specializing in lobbying governments with new, deep pocketed clients. SWFs also contract with investment/merchant banks to provide for the acquisition and sale of firms, in whole or in part, including via private parties or through the IPO route. Investment banks can also provide assistance in complex financial arrangements involving equity, debt, and partnership arrangements between the SWF and other parties, including other governments.

Thus, the growth of SWFs represents a significant new source of revenues for investment banks, accounting firms, lobbying firms and other types of legal firms, giving these entities a stake in the growth of the SWF sector. The broader the base of financial connections between SWFs and other multinational/transnational

---

58 As we have seen with the Chinese government, sovereign agencies also shape the rules of the game that determines the supply of private equity, bonds, and other securities. Thus, government has a broad impact on the supply side, even as SWFs make government active players on the demand side of the financial markets.

firms, the greater the likelihood that the SWFs can successfully push back against efforts to restrict or regulate their activities.

The political contradictions for China's sovereign wealth funds

As China's role in global financial markets expands, two contradictory processes will be fostered: on the one hand, transnational financial firms with contractual relationships with China will become increasingly reliant on China playing a major role in financial markets and will therefore support efforts to promote such continued participation by Chinese SWFs and, on the other hand, foreign governments may react negatively to the growing influence of Chinese state owned and operated financial institutions becoming major players in their financial markets or, more generally, the global financial markets and attempt to restrict such activities. This could generate some interesting political struggles, the resolution of which is not apparent at this early stage in the processes. In any event, in a WTO world, it might be difficult for governments, such as the U.S. government, to treat Chinese SWFs differently than those of nations considered friendlier, such as Norway or the oil exporting nations of the Middle East, excluding Iran.

On the other hand, pressure will inevitably mount on China and other active participants in the SWF game, but who have rather restrictive domestic financial markets, to open up their markets to foreign players. In other words, the more active China is in the SWF arena, the more likely the Chinese government will have to allow foreign financial firms greater freedom of operation within China. The same pressure will be applied to Russia and India, two other major players in the SWF game who are also relatively restrictive about foreign participation in their domestic financial markets.

Thus, the U.S., E.U., and other OECD nations with relatively open financial markets may gain from the growth of SWFs in terms of greater overall openness of global financial markets. Given that the most powerful financial firms tend to be headquartered in these nations, they may stand to gain more from the growth of SWFs than they might lose. And if this is not a sufficient argument in favor of the role of SWF's in the global economy, there is the fact that SWFs have played a positive role during the recent American initiated financial crisis. In fact, global financial markets have provided a doorway through which capital has flowed from SWFs to developed economies. In addition, Chinese firms have played an important role in supporting more developed economies by direct investments abroad.[59]

The establishment of SWF China Investment Corporation (CIC) and the problem of burgeoning foreign exchange reserves

The largest Chinese SWF was established by the State Council as the China Investment Corporation (CIC) on September 29, 2007. The initial capitalization of CIC was $200 billion, making it the fifth largest SWF in the world. This firm came into being as a direct consequence of debates within the CPC leadership about how to manage the burgeoning foreign exchange reserves, which were a result of running substantial yearly current account surpluses since the late 1990s, when the export boom began.

The large accumulation of foreign exchange reserves, mostly in U.S. dollar denominated bonds, did not provide the Chinese government with much in the way of a return on its accumulation, nor did the concentration in U.S. government (and agency) bonds provide much in the way of diversification. In addition, as Chinese firms exchanged U.S. dollars for RMB, the rising supply of dollars and the related rising demand for RMB put pressure on the government to allow the yuan to appreciate in value vis-à-vis the dollar. However, if this appreciation had been allowed to take place, it would have increased the price of Chinese made products and lowered the competitiveness of Chinese firms, reducing the very export boom that was fueling the growth in the foreign

---

59 According to *China Daily*, 17 December 2012, Chinese official statistics estimate that 888,000 foreign workers depended for their livelihood on jobs with Chinese enterprises operating abroad and these firms paid over $22 billion in taxes to foreign governments, providing a much needed boost to the global economy and job markets.

exchange reserves in the first place.

The Chinese government did not want to give up this accumulation of reserves; rather it wanted to use these reserves to modernize the Chinese economy. So, what to do? The PBOC needed to find a way to reduce the quantity of RMB in circulation within China (to lower the domestic money supply) despite the flood of dollars being exchanged for RMB. The fact that not only the central bank, the PBOC, but the large commercial banks remained under the direct influence of the Party-state provided a solution: the banks would purchase short-term bonds from the PBOC, removing some of the RMB from circulation, and the banks would at the same time maintain a high required reserve ratio, further maintaining a tight money supply. Thus, the potential inflationary impact of the accumulating foreign exchange reserves with the concomitant growth in RMB being paid by the PBOC for U.S. dollars was short circuited.

This solution would not be possible under a more liberalized financial system because the tight monetary policies would drive up interest rates, which would then negatively impact investment. As discussed previously a slowdown in investment could trigger a sharp slowdown in the Chinese economy and an economic and social crisis. However, the Chinese government retained the authority to restrict interest rates in the system, and thus used interest rate repression to protect domestic firms from the effect of higher interest rates. Thus, the sterilization of the foreign exchange reserve accumulation was possible largely because the Chinese government retained extraordinary powers over the financial system and exercised those powers to 1) maintain a relatively weak exchange rate, 2) counteract inflationary pressures from the buildup of the domestic money supply, and 3) repress interest rates to maintain investment growth rates that have been a key driver in the overall rapid economic growth of the economy. This is, nevertheless, a delicate balancing act and one that has not only created its own internal costs in the Chinese economy but has sparked political tensions with the United States, where politicians have been hammering the "currency manipulation" aspects of this policy.

The decision to fund a SWF came from recognition that the accumulated reserves needed to generate a higher rate of return, mitigate the potential impact of a slowdown in exports, and provide a means for strategic investments that would promote the long-run economic development of the nation. Diversification would both reduce the risk of the holdings being concentrated in U.S. bonds and systemic risks associated with relying solely on the domestic economy as a source of long-run value creation.

The use of CIC for strategic investments and reduced agency costs

Strategic use of the reserves for acquisitions of certain types of assets, including partial or total acquisition of foreign corporations to access raw materials, sources of energy, or technology, could further the modernization project of the current leadership. The ability to direct these capital investments (and loans) to nations that had difficulty raising funds from OECD-based firms, such as Venezuela, was perceived as an advantage. Furthermore, CIC stakes in domestic firms could provide a mechanism through which financial technocrats within CIC, mandated to find ways to improve the value of direct investments, could push domestic firm management to adopt "best practices," including improvements to technologies deployed and operating algorithms. Thus, the CIC could contribute to reducing agency costs in SOEs and state owned financial institutions.

The State Council appointed the CIC board of directors by selecting representatives from the various state agencies whose funds would be used as initial capital, providing a mechanism for each of these agencies to provide input into the strategies and management of the fund, including the choices of fund senior executives. While the CIC may provide a way to reduce agency costs at those firms with CIC investment stakes, the competition among various state agencies could present a problem if there are disagreements over the appropriate strategies for the use of CIC and these disagreements are reflected in the voting patterns of directors. The State Council cannot monitor CIC closely, since doing so would require allocating personnel to such a purpose and thus reduce the effectiveness of CIC as a way to generate value for the state (since surveillance costs would reduce returns), and therefore must find other means for pushing CIC's directors to remain focused on value creation. One way to do this is to push CIC into competition with other state agencies for certain types of investments and to compare CIC returns to private fund management companies.

Ensuring CIC competitiveness

CIC was required to pay a minimal interest rate on the initial funds and allowed a great deal of latitude on the assets that could be secured: bonds and other fixed income securities, equities, including IPOs, private investment funds, including mutual funds, PE firms, hedge funds, real estate investment funds, direct investments in real estate, and other direct investments. Li Rongrong, head of the State Assets Supervision and Administration Commission, a key state agency involved in finding solutions for the debt problems of troubled SOES, viewed CIC as a potential source of capital for these firms and lobbied for such investments. The struggles over the appropriate strategy for CIC highlight the problems of SWFs, trying to serve both economic and political objectives. Indeed, CIC has made substantial investments in SOEs, China's state owned banks, and other domestic financial institutions. One of the criticisms of CIC is that it has such substantial stakes in financial institutions and select SOEs that it has gained the power to channel funds from the banks to favored firms, replicating one of the problems of the old bureaucratic structure, as well as raising the potential for corruption, at worse, and unfair competitive advantages for CIC funded firms, at the least.

In its foreign investments, CIC has made two very prominent investments in U.S. based financial firms: the PE firm, Blackstone Group, LP, and the investment banking firm, Morgan Stanley. The CIC investment in these major financial firms provides the Party-state with a direct line to information that could prove valuable to state firm and state banks, given that one of the most important raw materials of PE and investment banking operations is information. Other acquisitions carried out by CIC and other state firms have provided access to natural resources, access to markets, improvements in supply-chain management, access to technology, and technology diffusion.

The role of CIC and other SWFs as sources of "emergency" capital for financial institutions based in the U.S. and other OECD nations highlights the way the globalized financial and economic structures have changed the dynamics of both crisis and crisis resolution. It is clear that these SWFs played a stabilizing role at a critical moment in the reproductive life of the global capitalist system, but perhaps more importantly in the reproductive life of specific corporations, whose failure to meet contractual obligations without this capital infusion could have greatly deepened the systemic crisis. The injections of capital from the SWFs helped to moderate market sentiment, as well, which may have worked to reduce the degree of capital flight from the financial markets, which were also exacerbating the crisis.

The economic system that prevailed in China prior to the economic reforms of late 1978 to the present was one in which NPV negative investments were far too common. The long-held goal of The Great Renewal of the Chinese Nation (strengthening China's economy and recovering from the deep humiliations of the Qing and Nationalist periods) could not be achieved without a dramatic turnaround in the creation and effective deployment of capital. Economic reforms in agriculture demonstrated that systemic restructuring and changing economic incentives could result in value creation and capital mobilization. The extension of reforms to the industrial sector reinforced this conclusion. Today, the Chinese economy has been fundamentally restructured. In particular, the Party-state leadership has come to the realization that the financial sector must play a critical role in continued economic growth and modernization by providing the necessary increased availability of capital, as well as the incentives for firms to properly deploy capital.

China's state centered capitalism, with a financial sector dominated by state owned banks, has provided relative systemic stability, even during periods of global economic crisis. The close interrelationship between the Party-state, state owned banks, and SOEs, in conjunction with rapid export growth, has provided the basis for wide-scale investments in long-term assets and the modernization of the Chinese economy. This strategy has been reinforced by financial restructuring and expansion focused primarily on providing more capital to SOEs and, only to a lesser extent, to farmers and other rural businesses, SMEs, and other NSOEs. The overall result has been to achieve meaningful progress on Zhou Enlai's Four Modernizations.

The drive to modernization has borne important fruit, as evidenced by income growth that has changed China's status from that of a low to a middle income nation. China's infrastructure has been upgraded to such a significant extent that, in many areas, it rivals that of many OECD countries, including the United States. There has been steady progress in developing a more robust educational system, one that produces more innovative graduates. And the brain drain of students studying abroad and not returning home has reversed, helping to provide talent for domestically based enterprises and other institutions, as well as to add to the cultural mix that is changing social mores in China. The advance of invention and innovation, fruits of these processes, is reflected in China now ranking in the top third of nations in patent applications. When I lived in Nanjing in the mid to late 1990s, the country was not even on the patent map. Chinese inventiveness, once at the apex of human technological evolution, is once again a force to be recognized. This bodes well for improvements in the competitiveness of China's enterprises and institutions. More talented managers and specialized personnel contributes to future cash flow generation, both through domestic market expansion and making inroads into more high value export markets.

However, the same factors that encourage long-term investments and make Chinese capitalism less prone to volatility and crises generate moral hazard and agency problems. The solution may be to shift more economic activity to the rapidly expanding private sector, particularly SMEs, and to deregulate to a greater extent. Shifting the focus of the financial sector towards NSOEs, more generally, would likely help generate the employment growth necessary to minimize future unemployment and underemployment problems, which could add to instability conditions, given that the NSOE sector provides approximately 80 percent of total employment and an even larger percentage of employment growth. This strategy would intensify competition in the Chinese economy, which could force SOEs to become even more focused on NPV positive investments which would add to social wealth and help fund further modernization. On the other hand, increased competition could also result in Schumpeterian creative destruction, which would raise unemployment risks for workers and potentially generate related social problems. The Chinese government has worked diligently to avoid such an outcome and is unlikely to carry out actions that would result in greater social instability.

Nevertheless, factors that point towards an eventual economic crisis in China are numerous and include the dramatic growth in income and asset inequality, the unsustainable housing and construction boom, and overinvestment. The contradiction between rapidly rising overall wealth and the relative lag in the development of the mass consumption market is one of the problems that must be solved to avoid a crisis: more domestic demand has been widely recognized as a necessary condition for China's economic growth path to be sustained, given that there is a clear problem with trying to maintain past rates of export growth. However, despite rhetoric from previous President Hu that more would be done to diminish income inequality, there appears to be an internal dynamic in the country that favors more, rather than less, inequality. Those with greater economic power along the Eastern seaboard, and particularly in Shanghai, southern Jiangsu Province, Guangdong Province, and Beijing, have accumulated inordinate political clout within the CPC and over public policies. In a political system where factional alliances rule the day, politicians with allegiances to these areas appear to wield the greater influence. It is not in their interest to shift towards a more egalitarian system of income distribution (or redistribution), although certainly some steps will be taken to strengthen social insurance to minimize the possibility of social unrest.

Overinvestment and inventory accumulation are clearly problems, given the rate at which capital budgets have expanded based on expectations of continued abnormally high rates of economic growth. The current strategy of shifting the Chinese economy towards more domestic demand related revenue growth has some serious hurdles to overcome. Perhaps the most serious is the aforementioned growth in income inequality. Luxury goods markets in China are actually growing at robust rates, whether for luxury homes, automobiles, or consumer goods. However, this market is unlikely to generate the sort of domestic growth in employment required to avoid rising unemployment. For example, the SOEs in the automobile sector in China are major employers but it is unlikely that the richest 1% of the Chinese population will purchase domestically produced automobiles, rather than continue the current proclivity for foreign luxury automobiles. And even if they shifted more of their purchases to domestically produced automobiles, it is unlikely they can buy enough automobiles to sustain growth of the Chinese automobile industry and related employment. However, if income growth among the top 20% expands sufficiently this may sustain such growth for a long period of time. Eventually, income growth must spread to the next 40% and 60% to keep the economy on a long-run path for expansion in the automobile industry. In other words, the rise in the Gini coefficient over the period of the reforms must be reversed if domestic-led demand is to become the engine of growth over the long-run. In the meantime, the rising Gini coefficient becomes another risk factor, one that is pointing in the direction of a demand shortfall that will contribute to disappointing cash flow growth for firms (other than luxury goods firms) selling into the Chinese market.

It is clear that an economic crisis in China in the not too distant future is more than a low probability event, but hardly a certainty. The Party-state still holds a lot of options for intervening to reduce systemic risks. But even if a major domestic economic crisis erupts, this does not necessitate a broader social crisis that threatens the continued dominance of the CPC, as some might assume. An economic crisis in China need not augur the coming of a Chinese version of one of the Jasmine revolutions in the Middle East. Nevertheless, expectations that such a cataclysmic crisis will occur remains a talking point for many academics. The assumption is that the Party-state is innately fragile.

China's economic and social structures are more complex than is often recognized in simplistic analyses. The overdetermined nature of China's mixture of state and private capitalism, in the context of globalization, one-party political concentration, and an ever changing Chinese cultural mosaic (which increasingly influences and is influenced by external cultural influences) has resulted in this complexity. Greater complexity generates less predictability and therefore more uncertainties.

For corporations and for government, uncertainty represents risk, the possibility that predicted outcomes will not be forthcoming and the potential for unexpected outcomes. For corporations and other businesses, uncertainties are translated into greater volatility in project cash flows and higher required returns of capital providers. As these factors become more important, investment spending may eventually be put under pressure, raising the risk of economic crisis. Ironically, increased volatility is both a product and cause of greater risk for firms – uncertain investors are not the only economic actors who respond to higher levels of volatility, even customers and clients may respond negatively to an environment where future outcomes are more difficult to predict.

Perhaps one of the more problematic systemic risks that arise under conditions of greater uncertainty about future cash flows of firms is the web of interconnected contractual obligations that serve as nexus between the so-called real and the financial sectors. When firms suffer cash flow shortfalls, they may be unable to satisfy financial obligations, such as interest payments and principal repayments outlined in bond indentures. The failure to meet such obligations may force a firm into bankruptcy, unless the state intervenes, threatening firms with which that firm had other contractual relationships to have to adjust. These adjustments can be quite unpleasant for the firms in question, their workers, customers, and governments expecting higher tax payments than may be forthcoming. The strong Party-state has served as a guardian of the economy, keeping this volatility in check by directly intervening to protect certain SOEs and certain markets. By playing this interventionist role, in many cases in the guise of activist owner, the Party-state has reduced the level of uncertainty (and risk) in the Chinese economy.

However, the pressures to *liberalize* the Chinese economy, by weakening state intervention in the economy, particularly institutionalized interventions, continue to be exerted by forces both internal and external to the Party. One of the arguments made for liberalization is that it is necessary if Chinese firms are to become more competitive and take greater advantage of market opportunities. It is further argued that liberalized markets are the key to the objective of modernization through innovation. But as indicated above, it is the Party-state's interventionism that has been a critical source of stability, even in crisis conditions. Thus, liberalization carries a degree of risk. If other capitalist transitions are any indication, the nature of capitalism is that as capitalist firms gain in market power and cash flow strength, they will also gain in political clout. This is one reason that in capitalist economies over time, more liberal political policies have tended to evolve. Relatively autonomous corporations breed internal dynamics that promote even greater autonomy, less government interference in the practices of corporations. Will this be different in China, given the continued importance of SOEs and state owned banks? Perhaps, but there are counter trends, such as the slow erosion in the SOE share of the Chinese economy, measured in terms of revenues or employment shares. The private sector is growing, so even if the SOEs should be supportive of an activist government, the private sector may be growing more important and would likely have a different tendency.

One possibility is that China will drift slowly in the direction of liberalization. If so, and it follows the course of other economies that have transitioned to capitalism, there will come an eventual inflection point when the balance between state control and market flexibility tips so much in the direction of deregulation that a crisis becomes not only likely but probable. The more deregulated an economy, the higher the risk of an economic crisis. Given the size and fragility of the Chinese social formation and the interconnections in the globalized economy, this crisis could potentially be massive and worldwide in its effects.

The U.S. initiated 2007-2009 economic crisis highlights the dangers of a globalized financial system interacting with deregulation and macroeconomic disequilibria. As China globalizes and liberalizes its financial systems, creating more channels for capital inflows and outflows, as well as greater decentralization in control over various cash flow distributions, uncertainties increase and along with these uncertainties comes greater risk that cash flows within the domestic and global economic networks may fail to meet expectations or even contractual obligations resulting in major financial/economic crisis with far reaching implications.

In one scenario, Xi Jinping and successive modernist leaders maintain the balance between a strong state role in the economy and the advance of market capitalism such that crises are averted. The disequilibria are manageable and growth continues.

In a second scenario, the leadership continues to weaken the state. This is pushed by ever more powerful and autonomous domestic corporate structures and foreign corporations that have become an even more important player in China's domestic economy.

In a third scenario, the crisis happens. It may be triggered by domestic problems that result in breaks in the cash flow nexus described in earlier chapters or it may be triggered by external events or both. China's growth has not put every other country to sleep, after all, and actions are being taken by other nations, including the still quite powerful United States, to take advantage of China's weaknesses and their own strengths. Signs of a modest rebirth of industrial growth are even beginning to appear on the American landscape and the creativity of America's scientists and engineers continue to give that nation a competitive edge that can be exploited. Thus, China could face serious problems. If a crisis occurs and unemployment grows too large or stays above a critical level for too long, a socialist backlash could occur and result in a push back against the tide of reforms, reversing significant aspects of liberalization. Some believe the fall of Bo Xilai was, in part, the result of fears on the part of the reformist factions that more radical elements in the Party could rise to the fore if things do not go well over the next few years.

The global economic crisis that started in the United States in 2007 and spread into Europe has also opened an enormous set of opportunities for China. In particular, Chinese banks and investment companies can fill the void left by weakened American and European banks in Africa, Latin America, and Asia, where the hunger for capital is growing. Indeed, rapid economic growth in what used to be called "The Third World" is becoming more widespread at just the time when the large financial institutions of the West are least capable of meeting the growing needs for capital. By opening new channels of capital flow from China into these emerging economies, China would gain in both economic and political terms.

APPENDIX: CHINESE EXTERNAL MERGERS AND ACQUISITIONS

Table 5.1

Year	Buyer	Seller	Industry	Investment ($ millions)
2007				
	Husky Inc.	Lima Refinery	Oil and gas	1,900
	CITIC	Delta Tech Controls	Electric components	10
	China Investment Corporation	Blackstone (12.5%)	Misc. investment	4,000
	CIC	Morgan Stanley (7.9%)	Misc. business services	5,600
	China Development Bank	Barclays (3%)	Misc. investments	3,000
	Ping'an Bank	Fortis (4.2%)	Banking and life ins.	2,700
	ICBC	ICBC Asia (8.2%)	Banking	245
	China Mobile	Paktel	Telecommunications	460
	Chinalco	Peru Copper	Copper ores	790
	Sinopec	Iranian National	Oil and gas	2000
	Haier	Thailand Refrigerator	Appliances	20
	Haier	India Refrigerator	Appliances	undisclosed
	ICBC	Seng Heng Bank (Macao) (80%)	Foreign banks	586
	ICBC	South Africa Standard (20%)	Foreign banks	5,000
	ICBC	Thai ACL Bank (19%)	Foreign banks	33
	China Development Bank	PakChina Investment Corp.	Misc. investments	100
Total				26,444
2008				
	SAFE	Total (1.6%)	Crude oil and gas	2,820
	SAFE	BP (1%)	Crude oil and gas	2,000
	CNOOC	Norwegian Awilco	Oil and gas services	2,490
	Bank of China	Swiss Heritage Fund	Misc. investments	8.7
	Husky Inc.	Toledo Refinery	Oil and gas services	2500
	Mindray Medical	Datascope Corp.	Electromedical equip.	202
	Grace Semiconductor	STM Microelectronics	Electronic components	undisclosed
	CITIC	Citizens Mutual Telephone	Telecom equipment	33
	Wuxi Pharmatech	AppTec Lab Services	Testing laboratories	151
	Spreadtrum Communications	Quorum Systems	Semiconductors	7
	CIC	Visa (<1%)	Business services	100
	China Life	Visa (1%)	Business services	300
	CIC	JC Flowers	Misc. investment	4,000
	SAFE	Texas Pacific Group	Misc. investment	5,600

Year	Buyer	Seller	Industry	Investment ($millions)
	Chinalco	Toromach Copper Mine	Copper ores	2160
	Xinxing and China Metal	Indian JV	Metal mining services	1200
	Suntech Power	Japan MSK Solar (33%)	Misc. electric machinery	107
	China Aluminum International Engineering	Vietnam bauxite mine	Misc. metal ores	466
	Shanghai Automotive	Sangyong Automotive (2.1%)	Motor vehicles	50
	China Merchant Bank	HK Wing Lung Bank (53.1%)	Foreign banking services	2500
Total				26,695
2009				
	Beijing West Ind.	Delphi Auto Parts	Motor vehicles parts	100
	Airtime DSL	TAG Industries	Lighting equipment	27
	Qiaoxing Group	Freescale Semiconductors	Communications equip.	100
	CIC	Morgan Stanley (2%)	Business services	1,200
	China MinMetals	OZ Metals (Australia)	Copper, lead, zinc, other ores	1200
	CNPC	Singapore Petroleum (45.5%)	Oil and gas	1,000
	Hunan Valin	Fortescue (17%)	Iron ores	462
	Haier	Prachin Buri Refrigerator Thailand	Appliances	5
	SAFE	Total (1.6%)	Crude oil and gas	705
Total				4,799
2010				
	Sinopec	Repsol YPF Brazil SA	Oil and gas (40%)	7111
	Sinochem Group	Peregrino Project, Campos Basin	Oil field (40%)	3070
	Tencent Holdings Ltd.	Digital Sky Technologies	Internet investment (10%)	300
	East China Mineral Exploration	Itaminas Comercio de Minerios	Iron ore mine	1220
Total				11,701
2011				
	Jinchuan Group	Metorex	Copper and cobalt mine	1328
	CIC	Shanduka Group Pty Ltd	Diversified investment (25%)	244
	China Niobium Investment	CBMM	Niobium producer (15%)	1950
	Chongqing Huapont Pharm	CCAB Agro	Agriculture, chemicals (7.5%)	20
Total				3542

Source: Deloitte (2012), Wolf, et al. (2011). Note: (%) indicates ownership stake. The absence of percentages implies 100 percent acquisition.

BIBLIOGRAPHY

Barma, N. and Ratner, E. (2006). China's illiberal challenge: the real threat posed by China isn't economicor military—it's ideological. *Democracy: A Journal of Ideas* 2, 56–68.

Bergström, C. and Tang, E. (2001). Price differentials between different classes of stocks: an empirical study on Chinese stock markets. *Journal of Multinational Financial Management* 11, 407–426.

Bhattacharyay, B. N. (2013). Determinants of bond market development in Asia. *Journal of Asian Economics* 24, 124-137.

Bowles, P. and White, G. (1992). The dilemmas of market socialism: Capital market reform in China - part I: bonds. *The Journal of Development Studies* 28(3), 363-385.

Bramall, C. (2000). *Sources of Chinese Economic Growth, 1978-1996*. Oxford (UK): Oxford University Press.

Breslin, S. (2011). The 'China model' and the global crisis: from Friedrich List to a Chinese mode of governance?. *International Affairs* 87(6), 1323–1343.

Bulman, D. J. (2010). China and the financial crisis. *Stanford Journal of East Asian Affairs* 10(2), 20-38.

Cauley, J. and Sandler, T. (2001). Agency cost and the crisis of China's SOEs: A comment and further observations. *China Economic Review* 12, 293–297.

Chen, C., Jin, Q., & Yuan, H. (2011). Agency problems and liquidity premium: Evidence from China's stock ownership reform. *International Review of Financial Analysis* 20, 76-87.

Chen, J. and Thomas, S. (2005). China's bond market matures, slowly. *The China Business Review*, 30-33.

Chen, X. and Sun, C. (2000). Technology transfer to China: alliances of Chinese enterprises with western technology exporters. *Technovation* 20, 353–362.

Chen, Z., Ge, Y., & Lai, H. (2011). Foreign Direct Investment and Wage Inequality: Evidence from China. *World Development* 39(8), 1322–1332.

China Internet Network Information Center (CNNIC). (2012,

January). *The 29th Statistical Report on Internet Development in China*. Retrieved from http://www1.cnnic.cn/IDR/ReportDownloads/201209/P020120904421720687608.pdf

CIA World Factbook. (2008). Retrieved from https://www.cia.gov/library/publications/the-world-factbook/.

CIA World Factbook. (2012). Retrieved from https://www.cia.gov/library/publications/the-world-factbook/.

Ciocchini, F., Durbin, E., & Ng, D. T. C. (2003). Does corruption increase emerging market bond spreads? *Journal of Economics and Business* 55, 503–528.

Cui, Y., Tani, M., & Nahm, D. (2012). The determinants of employment choice of rural migrant workers in China: SOEs and non-SOEs. *Procedia Economics and Finance* 1, 98–107.

Cull, R. and Xu, L. C. (2003). Who gets credit? The behavior of bureaucrats and state banks in allocating credit to Chinese state-owned enterprises. *Journal of Development Economics* 71, 533-559.

Das, D. K. (2008). Repositioning the Chinese economy on the global economic stage. *Int Rev Econ* 55, 401–417.

Davis, A. (2012, October). Building China's bond market. *Asiamoney*.

De Haan, A. (2011). Will China change international development as we know it?. *Journal of International Development* 23, 881–908.

Deloitte Chinese Services Group. (2012) *Lateral Trades: Breathing fire into the BRICs*.

Dong, H. E. and Wang, H. (2012). Dual-track interest rates and the conduct of monetary policy in China. *China Economic Review* 23, 928-947.

Dong, X. and Putterman, L. (2003). Soft budget constraints, social burdens, and labor redundancy in China's state industry. *Journal of Comparative Economics* 31, 110–133.

Dong, X., Putterman, L., & Unel, B. (2006). Privatization and firm performance: A comparison between rural and urban enterprises in China. *Journal of Comparative Economics* 34, 608–633.

Fan, L. and Johansson, A. C. (2010). China's official rates and bond yields. *Journal of Banking & Finance* 34, 996–1007.

Fan, L., Tian, S., & Zhang, C. (2012). Why are excess returns on China's Treasury bonds so predictable? The role of the monetary system.

Journal of Banking and Finance 36, 239-248.

Firth, M., Oliver M. Rui, O. M., & Wu, W. (2011). Cooking the books: Recipes and costs of falsified financial statements in China. *Journal of Corporate Finance* 17, 371-390.

Gabriel, S. (2006) *Chinese Capitalism and the Modernist Vision.* London: Routledge.

Gabriel, S., Resnick, S. A., & Wolff, R. (2008). State capitalism versus communism: What happened in the USSR and the PRC?. *Critical Sociology* 34, 539-556.

Gabriel, S., Resnick, S. A., & Wolff , R. (2011). State capitalism in the USSR. In Vincent Pollard (Ed.), *State Capitalism: Contentious Politics and Large-Scale Social Change.* Leiden: Brill Publishers.

Gabriele, A. (2010). The role of the state in china's industrial development: a reassessment. *Comparative Economic Studies* 52, 325-350.

Gamble, W. (2000). The Middle Kingdom runs dry. *Foreign Affairs* 79(6), 16.

Gonzalez-Vicente, R. (2011). The internationalization of the Chinese state. *Political Geography* 30, 402-411.

Green, S. (2003). *China's Stockmarket: A Guide to its Progress, Players and Prospects.* London: Profile Books/The Economist.

Groenewolda, N., Tang,S. H. K., & Wu, Y. (2003). The efficiency of the Chinese stock market and the role of the banks.*Journal of Asian Economics* 14, 593–609.

Hong, S. (2014). China tops US in corporate debt issuance. Retrieved from

Hung, M., Wong, T. J., & Zhang, T. (2012). Political considerations in the decision of Chinese SOEs to list in Hong Kong. *Journal of Accounting and Economics* 53, 435-449.

International Energy Agency. (2012). *Key World Energy Statistics.* Paris, France: IEA.

International Labor Office (ILO). (2013). *Global Wage Report 2012/13: Wages and equitable growth.* Geneva: International Labour Office.

International Labor Office (ILO). (2010). *Global Wage Report 2010/11: Wage policies in times of crisis.* Geneva: International Labour Office.

Ip, E. C. and Law, M. K. H. (2011). Decentralization, agency costs, and the new economic constitution of China. *Const Polit Econ* 22, 355–372.

Jiang, Y. (2011). Understanding openness and productivity growth in China: An empirical study of the Chinese provinces. *China Economic Review* 22, 290-298.

Jusi, W. (1989). Water pollution and water shortage problems in China. *Journal of Applied Ecology* 26(3), 851-857.

King, R. G. and Levine, R. (1993). Finance and growth: Schumpeter might be right. *The Quarterly Journal of Economics* 108(3), 717-737.

Kotter, J. and Lel, U. (2011). Friends or foes? Target selection decisions of sovereign wealth funds and their consequences. *Journal of Financial Economics* 101, 360-381.

Lau, L. J. and Li, K. (2012, March 15). The Chinese economy: A critical decade. [Presentation]. Standard Chartered Hong Kong Forum, Hong Kong, China.

Lee, C. J. (2001). Financial restructuring of state owned enterprises in china: the case of shanghai sunve pharmaceutical corporation. *Accounting, Organizations and Society* 26, 673-689.

Lee, Y. (1997). Bank loans, self-financing, and grants in Chinese SOEs: Optimal policy under incomplete information. *Journal of Comparative Economics* 24, 140–160.

Linton, K. C. (2008). Access to capital in China: Competitive conditions for foreign and domestic firms. *United States International Trade Commission Journal of International Commerce & Economics* I, 27-49.

Liu, C., Uchida, K., & Yang, Y. (2012). Corporate governance and firm value during the global financial crisis: Evidence from China. *International Review of Financial Analysis* 21, 70-80.

Lu, Z., Zhu, J., & Zhang, W. (2012). Bank discrimination, holding bank ownership, and economic consequences: Evidence from China. *Journal of Banking and Finance* 36, 341-354.

Masood,O. and Sergi, B. S. (2011). China's banking system, market structure, and competitive conditions. *Front. Econ. China* 6(1): 22–35.

Mauro, P. (1995). Corruption and growth. *Quarterly Journal of Economics* 110(3), 681-712.

Mehrotra, A. and Pääkkönen, J. (2011). Comparing China's GDP statistics with coincident indicators. *Journal of Comparative Economics* 39, 406-411.

Meyer, C. (2011). *China or Japan: Which Will Lead Asia.* New York: Columbia University Press.

Mihai, I. (2013). The evolution of sovereign wealth funds and their influence in the global economy: The case of China. *Theoretical and Applied Economics* 20(5), 93-106.

Mizen, P. and Tsoukas, S. (2012). The response of the external finance premium in Asian corporate bond markets to financial characteristics, financial constraints and two financial crises. *Journal of Banking and Finance* 36, 3048-3059.

National Bureau of Statistics China. (2012). Urbanization. Retrieved from NBSC website http://www.stats.gov.cn/english/

Naughton, B. (2007). *The Chinese Economy.* Cambridge, MA: MIT Press.

Niquet, V. (2009). China in the face of economic crisis. *China Perspectives* 3, 80-86.

O'Connor, N. G., Chow, C. W., & Wu, A. (2004). The adoption of "Western" management accounting/controls in China's state-owned enterprises during economic transition. *Accounting, Organizations and Society* 29, 349–375.

OECD. (2012a). Country statistical profile: China 2011-2012. Retrieved from OECD website http://www.oecd-ilibrary.org/statistics

OECD. (2012b). *OECD Factbook 2011-2012: Economic, Environmental and Social Statistics.* OECD Publishing.

Paus, E., Prime, P., &Western, J. (2009). China rising: a global transformation?. in Eva Paus, Penelope Prime and Jon Western (Eds.), *Global giant: is China changing the rules of the game?* Basingstoke: PalgraveMacmillan.

Peng, M. W., Zhang, S., & and Li, X., (2007). CEO duality and firm performance during China's institutional transitions. *Management and Organization Review* 3(2), 205–225.

Peng, Y. (2007). *The Chinese Banking Industry.* London: Routledge.

People's Bank of China. (2012). Statistics. Retrieved from website http://www.pbc.gov.cn/publish/english/963/index.html

Ping, He Wei. (2013). Regulatory capture in China's banking sector.

Journal of Banking Regulation. 14(1), 80-90.

Piovani, C. and Li, M. (2011). One hundred million jobs for the Chinese workers! Why China's current model of development is unsustainable and how a progressive economic program can help the Chinese workers, the Chinese economy, and China's environment. *Review of Radical Political Economics* 43(1) 77–94.

PwC. (2013). Private equity 2013 review and 2014 outlook. Retrieved from website http://www.pwccn.com/webmedia/doc/635301401296400508_pe_china_review_feb2014.pdf

Rawski, T. G. (2001). What is happening to China's GDP statistics?. *China Economic Review* 12(4), 347-354.

Rawski, T. G. (2002). Will investment behavior constrain China's growth?. *China Economic Review* 13(4), 361-372.

Resnick, S. A. and Wolff, R. D. (1989). *Knowledge and Class.* Chicago, IL: University of Chicago Press.

Resnick, S. A. and Wolff, R. D. (2002). *Class Theory and History: Capitalism and Communism in the USSR.* London: Routledge.

Ronen,T. and Zhou, X. (2013). Trade and information in the corporate bond market. *Journal of Financial Markets* 16(1), 61-103.

Rozelle, S. and Swinnen, J. F. M. (2009). Why did the communist party reform in China, but not in the Soviet Union? The political economy of agricultural transition. *China Economic Review* 20, 275–287.

Shanghai Stock Exchange. (2012). *Fact Book.* Retrieved from website http://www.sse.com.cn/sseportal/en/pages/p1005/p1005_content/factbook_us2012.pdf

Shenzhen Stock Exchange. (1998). *Fact Book.*

Shenzhen Stock Exchange. (2000). *Fact Book.*

Shenzhen Stock Exchange. (2004). *Fact Book.*

Shenzhen Stock Exchange. (2011). *Fact Book.*

Soros, G. (2008). *The New Paradigm for Financial Markets.* New York: Public Affairs Publishers.

State Administration of Foreign Exchange. (2012). Forex reserves. Retrieved from SAFE website http://www.safe.gov.cn/

Stubbs, R. (2011). The East Asian developmental state and the Great Recession: Evolving contesting coalitions. *Contemporary Politics* 17(2), 151–66.

Sui, H. (2011). Factors influencing the development of China's corporate bond market and relevant suggestions. *International Journal of Business and Management* 6(9). Retrieved from http://www.ccsenet.org/journal/index.php/ijbm/article/view/12084

Taleb, N. (2010). *The Black Swan: the impact of the highly improbable*. New York: Random House.

Tan, J. and Wang, L. (2010). Flexibility–efficiency tradeoff and performance implications among Chinese SOEs. *Journal of Business Research* 63, 356–362.

Tan, Q. (2004). State, institution building, and emerging stock markets in China. *Communist and Post-Communist Studies* 37, 373–394.

Tian, G. (2011). On deep-rooted problems in China's economy. *Front. Econ. China* 6(3), 345–358.

Tong, Y. (2011). Morality, benevolence, and responsibility: Regime legitimacy in China from past to the present. *Journal of Chinese Political Science* 16, 141–159.

Truman, E. (2007). Sovereign wealth funds: The need for greater transparency and accountability. *Peterson Institute for International Economics Policy Brief* 07-6. Washington: Peterson Institute for International Economics.

UNCTAD. (2012, October 23). *Global Investment Trends Monitor* 10.

UNDP. (2012). *One Planet to Share: Sustaining Human Progress in a changing climate*: *Asia Pacific Human Development Report*. Retrieved from http://hdr.undp.org.

US Census Bureau. (2012). China trade surplus with the US. Retrieved from the US Cenus Bureau website http://www.census.gov/foreign-trade/balance/c5700.html

USChina.org. (2012). US-China trade statistics and China's world trade statistics. Retrieved from USChina.org website https://www.uschina.org/statistics/tradetable.html

Wade, R. (2010). After the crisis: industrial policy and the developmental state in low-income countries. *Global Policy* 1(2), pp. 150–61.

Wan, J. and Yuce, A. (2007). Listing regulations in China and their effect on the performance of IPOs and SOEs. *Research in International Business and Finance* 21(3), 366-378.

Wang, X. and Wen, Y. (2011). Can rising housing prices explain China's high household saving rate?. *Federal Reserve Bank of St. Louis Review* 93(2), pp. 67-87.

Whalley, J. and Xin, X. (2010). China's FDI and non-FDI economies and the sustainability of future high Chinese growth. *China Economic Review* 21, 123–135.

Wolf, C. and Chow, B., Jones, G, & Harold, S. (2011). China's expanding role in global mergers and acquisitions. Santa Monica, CA: Rand, 2011.

Woo, Jaejoon. (2012). Technology upgrading in China and India: What do we know?. OECD Development Center Working Paper no. 308. Paris, France: OECD Development Center.

World Bank. (2012) National accounts data. Retrieved from World Bank website http://data.worldbank.org/data-catalog

World Bank. (2012b). *China 2030: Building a Modern, Harmonious, and Creative High-Income Society*. Washington, D.C.: World Bank.

Xu, C. K. (2000). The microstructure of the Chinese stock market. *China Economic Review* 11, 79-97.

Xu, L. and Ohb, K. B. (2011). The stock market in China: An endogenous adjustment process responding to the demands of economic reform and growth. *Journal of Asian Economies* 22, 36-47.

Yang, W. (2006). Reforms, structural adjustments, and rural income in China. *China Perspectives*, [online] 63.

Yinghua Jin, Y., Ligthart, J., & Rider, M. (2011). The evolution of fiscal decentralization in China and India: A comparative study of design and performance. *Journal of Emerging Knowledge on Emerging Markets* 3

Yuxiang, K. and Chen, Z. (2010). Government expenditure and energy intensity in China. *Energy Policy* 38, 691–694.

Zhang, L. (2004). The roles of corporatization and stock market listing in reforming China's state industry. *World Development* 32(12), 2031–2047.

Ziesemer, T. H. W. (2012). Worker remittances, migration, accumulation and growth in poor developing countries: Survey and analysis of direct and indirect effects. *Economic Modeling* 29, 103-118.

Index